D1067704

Item Response Theory

Evaluation in Education and Human Services series

Editors:

George F. Madaus, Boston College
Daniel L. Stufflebeam, Western Michigan University

Previously published:

Kellaghan, Thomas; Madaus, George F.; Airasian, Peter W.: THE
EFFECTS OF STANDARDIZED TESTING
Madaus, George F.: THE COURTS, VALIDITY AND MINIMUM
COMPETENCY TESTING
Madaus, George F.; Scriven, Michael S.; Stufflebeam, Daniel L.:
EVALUATION MODELS: VIEWPOINTS ON EDUCATIONAL AND
HUMAN SERVICES EVALUATION
Brinkerhoff, Robert O.; Brethower, Dale M.; Hluchyj, Terry; Nowakowski,
Jeri Ridings: PROGRAM EVALUATION: A PRACTITIONER'S GUIDE
FOR TRAINERS AND EDUCATORS, A SOURCEBOOK/CASEBOOK
Brinkerhoff, Robert O,; Brethower, Dale M.; Hluchyj, Terry; Nowakowski,
Jeri Ridings: PROGRAM EVALUATION: A PRACTITIONER'S GUIDE
FOR TRAINERS AND EDUCATORS, A SOURCEBOOK
Brinkerhoff, Robert O.; Brethower, Dale M.; Hluchyj, Terry; Nowakowski,
Jeri Ridings: PROGRAM EVALUATION: A PRACTITIONER'S GUIDE
FOR TRAINERS AND EDUCATORS, A DESIGN MANUAL

Item Response Theory

Principles and Applications

Ronald K. Hambleton

Hariharan Swaminathan

Kluwer·Nijhoff Publishing
a member of the Kluwer Academic Publishers Group
Boston/Dordrecht/Lancaster

Distributors for North America:
Kluwer Boston, Inc.
190 Old Derby Street
Hingham, MA 02043, U.S.A.

Distributors Outside North America:
Kluwer Academic Publishers Group
Distribution Centre
P.O. Box 322
3300AH Dordrecht, The Netherlands

Library of Congress Cataloging in Publication Data

Hambleton, Ronald K.
  Item response theory.

  (Evaluation in education and human services)
  Includes bibliographical references and index.
  1. Item response theory. I. Swaminathan, Hariharan.
II. Title. III. Series.
BF176.H35 1984   150'.28'7   83-11385
ISBN 0-89838-065-0

Printed in the United States of America

To Else and Fran

Contents

List of Figures

PREFACE

In the decade of the 1970s, item response theory became the dominant topic for study by measurement specialists. But, the genesis of item response theory (IRT) can be traced back to the mid-thirties and early forties. In fact, the term "Item Characteristic Curve," which is one of the main IRT concepts, can be attributed to Ledyard Tucker in 1946. Despite these early research efforts, interest in item response theory lay dormant until the late 1960s and took a backseat to the emerging development of strong true score theory. While true score theory developed rapidly and drew the attention of leading psychometricians, the problems and weaknesses inherent in its formulation began to raise concerns. Such problems as the lack of invariance of item parameters across examinee groups, and the inadequacy of classical test procedures to detect item bias or to provide a sound basis for measurement in "tailored testing," gave rise to a resurgence of interest in item response theory.

Impetus for the development of item response theory as we now know it was provided by Frederic M. Lord through his pioneering works (Lord, 1952; 1953a, 1953b). The progress in the fifties was painstakingly slow due to the mathematical complexity of the topic and the nonexistence of computer programs. Additional work by Lord (1968), the appearance of five chapters on the topic of item response theory in Lord and Novick's *Statistical Theories of Mental Test Scores* in 1968, and the work of Benjamin Wright and Darrell Bock and their students at the University of Chicago signaled renewed interest in the area and resulted in an explosion of research articles and applications of the theory. Special issues of the *Journal of Educational Measurement* (1977) and *Applied Psychological Measurement* (1982) were devoted to item response theory and applications. A handbook on Rasch model analysis, *Best Test Design*, was published by Wright and Stone (1979). Crowning these efforts, a book by Lord was published on the subject in 1980, a book that must be considered an intimate and a personal statement of the most influential personage in the field.

Given the existence of these sources, is there a need for another book in this area? Lord (1980a, p. xii) notes that "reviewers will urge the need for a book on item response theory that does not require the mathematical understanding required [in my book]." The book by Lord (1980a) requires considerable mathematical maturity and centers on the three-parameter logistic model. Wright and Stone (1979) have aimed their work at the practitioner and do not require the same level of mathematical sophistication. They have, however, focused their attention on the Rasch model and its applications. The need for a book that provides a not too technical discussion of the subject matter and that simultaneously contains a treatment of many of the item response models and their applications seems clear.

The purpose of this book is threefold. We have attempted to provide a nontechnical presentation of the subject matter, a comprehensive treatment of the models and their applications, and specific steps for using the models in selected promising applications. Although our aim is to provide a nontechnical treatment of the subject, mathematical and statistical treatment is unavoidable at times, given the nature of the theory. We have, however, attempted to keep the level of mathematics and statistics to a minimum so that a reader who has had basic courses in statistics will be able to follow most of the discussion provided. The mathematical analyses found in parts of chapters 5, 6, and 7 could be omitted without loss of continuity. Familiarity with classical test theory and principles of measurement is, however, desirable.

The book is organized into four parts:

- Introduction to item response theory, models, and assumptions;
- Ability scales, estimation of ability, information functions, and calibration of tests;
- Investigations of model-data fit;
- Equating, test development, and several other promising applications.

The level of mathematical treatment is clearly higher in the second part of the textbook than it is in the other parts. We consider this necessary and valid. Where it was felt that a reasonable example was not possible or could not be provided to illustrate the principles, illustrations of applications are provided.

One problem that we faced concerned notation. In a rapidly expanding field such as item response theory, uniformity of notation cannot be expected. Rather than contribute to the profusion of notation, we have attempted to adhere to the notational scheme employed by Lord (1980a). We hope this will reduce somewhat the problem of notational diversity in the future.

Considerations of manuscript length and cost were factors in our selection of content and depth of coverage. Hence, we were not always able to allocate an appropriate amount of space to deserving topics. Presently, the one-, two-, and three-parameter logistic test models are receiving the most attention from researchers and test builders. Since more technical information is available on these three logistic models and presently they are receiving substantial use, they were emphasized in our work. However, we have no reservations about predicting that other item response models may be produced in the future to replace those models emphasized in our book. Also, while detailed descriptions of test equating, test development, and item bias are included, promising and important applications of item response models to adaptive testing, criterion-referenced measurement, and inappropriateness measurement, were given limited or no coverage at all. Readers are referred to Harnisch and Tatsuoka (1983), Levine and Rubin (1979), Lord (1980a), and Weiss (1980, 1983) for technical information on these latter topics.

Our dependence on the works of Frederic M. Lord is evident throughout. We have been inspired by his guidance and have benefited immensely from discussions with him. Our introduction to the subject, however, must be traced to our mentors, Ross E. Traub and Roderick P. McDonald, who, through their concern for our education and through their exemplary scholarship, influenced our thinking. We tried to be faithful to Roderick McDonald's dictum that a person who learned the subject matter from our work should not "be a danger to himself and a nuisance to others." Several former graduate students of ours—Linda Cook, Daniel Eignor, Janice A. Gifford, Leah Hutten, Craig Mills, Linda N. Murray, and Robert Simon— further contributed to our understanding of item response theory by working with us on several research projects. Janice A. Gifford and Linda N. Murray provided valuable service to us by performing many of the computations used in the examples and by proofreading the manuscript. We are especially indebted to Bernadette McDonald and Cindy Fisher, who patiently and painstakingly typed numerous revisions of the text, formulas, and tables. The errors that remain, however, must, unfortunately, be attributed to us.

Most of the developments and studies reported here attributed to us were made possible by the support of the Personnel and Training Branch, Office of Naval Research (Contract No. N0014–79–C–0039), Air Force Human Resources Laboratory (Contract No. FQ7624–79–0014), Air Force Office of Scientific Research (Contract No. F49620–78–0039), and the National Institute of Education (Contract No. 02–81–20319). We are deeply grateful to these agencies, and in particular to Charles Davis, Malcolm Ree, Brian Waters, Phil DeLeo, and Roger Pennell for their support and encouragement.

1 SOME BACKGROUND TO ITEM RESPONSE THEORY

1.1 Shortcomings of Standard Testing Methods

The common models and procedures for constructing tests and interpreting test scores have served measurement specialists and other test users well for a long time. These models, such as the classical test model, are based on weak assumptions, that is, the assumptions can be met easily by most test data sets, and, therefore, the models can and have been applied to a wide variety of test development and test score analysis problems. Today, there are countless numbers of achievement, aptitude, and personality tests that have been constructed with these models and procedures. Well-known classical test model statistics, such as the standard error of measurement, the disattenuation formulas, the Spearman-Brown formula, and the Kuder-Richardson formula-20, are just a few of the many important statistics that are a part of the classical test model and related techniques (Gulliksen, 1950; Lord & Novick, 1968).

Still, there are many well-documented shortcomings of the ways in which educational and psychological tests are usually constructed, evaluated, and used (Hambleton & van der Linden, 1982). For one, the values of commonly used item statistics in test development such as item difficulty and item

1

discrimination depend on the particular examinee samples in which they are obtained. The average level of ability and the range of ability scores in an examinee sample influence, often substantially, the values of the item statistics. For example, item difficulty levels (typically referred to as p-values) will be higher when examinee samples used to obtain the statistics have higher ability than the average ability level of examinees in that population. Also, item discrimination indices tend to be higher when estimated from an examinee sample heterogeneous in ability than from an examinee sample homogeneous in ability. This result is obtained because of the well-known effect of group heterogeneity on correlation coefficients (Lord & Novick, 1968). The net result is that item statistics are useful only in item selection when constructing tests for examinee populations that are very similar to the sample of examinees in which the item statistics were obtained. Finally, the assessment of classical test reliability is not unrelated to the variability of test scores in the sample of examinees. Test score reliability is directly related to test score variability.

Another shortcoming of classical test theory, which for our purposes refers to commonly used methods and techniques for test design and analysis, is that comparisons of examinees on an ability measured by a set of test items comprising a test are limited to situations in which examinees are administered the same (or parallel) test items. One problem, however, is that because many achievement and aptitude tests are (typically) most suitable for middle-ability students, the tests do not provide very precise estimates of ability for either high- or low-ability examinees. Increased test score validity can be obtained when the test difficulty is matched to the approximate ability level of each examinee (Lord, 1980a; Weiss, 1983), Alternately, tests can often be shortened without any decrease in test score validity when test items are selected to match the ability levels of examinees to whom tests are administered. However, when several forms of a test that vary substantially in difficulty are used, the task of comparing examinees becomes a difficult problem. Test scores no longer suffice. Two examinees who perform at a 50 percent level on two tests that differ substantially in difficulty level cannot be considered equivalent in ability. Is the student scoring 60 percent on an easy test higher or lower in ability than the student scoring 40 percent on a difficult test? The task of comparing examinees who have taken samples of test items of differing difficulty cannot easily be handled with standard testing models and procedures.

A third shortcoming of classical test theory is that one of the fundamental concepts, test reliability, is defined in terms of parallel forms. The concept of parallel measures is difficult to achieve in practice: Individuals are never exactly the same on a second administration of a test. They forget things, they develop new skills, their motivational or anxiety level may change, etc. (Hambleton & van der Linden, 1982). Since classical test theory relies heavily on the concept of parallel-forms, it is not too surprising that problems are encountered in the application of classical test theory. As Hambleton and van der Linden (1982) have noted, researchers must be content with either lower-bound estimates of reliability or reliability estimates with unknown biases.

A fourth shortcoming of classical test theory is that it provides no basis for determining how an examinee might perform when confronted with a test item. Having an estimate of the probability that an examinee will answer a particular question correctly is of considerable value when adapting a test to match the examinee's ability level. Such information is necessary, for example, if a test designer desires to predict test score characteristics in one or more populations of examinees or to design tests with particular characteristics for certain populations of examinees.

A fifth shortcoming of the classical test model is that it presumes that the variance of errors of measurement is the same for all examinees. It is not uncommon to observe, however, that some people perform a task more consistently than others and that consistency varies with ability. In view of this, the performance of high-ability examinees on several parallel forms of a test might be expected to be more consistent than the performance of medium-ability examinees. What is needed are test models that can provide information about the precision of a test score (ability estimate), information that is specific to the test score (ability estimate) and that is free to vary from one test score (ability estimate) to another.

In addition to the five shortcomings of classical test theory mentioned above, classical test theory and associated procedures have failed to provide satisfactory solutions to many testing problems, for example, the design of tests, the identification of biased items, and the equating of test scores. Classical item statistics do not inform test developers about the location of maximum discriminating power of items on the test score scale; classical approaches to the study of item bias have been unsuccessful because they fail to adequately handle true ability differences among groups of interest: and test score equating is difficult to handle with classical methods, again because of the true ability differences of those examinees taking the tests. For these and other reasons, psychometricians have been concerned with the development of more appropriate theories of mental measurements. The purpose of any test theory is to describe how inferences from examinee item responses and/or test scores can be made about unobservable examinee characteristics or traits that are measured by a test. Presently, perhaps the most popular set of constructs, models, and assumptions for inferring traits is organized around *latent trait theory*. Consequently, considerable attention is being directed currently toward the field of *latent trait theory, item characteristic curve theory* or *item response theory* as Lord (1980a) prefers to call the theory. The notion of an underlying latent ability, attribute, factor, or dimension is a recurring one in the psychometric literature. Hence, the term latent trait theory, while appropriate, may not adequately convey the distinctions that exist between the family of procedures which include factor analysis, multidimensional scaling, and latent structure analysis, and the procedure for studying the characteristics of items relative to an ability scale. The term item characteristic curve theory or item response theory may be more appropriate. Presently, albeit arguably, the most popular term is *item response theory* (IRT), and so that term will be used throughout this book.

1.2 Historical Perspective

Figure 1–1 provides a graphical representation with a short synopsis of the major contributions to the IRT field. Item response theory can be traced to the work of Richardson (1936), Lawley (1943, 1944), and Tucker (1946). In fact, Tucker (1946) appears to have been the first psychometrician to have

Figure 1-1. Important Theoretical and Practical Contributions in the History of Item Response Theory

1916	Binet and Simon were the first to plot performance levels against an independent variable and use the plots in test development.
1936	Richardson derived relationships between IRT model parameters and classical item parameters, which provided an initial way for obtaining IRT parameter estimates.
1943, 44	Lawley produced some new procedures for parameter estimation.
1952	Lord described the two-parameter normal ogive model, derived model parameter estimates, and considered applications of the model.
1957, 58	Birnbaum substituted the more tractable logistic models for the normal ogive models, and developed the statistical foundations for these new models.
1960	Rasch developed three item response models and described them in his book, *Probabilistic Models for Some Intelligence and Attainment Tests*. His work influenced Wright in the United States and psychologists such as Andersen and Fischer in Europe.
1967	Wright was the leader and catalyst for most of the Rasch model research in the United States throughout the 1970s. His presentation at the ETS Invitational Conference on Testing Problems served as a

Figure 1-1 *(continued)*

	major stimulus for work in IRT, especially with the Rasch model. Later, his highly successful AERA Rasch Model Training programs contributed substantially to the understanding of the Rasch model by many researchers.
1968	Lord and Novick provided five chapters on the theory of latent traits (four of the chapters were prepared by Birnbaum). The authors' endorsement of IRT stimulated a considerable amount of research.
1969	Wright and Panchapakesan described parameter estimation methods for the Rasch model and the computer program *BICAL*, which utilized the procedures described in the paper. BICAL was of immense importance because it facilitated applications of the Rasch model.
1969	Samejima published her first in an impressive series of reports describing new item response models and their applications. Her models handled both polychotomous and continuous response data and extended unidimensional models to the multidimensional case.
1972	Bock contributed several important new ideas about parameter estimation.
1974	Lord described his new parameter estimation methods, which were utilized in a computer program called *LOGIST*.
1974	Fischer described his extensive research progam with linear logistic models.
1976	Lord et al. made available LOGIST, a computer program for carrying out parameter estimation with logistic test models. LOGIST is one of the two most commonly used programs today (the other is BICAL).
1977	Baker provided a comprehensive review of parameter estimation methods.
1977	Researchers such as Bashaw, Lord, Marco, Rentz, Urry, and Wright in the *Journal of Educational Measurement* special issue of IRT applications described many important measurement breakthroughs.
1979	Wright and Stone in *Best Test Design* described the theory underlying the Rasch model, and many promising applications.
1980	Lord in *Applications of Item Response Theory to Practical Testing Problems* provided an up-to-date review of theoretical developments and applications of the three-parameter model.
1980	Weiss edited the *Proceedings of the 1979 Computerized Adaptive Testing Conference*. These *Proceedings* contained an up-to-date collection of papers on adaptive testing, one of the main practical uses of IRT.
1982	Lord and his staff at ETS made available the second edition of LOGIST. This updated computer program was faster, somewhat easier to set up, and had more additional worthwhile output than the 1976 edition of the program.

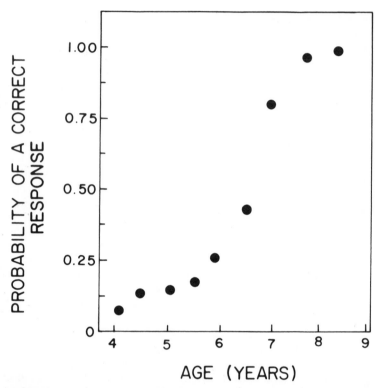

Figure 1-2. Average Performance of Children on a Cognitive Task as a Function of Age

used the term "item characteristic curve" (ICC), which is the key concept in the IRT field. Basically, an ICC is a plot of the level of performance on some task or tasks against some independent measure such as ability, age, etc. Usually, a smooth non-linear curve is fitted to the data to remove minor irregularities in the pattern of the data, and to facilitate subsequent uses of the relationship in test design and analysis. While the term was not used by them, Binet and Simon (1916) may have been the first psychologists to actually work with ICCs. Binet and Simon considered the performance of children of increasing age on a variety of cognitive tasks. They used plots like the one shown in figure 1-2 to help them select tasks for their first intelligence tests. These plots today are called *item characteristic curves*, which serve as the key element in the theory of latent traits or item response theory.

Lawley (1943, 1944) provided a number of initial theoretical developments in the IRT area. Frederic Lord himself, the most influential contributor to the IRT literature over the last 30 years, seemed to have been greatly influenced early in his career by Lawley's pioneering work. Lawley related parameters in item response theory to classical model parameters and advanced several promising parameter estimation methods. But Lawley's models were highly restrictive. For example, his work was based on such assumptions as (1) item intercorrelations are equal and (2) guessing is not a factor in test performance. Richardson (1936) and Tucker (1946) developed relationships between classical model parameters and the parameters associated with item characteristic curves.

Lazarsfeld (1950), who carried out the bulk of his research in the field of attitude measurement, was perhaps the first to introduce the term "latent traits." The work of Lord (1952, 1953a, 1953b), however, is generally regarded as the "birth" of item response theory (or modern test theory as it is sometimes called). Perhaps this is because he was the first to develop an item response model and associated methods for parameter estimation and to apply this model (called the "normal ogive" model) successfully to real achievement and aptitude test data. More recently, the extentions of item response theory from the analysis of dichotomous data to polychotomous and continuous response data, and from unidimensional models to multidimensional models by Samejima (1969, 1972), have served as important theoretical breakthroughs in IRT that may eventually be useful practically (see, for example, Bejar, 1977).

Birnbaum (1957, 1958a, 1958b) substituted the more tractable logistic curves for the normal-ogive curves used by Lord (1952) and others and provided the necessary statistical developments for the logistic models to facilitate the use of these models by other psychometricians. Birnbaum's substantial work is of paramount importance to IRT. But progress in the 1950s and 1960s was painstakingly slow, in part due to the mathematical complexity of the field, the lack of convenient and efficient computer programs to analyze the data according to item response theory, and the general skepticism about the gains that might accrue from this particular line of research. However, important breakthroughs recently in problem areas such as test score equating (Lord, 1980a; Rentz & Bashaw, 1975; Wright & Stone, 1979), adaptive testing (Lord, 1974b, 1977a, 1980b; Weiss, 1976, 1978, 1980, 1982, 1983), test design and test evaluation (Lord, 1980a; Wright & Stone, 1979) through applications of item response theory have attracted considerable interest from measurement specialists. Other factors that have contributed to the current interest include the pioneering work of Georg Rasch (1960, 1966a, 1966b) in Denmark, the AERA instructional workshops on the Rasch model by Benjamin Wright and his colleagues and students for over 12 years, the availability of a number of useful computer programs (Wright & Mead, 1976; Wingersky, 1983; Wingersky, Barton, & Lord, 1982), publication of a variety of successful applications (Hambleton *et al.*, 1978; Lord, 1968; Rentz & Bashaw, 1977; Wright, 1968), and the strong endorsement of the field by authors of the last four reviews of test theory in *Annual Review of Psychology* (Keats, 1967; Bock & Wood, 1971; Lumsden, 1976; Weiss & Davidson, 1981). Another important stimulant for interest in the field was the publication of Lord and Novick's *Statistical Theories of Mental Test Scores* in 1968. They devoted five chapters (four of them written by Allen Birnbaum) to the topic of item response theory.

A clear indication of the current interest and popularity of the topic is the fact that the *Journal of Educational Measurement* published six invited papers on item response theory and its applications in the summer issue of 1977, *Applied Psychological Measurement* published a special issue in 1982 with seven technical advances in IRT (Hambleton & van der Linden, 1982), the Educational Research Institute of British Columbia published a monograph in early 1983 which described many promising applications of IRT (Hambleton, 1983a), several other IRT books are in preparation, and numerous theory and applications papers have been presented at the annual meetings of the American Educational Research Association and National Council on Measurement in Education over the last ten years (but especially the last five years).

Today, item response theory is being used by many of the large test publishers (Yen, 1983), state departments of education (Pandey & Carlson, 1983), and industrial and professional organizations (Guion & Ironson, 1983), to construct both norm-referenced and criterion-referenced tests, to investigate item bias, to equate tests, and to report test score information. In fact, the various applications have been so successful that discussions of item response theory have shifted from a consideration of their advantages and disadvantages in relation to classical test models to consideration of such matters as model selection, parameter estimation, and the determination of model-data fit. Nevertheless, it would be misleading to convey the impression that issues and technology associated with item response theory are fully developed and without controversy. Still, considerable progress has been made since the seminal papers by Frederic Lord (1952, 1953a, 1953b) for applying IRT to achievement and aptitude tests. It would seem that item response model technology is more than adequate at this time to serve a variety of uses (see, for example, Lord 1980a) and there are several computer programs available to carry out item response model analyses (see Hambleton & Cook, 1977).

1.3 Item Response Theory

Any theory of item responses supposes that, in testing situations, examinee performance on a test can be predicted (or explained) by defining examinee characteristics, referred to as *traits*, or *abilities*; estimating scores for examinees on these traits (called "ability scores"); and using the scores to predict or explain item and test performance (Lord & Novick, 1968). Since traits are not directly measurable, they are referred to as *latent traits* or *abilities*. An item response model specifies a relationship between the *observable* examinee test performance and the *unobservable* traits or abilities assumed to underlie performance on the test. Within the broad framework of item response theory, many models can be operationalized because of the large number of choices available for the mathematical form of the item characteristic curves. But, whereas item response theory cannot be shown to be correct or incorrect, the appropriateness of particular models with any set of test data can be established by conducting a suitable goodness of fit investigation. Assessing model-test data fit will be addressed in chapters 8 and 9. Characteristics of an item response model are summarized in figure 1–3.

The relationship between the "observable" and the "unobservable" quantities is described by a *mathematical function*. For this reason, item response models are *mathematical models*, which are based on specific assumptions about the test data. Different models, or item response models as they are called, are formed through specifying the assumptions one is willing to make about the test data set under investigation. For example, it

Figure 1–3. Characteristics of an Item Response Model

- It is a model which supposes that examinee performance on a test can be predicted (or explained) in terms of one or more characteristics referred to as traits.
- An item response model specifies a relationship between the observable examinee item performance and the traits or abilities assumed to underlie performance on the test.
- A successful item response model provides a means of estimating scores for examinees on the traits.
- The traits must be estimated (or inferred) from observable examinee performance on a set of test items. (It is for this reason that there is the reference to latent traits or abilities.)

may be reasonable to assume that a set of data can be fit by a model that assumes only one examinee factor or trait is influencing item performance.

In a general theory of latent traits, one supposes that underlying test performance is a set of traits that impact on that performance. An examinee's position or ability level on the ith trait is often denoted θ_i. The examinee's position in a k-dimensional latent space is represented by a vector of ability scores, denoted $(\theta_1, \theta_2, \theta_3, \ldots, \theta_k)$. It also is essential to specify the relationships between these traits and item and test performance. When the mathematical form of this relationship is specified, we have what is called a "model," or, more precisely, an "item response model." Change the mathematical form of the relationship and a new item response model emerges. There are, therefore, an infinite variety of item response models that might be considered under the framework of item response theory. McDonald (1982) provided a general framework not only for organizing existing models but also for generating many new models. His framework includes the consideration of (1) unidimensional and multidimensional models, (2) linear and non-linear models, and (3) dichotomous and multi-chotomous response models. Some of the most popular models to date will be presented in chapter 3.

1.4 Features of Item Response Models

In view of the complexities involved in applying item response models as compared to classical test models and procedures, and (as will be seen later) the restrictiveness of the assumptions underlying IRT models, one may ask: Why bother? After all, classical test models are well developed, have led to many important and useful results, and are based on *weak* assumptions. Classical test models can be applied to most (if not all) sets of mental test data. In contrast, item response models are based on *strong* assumptions, which limit their applicability to many mental test data sets.

Perhaps the most important advantage of unidimensional item response models (Wright, 1968; Bock & Wood, 1971) is that, given a set of test items that have been fitted to an item response model (that is, item parameters are known), it is possible to estimate an examinee's ability on the same ability scale from *any* subset of items in the domain of items that have been fitted to the model. The domain of items needs to be homogeneous in the sense of measuring a single ability: If the domain of items is too heterogenous, the ability estimates will have little meaning. Regardless of the number of items administered (as long as the number is not too small) or the statistical characteristics of the items, the ability estimate for each examinee will be an asymptotically unbiased estimate of true ability, provided the item response model fits the data set. Any variation in ability estimates obtained from different sets of test items is due to measurement errors only. Ability estimation independent of the particular choice (and number) of items represents one of the major advantages of item response models. Hence, item response models provide a way of comparing examinees even though they may have taken quite different subsets of test items. Once the assumptions of the model are satisfied, the advantages associated with the model can be gained.

There are three primary advantages (summarized in figure 1-4) of item response models: (1) Assuming the existence of a large pool of items all measuring the same trait, the estimate of an examinee's ability is independent of the particular sample of test items that are administered to the examinee, (2) assuming the existence of a large population of examinees, the descriptors of a test item (for example, item difficulty and discrimination indices) are independent of the particular sample of examinees drawn for the purpose of calibrating the item, and (3) a statistic indicating the precision with which each examinee's ability is estimated is provided. This statistic is free to vary from one examinee to another. Needless to say, the extent to which the three advantages are gained in an application of an item response model depends on the closeness of the "fit" between a set of test data and the model. If the fit is poor, these three desirable features either will not be obtained or will be obtained in a low degree. An additional desirable feature is that the concept of parallel forms reliability is replaced by the concept of statistical estimation and associated standard errors.

The feature of item parameter invariance can be observed in figure 1-5. In the upper part of the figure are three item characteristic curves; in the lower part are two distributions of ability. When the chosen model fits the data set, the same ICCs are obtained regardless of the distribution of ability in the sample of examinees used to estimate the item parameters. Notice that an

Figure 1-4.   Features of Item Response Models

When there is a close fit between the chosen item response model and the test data set of interest:

- Item parameter estimates are independent of the group of examinees used from the population of examinees for whom the test was designed.
- Examinee ability estimates are independent of the particular choice of test items used from the population of items which were calibrated.
- Precision of ability estimates are known.

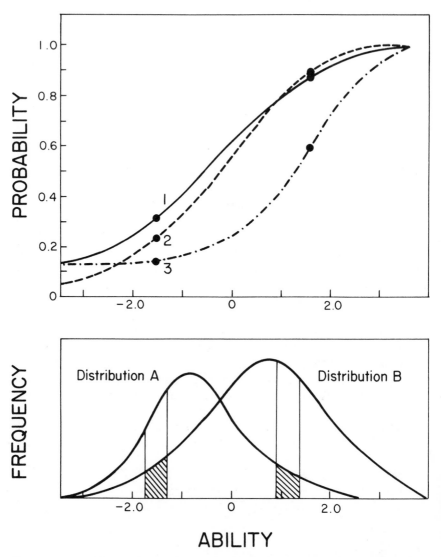

Figure 1-5. Three Item Characteristic Curves for Two Examinee Groups

ICC provides the probability of examinees at a given ability level answering each item correctly but the probability value does *not* depend on the number of examinees located at the ability level. The number of examinees at each ability level is different in the two distributions. But, the probability value is the same for examinees in each ability distribution or even in the combined distribution.

The property of invariance is not unique to IRT. It is a property which is obtained, for example whenever we study, the linear relationship (as reflected in a regression line) between two variables, X and Y. The hypothesis is made that a straight line can be used to connect the average Y scores conditional on the X scores. When, the hypothesis of a linear relationship is satisfied, the same linear regression line is expected regardless of the distribution of X scores in the sample drawn. Of course proper estimation of the line will require that a suitability heterogeneous group of examinees be chosen. The same situation arises in estimating the parameters for the item characteristic curves which are also regression lines (albeit, non-linear).

1.5 Summary

In review, item response theory postulates that (a) examinee test performance can be predicted (or explained) by a set of factors called traits, latent traits, or abilities, and (b) the relationship between examinee item performance and the set of traits assumed to be influencing item performance can be described by a monotonically increasing function called an *item characteristic function*. This function specifies that examinees with higher scores on the traits have higher expected probabilities for answering the item correctly than examinees with lower scores on the traits. In practice, it is common for users of item response theory to assume that there is one dominant factor or ability which explains performance. In the one-trait or one-dimensional model, the item characteristic function is called an *item characteristic curve* (ICC) and it provides the probability of examinees answering an item correctly for examinees at different points on the ability scale.

The goal of item response theory is to provide both invariant item statistics and ability estimates. These features will be obtained when there is a reasonable fit between the chosen model and the data set. Through the estimation process, items and persons are placed on the ability scale in such a way that there is as close a relationship as possible between the expected examinee probability parameters and the actual probabilities of performance for examinees positioned at each ability level. Item parameter estimates and examinee ability estimates are revised continually until the maximum agreement possible is obtained between predictions based on the ability and item parameter estimates and the actual test data.

The goal of this first chapter has been to provide an initial exposure to the topic of IRT. Several shortcomings of classical test theory that can be overcome by IRT were highlighted in the chapter. Also, basic IRT concepts, assumptions, and features were introduced. In the next two chapters, an expanded discussion of IRT models and their assumptions will be provided.

2 ASSUMPTIONS OF ITEM RESPONSE THEORY

2.1 Introduction

Any mathematical model includes a set of assumptions about the data to which the model applies, and specifies the relationships among observable and unobservable constructs described in the model. Consider as an example the well-known classical test model. With the classical test model, two unobservable constructs are introduced: true score and error score. The true score for an examinee can be defined as his or her expected test score over repeated administrations of the test (or parallel forms). An error score can be defined as the difference between true score and observed score. The classical test model also postulates that (1) error scores are random with a mean of zero and uncorrelated with error scores on a parallel test and with true scores, and (2) true scores, observed scores, and error scores are linearly related. Translating the above verbal statements into mathematical statements produces a test model with one equation:

$$x = t + e$$

where x, t, and e are observed, true, and error scores, respectively, and three assumptions are made:

1. $E(e) = 0$;
2. $\rho_{te} = 0$;
3. $\rho(e_1, e_2) = 0$, where e_1 and e_2 are error scores on two administrations of a test.

In this chapter, four common assumptions of item response models will be introduced along with some initial ideas on how the adequacy of the assumptions can be checked for any data set. One problem pointed out by Traub (1983) and which is endemic to social science research should be recognized at this juncture. There is no logical basis for ever concluding that the set of assumptions of a model are met by a dataset. In fact, the contrary situation applies. All of our statistical principles and methods for determining the viability of a set of assumptions are designed for rejecting the null-hypothesis about the appropriateness of assumptions for a dataset. The implication is that it must be recognized at the outset in working with IRT models that a logical basis does not exist for accepting the viability of a set of assumptions. Determining the adequacy with which a test dataset fits a particular set of model assumptions will be useful information to have when choosing a model. When the assumptions of a model cannot be met, the model-data fit will often be poor, and so the model will be of questionable value in any application. Readers are referred to Traub (1983) for an important discussion of the problems of model-data misfit, and the impact of systematic errors on various applications of the models. An extensive discussion of methods for assessing the adequacy of a set of assumptions will be presented in chapter 8.

2.2 Dimensionality of the Latent Space

In a general theory of latent traits, it is assumed that a set of k latent traits or abilities underlie examinee performance on a set of test items. The k latent traits define a k dimensional latent space, with each examinee's location in the latent space being determined by the examinee's position on each latent trait. The latent space is referred to as *complete* if all latent traits influencing the test scores of a population of examinees have been specified.

It is commonly assumed that only one ability or trait is necessary to "explain," or "account" for examinee test performance. Item response models that assume a single latent ability are referred to as *unidimensional*. Of course, this assumption cannot be strictly met because there are always other cognitive, personality, and test-taking factors that impact on test performance, at least to some extent. These factors might include level of motivation, test anxiety, ability to work quickly, knowledge of the correct use of answer sheets, other cognitive skills in addition to the dominant one measured by the set of test items, etc. What is required for this assumption to be met adequately by a set of test data is a "dominant" component or factor that influences test performance. This dominant component or factor is referred to as the ability measured by the test.

Often researchers are interested in monitoring the performance of individuals or groups on a trait over some period of time. For example, at the individual (or group) level, interest may be centered on the amount of individual (group) change in reading comprehension over a school year. National Assessment of Educational Progress is responsible for monitoring the growth on many educational variables over extended periods of time. The topic of measuring growth is a controversial one and fraught with substantive and technical problems. Our intent is *not* to draw special attention to these problems here but only to note that when IRT is used to define the underlying trait or ability scale on which growth is measured, the unidimensionality assumption must be checked at each time point *and* it must be determined that the *same* trait is being measured at *each* time point. Traub (1983) has described how the nature of training and education can influence the dimensionality of a set of test items. For example, with respect to education, Traub (1983) has noted:

> The curriculum and the method by which it is taught vary from student to student, even within the same class. Out-of-school learning experiences that are relevant to in-school learning vary widely over students. Individual differences in previous learning, quality of sensory organs, and presumably also quality of neural systems contribute to, if they do not totally define, individual differences in aptitude and intelligence. It seems reasonable then to expect differences of many kinds, some obvious, some subtle, in what it is different students learn, both in school and outside. How these differences are translated into variation in the performance of test items that themselves relate imperfectly to what has been taught and learned, and thus into the dimensionality of inferred latent space, is not well understood.

Models assuming that more than a single ability is necessary to adequately account for examinee test performance are referred to as *multidimensional*. The reader is referred to the work of Mulaik (1972) and Samejima (1974) for discussions of multidimensional item response models. These models will not be discussed further in this book because their technical developments are limited and applications not possible at this time.

The assumption of a unidimensional latent space is a common one for test constructors since they usually desire to construct unidimensional tests so as to enhance the interpretability of a set of test scores. What does it mean to say that a test is unidimensional in a population of examinees? Suppose a test consisting of n items is intended for use in r subpopulations of examinees (e.g., several ethnic groups). Consider the conditional distributions of test scores at a particular ability level for several subpopulations. Figure 2–1 provides an illustration of a conditional distribution at a particular ability level in one subpopulation of examinees. The curve shown is the nonlinear regression of test score performance on ability. Notice that there is a spread of test scores about the regression line. The variability is probably due, mainly, to measurement errors in the test scores. The distribution of test scores at each ability level is known as the conditional distribution of test scores for an ability level.

Next, consider the nonlinear regression lines for several subpopulations of examinees. These conditional distributions for the r subpopulations ($r = 3$ in figure 2-2) will be identical *if* the test is unidimensional. If the conditional

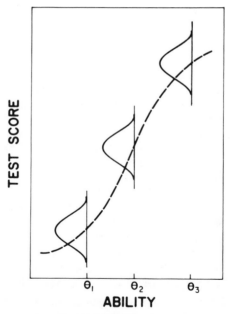

Figure 2-1. Conditional Distributions of Test Scores at Three Ability Levels

distributions vary across the several subpopulations, it can be only because the test is measuring something other than the single ability. No other explanation will suffice. Hence, the test cannot be unidimensional. In situation (1) in figure 2–2, the test is functioning differently in the three subpopulations (denoted, Groups A, B, and C). Since at a given ability level, the test is functioning differently (notice that the conditional distributions in the three groups are different), other abilities beside the one measured on the horizontal axis must be affecting test performance. Otherwise, the three regression lines would be equal. In situation (2) the test must be unidimensional since no difference in test performance is shown once the ability measured on the horizontal axis is controlled for.

It is possible for a test to be unidimensional within one population of examinees and not unidimensional in another. Consider a test with a heavy cultural loading. This test could appear to be unidimensional for all populations with the same cultural background, but, when administered to populations with varied cultural backgrounds, the test may in fact have more than a single dimension underlying test performance. Examples of this situation are seen when the factor structure of a particular set of test items varies from one cultural group to another. Another common example occurs when reading comprehension is a factor in solving math problems. In one subpopulation in which all examinees are able to comprehend the questions, the only trait affecting test performance is math ability. Suppose that reading proficiency is lower in a second subpopulation so that *not* all examinees will fully comprehend the questions. In this situation, both math ability and reading comprehension skill will impact on test performance. For a given math ability level, the conditional distribution of scores in the two subpopulations will differ.

Basically, there are two different views on the applications of item response models. Some researchers prefer to choose a model and then select test items to fit that chosen model, an approach for which advocates make extensive use of their preferred models in test development (e.g. Wright, Traub (1983) and others have spoken out strongly against such an approach. For example Traub (1983) says:

> It will be a sad day indeed when our conception of measurable educational achievement narrows to the point where it coincides with the criterion of fit to a unidimensional item response model, regardless of which model is being fitted.

An alternative perspective is one in which content domains of interest are specified by the test developer and then an item response model is located

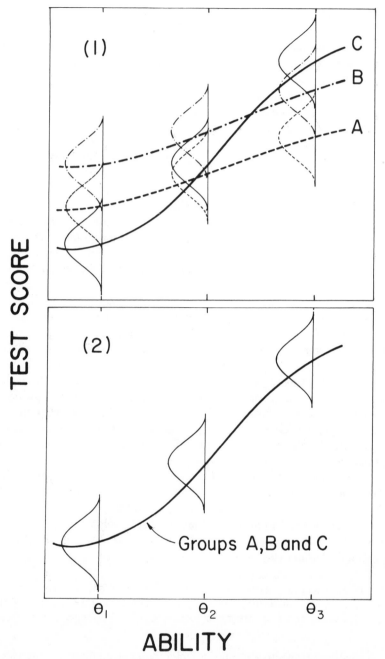

Figure 2-2. Conditional Distributions of Test Scores at Three Ability Levels for Three Groups (A, B, C) in Two Situations

later to fit the test as constructed. This approach will be described in detail in Chapter 8.

With respect to the former approach, Lumsden (1961) provided an excellent review of methods for constructing unidimensional tests. He concluded that the method of factor analysis held the most promise. Fifteen years later, he reaffirmed his conviction (Lumsden, 1976). Essentially, Lumsden recommends that a test constructor generate an initial pool of test items selected on the basis of empirical evidence and a priori grounds. Such an item selection procedure will increase the likelihood that a unidimensional set of test items within the pool of items can be found. If test items are not preselected, the pool may be too heterogeneous for the unidimensional set of items in the item pool to emerge. In Lumsden's method, a factor analysis is performed and items not measuring the dominant factor obtained in the factor solution are removed. The remaining items are factor analyzed, and, again, "deviant" items are removed. The process is repeated until a satisfactory solution is obtained. Convergence is most likely when the initial item pool is carefully selected to include only items that appear to be measuring a common trait. Lumsden proposed that the ratio of first-factor variance to second-factor variance be used as an "index of unidimensionality."

Factor analysis can also be used to check the reasonableness of the assumption of unidimensionality with a set of test items (Hambleton & Traub, 1973). This approach, however, is not without problems. For example, much has been written about the merits of using tetrachoric correlations or phi correlations (McDonald & Ahlawat, 1974). A phi correlation is a measure of the relationship between two dichotomous variables. The formula is a special case of the Pearson correlation coefficient. The common belief is that using phi correlations will lead to a factor solution with too many factors, some of them "difficulty factors" found because of the range of item difficulties among the items in the test. McDonald and Ahlawat (1974) concluded that "difficulty factors" are unlikely if the range of item difficulties is not extreme and the items are not too highly discriminating.

A tetrachoric correlation is a measure of the relationship between two dichotomous variables where it is assumed that performance underlying each variable is normally distributed. Except in the simple and unlikely situation in which 50 percent of the candidates receive each score for each variable, the computational formula for the tetrachoric correlation is very complex and, except in some special cases, involves numerical integration techniques. Tetrachoric correlations have one attractive feature: A sufficient condition for the unidimensionality of a set of items is that the matrix of tetrachoric item intercorrelations has only one common factor (Lord & Novick, 1968).

On the negative side, the condition is not necessary. Also, tetrachoric correlations do not necessarily yield a correlation matrix that is positive definite, a problem when factor analysis is attempted.

It may be useful to remind readers at this point that to say that a test measures a "unidimensional trait" does not in any way indicate what that trait is. For example, consider the following four item test:

1. What is your height? (Circle one)
    (a) less than two feet, (b) over two feet
2. What is the sum of $1 + 1$? _____
3. Name two presidents of the United States.
    (1) _____ (2) _____
4. Solve the integration problem

$$\int \frac{e^x}{\sqrt{x^2 + 1}} \, d_x.$$

Examinee performance on the four item test will be unidimensional, since apart from measurement error, only five response patterns will emerge:

1. 0 0 0 0
2. 1 0 0 0
3. 1 1 0 0
4. 1 1 1 0
5. 1 1 1 1

It is difficult to conceive of any other patterns emerging, except those patterns which were the result of carelessness on the part of examinees.

The data clearly fit the pattern of a unidimensional test (also known as a Guttman scale), but the researcher would have a difficult time in identifying what that unidimensional trait is. In chapter 4 the matter of identifying and validating traits will be considered.

2.3 Local Independence

There is an assumption equivalent to the assumption of unidimensionality known as the *assumption of local independence*. This assumption states that an examinee's responses to different items in a test are statistically independent. For this assumption to be true, an examinee's performance on one item must not affect, either for better or for worse, his or her responses to any other items in the test. For example, the content of an item must not provide clues to the answers of other test items. When local independence exists, the probability of any pattern of item scores occurring for an examinee is simply the product of the probability of occurrence of the scores on *each* test item. For example, the probability of the occurrence of the five-item response pattern $u = (1\ 0\ 1\ 1\ 0)$, where 1 denotes a correct response and 0 an incorrect response, is equal to $P_1 \cdot (1 - P_2) \cdot P_3 \cdot P_4 \cdot (1 - P_5)$, where P_i is the probability that the examinee will respond correctly to item i and $1 - P_i$ is the probability that the examinee will respond incorrectly. But test data must satisfy other properties if they are to be consistent with the assumption of local independence. The order of presentation of test items must not impact on test performance. Some research supports the position that item order can impact on performance (Hambleton & Traub, 1974; Yen, 1980). Also, test data must be unidimensional. Performance across test items at a fixed ability level will be correlated when a second ability or more than two abilities are being measured by the test items. For examinees located at an ability level, examinees with higher scores on a second ability measured by a set of test items are more apt to answer items correctly than examinees with lower scores on the second ability.

If U_i, $i = 1, 2, \ldots, n$, represent the binary responses (1, if correct; 0 if incorrect) of an examinee to a set of n test items, $P_i =$ the probability of a correct answer by an examinee to item i, and $Q_i = 1 - P_i$, then the assumption of local independence leads to the following statement:

$$\text{Prob}\,[U_1 = u_1,\ U_2 = u_2, \ldots,\ U_n = u_n \,|\, \theta] = \text{Prob}\,[U_1 = u_1 \,|\, \theta]$$
$$\text{Prob}\,[U_2 = u_2 \,|\, \theta] \ldots \text{Prob}\,[U_n = u_n \,|\, \theta].$$

If we set $P_i(\theta) = \text{Prob}\,[U_i = 1 \,|\, \theta]$ and $Q_i(\theta) = \text{Prob}\,[U_i = 0 \,|\, \theta]$, then

$$\text{Prob}\,[U_1 = u_1,\ U_2 = u_2, \ldots U_n = u_n \,|\, \theta]$$
$$= P_1(\theta)^{u_1} Q_1(\theta)^{1-u_1} P_2(\theta)^{u_2} Q_2(\theta)^{1-u_2} \ldots P_n(\theta)^{u_n} Q_n(\theta)^{1-u_n}$$
$$= \prod_{i=1}^{n} P_i(\theta)^{u_i} Q_i(\theta)^{1-u_i}. \tag{2.1}$$

In words, the assumption of local independence applies when the probability of the response pattern for each examinee is equal to the product of the probability associated with the examinee response to each item.

One result of the assumption of local independence is that the frequency of test scores of examinees of fixed ability (conditional distribution of test scores for a fixed ability), denoted θ, is given by

$$f(x\,|\,\theta) = \sum_{\Sigma u_i = x} \prod_{i\,=\,1}^{n} P_i(\theta)^{u_i} Q_i(\theta)^{1-u_i} \qquad (2.2)$$

where x is an examinee's test score, can take on values from 0 to n.

One should note that the assumption of local independence for the case when θ is unidimensional and the assumption of a unidimensional latent space are equivalent. First, suppose a set of test items measures a common ability. Then, for examinees at a fixed ability level θ, item responses are statistically independent. For fixed ability level θ, if items were not statistically independent, it would imply that some examinees have higher expected test scores than other examinees of the same ability level. Consequently, more than one ability would be necessary to account for examinee test performance. This is a clear violation of the original assumption that the items were unidimensional. Second, the assumption of local independence implies that item responses are statistically independent for examinees at a fixed ability level. Therefore, only one ability is necessary to account for the relationship among a set of test items.

It is important to note that the assumption of local independence does *not* imply that test items are uncorrelated over the total group of examinees (Lord & Novick, 1968, p. 361). Positive correlations between pairs of items will result whenever there is variation among the examinees on the ability measured by the test items. But item scores are uncorrelated at a fixed ability level.

Because of the equivalence between the assumptions of local independence and of the unidimensionality of the latent space, the extent to which a set of test items satisfies the assumption of local independence can also be studied using factor analytic techniques. Also, a rough check on the statistical independence of item responses for examinees at the same ability level was offered by Lord (1953a). His suggestion was to consider examinee item responses for examinees within a narrow range of ability. For each pair of items, a χ^2 statistic can be calculated to provide a measure of the independence of item responses. If the proportion of examinees obtaining each response pattern (00, 01, 10, 11) can be "predicted" from the marginals for the group of examinees, the item responses on the two items are statistically independent. The value of the χ^2 statistic can be computed for each pair of items, summed, and tested for significance. The process would be repeated for examinees located in different regions of the ability continuum.

In concluding this section it is desirable for us to draw attention to some recent work by McDonald (1980a, 1980b, 1982) on definitions for unidimensionality and the equivalence of assumptions concerning uni-dimensionality and local independence. In McDonald's judgment (and we concur), a meaningful definition of unidimensionality should be *based* on the principle (or assumption) of local independence. McDonald defined a set of test items as *unidimensional* if, for examinees with the same ability, the covariation between items in the set is zero. Since the covariation between items is typically non-linear, he recommended the use of non-linear factor analysis (see McDonald, 1967) to study the covariation between items. Some recent work by Hambleton and Rovinelli (1983) provides support for McDonald's recommendation of non-linear factor analysis. Readers are referred to an extensive review of the literature by Hattie (1981) on definitions of unidimensionality and approaches for assessing it.

2.4 Item Characteristic Curves

The frequency distribution of a binary item score for fixed ability θ can be written:

$$f_i(u_i \mid \theta) = P_i(\theta)^{u_i} Q_i(\theta)^{1-u_i}$$

since

$$f_i(u_i \mid \theta) = P_i(\theta) \quad \text{if } u_i = 1,$$

and

$$f_i(u_i \mid \theta) = Q_i(\theta) \quad \text{if } u_i = 0. \tag{2.3}$$

The "curve" connecting the means of the conditional distributions, repre-sented by equation (2.3), is the regression of item score on ability and is referred to as an *item characteristic curve* or *item characteristic function*. An item characteristic curve (ICC) is a mathematical function that relates the probability of success on an item to the ability measured by the item set or test that contains it. In simple terms, it is the nonlinear regression function of item score on the trait or ability measured by the test. The main difference to be found among currently popular item response models is in the mathematical form of $P_i(\theta)$, the ICC. It is up to the test developer or IRT user to choose one of the many mathematical functions to serve as the form of the ICCs. In doing so, an assumption is being made that can be verified later by how well the chosen model accounts for the test results. If both item and ability scores for a population of examinees were known, the form of an ICC could be discovered from a consideration of the distribution of item scores at fixed levels of ability. The mean of each distribution could be computed. The curve connecting the means of these conditional distributions would be the regression of item score on ability. When only one latent ability is being measured, this regression is referred to as an ICC; when the latent ability space is multidimensional, the regression has been referred to as the item characteristic function. It is usually expected that the regression of item scores on ability is nonlinear, but, as we will see very soon, this has not stopped theorists from developing an item response model having a linear ICC.

If the complete latent space is defined for the examinee population of interest, the conditional distributions of item scores at fixed ability levels must be identical across these populations. If the conditional distributions are identical, then the curves connecting the means of these distributions must be identical; i.e., the item characteristic curve will remain invariant across populations of examinees for which the complete latent space has been defined.

Since the probability of an individual examinee providing a correct answer to an item depends only on the form of the item characteristic curve, this probability is *independent* of the distribution of examinee ability in the population of examinees of interest. Thus, the probability of a correct response to an item by an examinee will not depend on the number of examinees located at the same ability level. This invariance property of item characteristic curves in the population of examinees for whom the items were calibrated is one of the attractive characteristics of item response models. The invariance of item response model parameters has important implications for tailored testing, item banking, the study of item bias, and other applications of item response theory.

It is common to interpret $P_i(\theta)$ as the probability of an examinee answering item i correctly. But such an interpretation may be incorrect. For example, consider a candidate of middle ability who knows the answer to a medium difficult item. The model would suggest that $P_i(\theta)$ for the examinee may be close to .50, but for this examinee across independent administrations of the test item, the estimated probability would be close to 1.0. Lord (1974a, 1980a) provided an example to show that this common interpretation of $P_i(\theta)$ leads to an awkward situation. Consider two examinees, A and B, and two items, i and j. Suppose examinee A knows the answer to item i and does not know the answer to item j. Consider the situation to be reversed for examinee B. Then, $P_i(\theta_A) = 1$, $P_j(\theta_A) = 0$, $P_i(\theta_B) = 0$, $P_j(\theta_B) = 1$. The first two equations suggest that item i is easier than item j. The other two equations suggest the reverse conclusion. One interpretation is that items i and j measure different abilities for the two examinees. Of course, this would make it impossible to compare the two students. One reasonable solution to the dilemma is to define the meaning of $P_i(\theta)$ differently. Lord suggests that $P_i(\theta)$ be interpreted as the probability of a correct response for the examinee across test items with nearly identical item parameters. An alternative interpretation of $P_i(\theta)$ is as the probability of a correct answer to item i across a group of examinees at ability level θ. Perhaps a third interpretation is the most useful; $P_i(\theta)$ can be viewed as the probability associated with a randomly selected examinee at θ answering item i correctly. In the remainder of this text, whenever a statement like "the probability of examinee A answering the item correctly is 50%" is made, assume that the student was chosen at random.

Each item characteristic curve for a particular item response model is a member of a family of curves of the same general form. The number of parameters required to describe an item characteristic curve will depend on the particular item response model. It is common, though, for the number of parameters to be one, two, or three. For example, the item characteristic curve of the latent linear model shown as illustration C in figure 2–3 has the general form $P_i(\theta) = b_i + a_i\theta$, where $P_i(\theta)$ designates the probability of a correct response to item i by a randomly-chosen examinee with ability level, θ. The function is described by two item parameters, item difficulty and item discrimination, denoted b and a, respectively. An item characteristic curve is defined completely when its general form is specified and when the parameters of the curve for a particular item are known. Item characteristic curves of the latent linear model will vary in their intercepts (b_i) and slopes (a_i) to reflect the fact that the test items vary in "difficulty" and "discriminating power." Notice that with higher values of b the probability of correct responses increases as well. If $b = -.25$, $a = .50$ and $\theta = 2$, $P(\theta) = .75$. When the value of b is increased by .15 to a value of $-.10$, $P(\theta) = .90$. The intercept parameter is directly related to the concept of item difficulty in classical test theory. Also, the "a" parameter functions in a

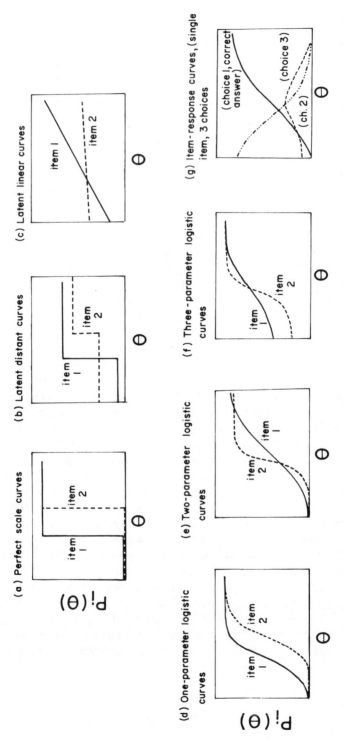

Figure 2-3. Seven Examples of Item Characteristic Curves (From Hambleton, R. K., & Cook, L. L. Latent trait models and their use in the analysis of educational test data. *Journal of Educational Measurement*, 1977, *14*, 76-96. Copyright 1977, National Council on Measurement in Education, Washington, D.C. Reprinted with permission.)

similar way to an item discrimination index in classical test theory. The difference between the probabilities of a correct response at any two ability levels increases directly with the value of a. For example, consider $P(\theta)$ for $\theta = 1$ and $\theta = 2$ with $b = -.10$, and $a = .20$, and then $a = .50$:

$$P(\theta)$$

		$\theta = 1$	$\theta = 2$
$b = -.10$	$a = .20$	.10	.30
$b = -.10$	$a = .50$	.40	.90

The discriminating power of the item is considerably better with the higher a value, or correspondingly, poorer with the lower a value.

A major problem with linear ICCs is that they cannot be too steep or they will result in probability estimates that are not on the interval $(0,1)$. For this reason, nonlinear ICCs have proven to be more useful. The latent linear model is developed in some detail by Lazarsfeld and Henry (1968) and Torgerson (1958).

Item characteristic curves for Guttman's *perfect scale model* are shown in figure 2–3(a). These curves take the shape of step functions; probabilities of correct responses are either 0 to 1. The critical ability level $\theta*$ is the point on the ability scale where probabilities change from 0 to 1. Different items lead to different values of $\theta*$. When $\theta*$ is high, we have a difficult item. Easy items correspond to low values of $\theta*$. Figure 2–3(b) describes a variation on Guttman's perfect scale model. Item characteristic curves take the shape of step functions, but the probabilities of incorrect and correct responses, in general, differ from 0 to 1. This model, known as the latent distance model, has been used also by social psychologists in the measurement of attitudes.

Illustrations (d), (e), and (f) in figure 2-3 show "S" shaped ICCs which are associated with the one-, two-, and three-parameter logistic models, respectively. With the *one-parameter logistic model*, the item characteristic curves are nonintersecting curves that differ only by a translation along the ability scale. Items with such characteristic curves vary only in their difficulty. With the *two-parameter logistic model*, item characteristic curves vary in both slope (some curves increase more rapidly than others; i.e., the corresponding test items are more discriminating than others) and translation along the ability scale (some items are more difficulty than others). Finally, with the *three-parameter logistic model*, curves may differ in slope, translation, *and* lower asymptote. With the one- and two-parameter logistic curves, the probabilities of correct responses range from 0 to 1. In the three-parameter model, the lower asymptote, in general, is greater than 0. When guessing is a factor in test performance, this feature of the item characteristic curve can improve the "fit" between the test data and the model. In other models such as the *nominal response model* and the *graded response model*, there are *item option characteristic curves*. A curve depicting the probability of an item option being selected as a function of ability is produced for *each* option or choice in the test item. An example of this situation is depicted in illustration (g) in figure 2-3.

It is common for IRT users to specify the mathematical form of the item characteristic curves before beginning their work. But, it is not easy to check on the appropriateness of the choice because item characteristic curves represent the regression of item scores on a variable (ability) that is *not* directly measurable. About the only way the assumption can be checked is to study the "validity" of the predictions with the item characteristic curves (Hambleton & Traub, 1973; Ross, 1966). If the predictions are acceptable, the ICC assumption was probably reasonable; if predictions are poor, the assumption probably was not reasonable.

2.5 Speededness

An implicit assumption of all commonly used item response models is that the tests to which the models are fit are not administered under speeded conditions. That is, examinees who fail to answer test items do so because of limited ability and not because they failed to reach test items. This assumption is perhaps seldom stated because it is implicit in the assumption of unidimensionality. When speed affects test performance, then at least *two* traits are impacting on test performance: speed of performance, and the trait measured by the test content. The extent to which a test is speeded can be assessed crudely by counting the number of examinees who fail to complete the set of administered test items.

2.6 Summary

The purpose of this chapter has been to provide an introductory discussion of the main assumptions of many item response models and describe some approaches for assessing the viability of these assumptions with real data. Mathematical equations for the item characteristic curves with several of the item response models introduced in this chapter will be given in the next chapter. Readers are also referred to the excellent chapter by Bejar (1983).

3 ITEM RESPONSE MODELS

3.1 Introduction

The purpose of this chapter is to introduce a wide array of mathematical models that have been used in the analysis of educational and psychological test data. Each model consists of (1) an equation linking (observable) examinee item performance and a latent (unobservable) ability and (2) several of the assumptions described in chapter 2 plus others that will be described. To date, most of the IRT models have been developed for use with binary-scored aptitude and achievement test data. In this chapter, models that can be applied to multicategory scored items (e.g., Likert five-point attitude scales) and continuous data will be briefly described.

3.2 Nature of the Test Data

One of the ways in which IRT models can be classified is on the basis of the examinee responses to which they can be applied. Three response levels are common: dichotomous, multi-chotomous, and continuous.

Over the years multiple-choice test items with dichotomous scoring have become the main mode through which educational assessments have been made. However, there are other types of items for which dichotomous scoring systems are used: true-false, short answer, sentence completion, and matching items. With psychological assessments, again, dichotomous data are often obtained but from "true-false," "forced-choice" or "agree-disagree" rating scales. Even free-response data can be subjected to a dichotomous scoring system. The majority of the presently available item response models handle binary-scored data. To use these models, we sometimes force a binary scoring system on multichotomous response data. This may be done by combining the available scoring categories so that only two are used.

Somewhat less common in present measurement practices are multichotomous or polychotomous scoring systems. These systems arise, for example, when scoring weights are attached to the possible responses to multiple-choice test items. The scoring system for essay questions is usually polychotomous as is the scoring system for Likert scales. With essay questions, points are assigned either to reflect the overall quality of an essay or to reflect the presence of desirable characteristics such as correct spelling, grammatical structure, originality, and so on. The nominal response and graded response models are available to handle polychotomous response data.

Finally, continuous scoring systems occasionally arise in practice. Here, an examinee or rater places a mark ($\sqrt{}$) at a point on some continuous rating rating scale. Even though the responses from this type of rating scale can easily be categorized and fit a polychotomous response model, some information is lost in the process (Samejima, 1972).

3.3 Commonly Used Item Response Models

The purpose of this section is to introduce several of the commonly used item response models. These models, along with the principal developers, are identified in figure 3–1. All models assume that the principle of local independence applies and (equivalently) that the items in the test being fitted by a model measure a common ability. A significant distinction among the models is in the mathematical form taken by the item characteristic curves. A second important distinction among the models is the scoring.

Deterministic models (for example, Guttman's perfect scale model) are of no interest to us here because they are not likely to fit most achievement and

Figure 3-1.   Summary of Commonly Used Unidimensional Models

Nature of the Data	Model	References
Dichotomous	Latent Linear	Lazarsfeld & Henry (1968)
	Perfect Scale	Guttman (1944)
	Latent Distance	Lazarsfeld & Henry (1968)
	One-, Two-, Three- Parameter Normal Ogive	Lord (1952)
	One-, Two-, Three- Parameter Logistic	Birnbaum (1957, 1958a, 1958b, 1968), Lord & Novick (1968), Lord (1980a), Rasch (1960), Wright & Stone (1979)
	Four-Parameter Logistic	McDonald (1967), Barton & Lord (1981)
Multicategory Scoring	Nominal Response	Bock (1972)
	Graded Response	Samejima (1969)
	Partial Credit Model	Master (1982)
Continuous	Continuous Response	Samejima (1972)

aptitude test data very well. Test items rarely discriminate well enough to be fit by a deterministic model (Lord, 1974a).

3.3.1 Two-Parameter Normal Ogive Model

Lord (1952, 1953a) proposed an item response model (although he was not the first psychometrician to do so) in which the item characteristic curve took the form of a two-parameter normal ogive:

$$P_i(\theta) = \int_{-\infty}^{a_i(\theta - b_i)} \frac{1}{\sqrt{2\pi}} e^{-z^2/2} dz, \qquad (3.1)$$

where $P_i(\theta)$ is the probability that a randomly selected examinee with ability θ answers item i correctly, b_i and a_i are parameters characterizing item i, and

z is a normal deviate from a distribution with mean b_i and standard deviation $1/a_i$. The result is a monotonically increasing function of ability. The parameter b_i is usually referred to as the index of *item difficulty* and represents the point on the ability scale at which an examinee has a 50 percent probability of answering item i correctly. The parameter a_i, called *item discrimination*, is proportional to the slope of $P_i(\theta)$ at the point $\theta = b_i$.

When the ability scores for a group are transformed so that their mean is zero and the standard deviation is one, the values of b vary (typically) from about -2.0 to $+2.0$. Values of b near -2.0 correspond to items that are very easy, and values of b near 2.0 correspond to items that are very difficult for the group of examinees. For the same reasons that z-scores are usually transformed to more convenient scales (to avoid decimals and negatives), transforming ability scores and/or item parameter estimates to more convenient scales is common. A method for accomplishing the transformation correctly is described in the next chapter.

The item discrimination parameter, a_i, is defined, theoretically, on the scale $(-\infty, +\infty)$. However, negatively discriminating items are discarded from ability tests. Also, it is unusual to obtain a_i values larger than two. Hence, the usual range for item discrimination parameters is (0, 2). High values of a_i result in item characteristic curves that are very "steep," while low values of a_i lead to item characteristic curves that increase gradually as a function of ability.

3.3.2 Two-Parameter Logistic Model

Birnbaum (1957, 1958a, 1958b, 1968) proposed an item response model in which the item characteristic curves take the form of two-parameter logistic distribution functions:

$$P_i(\theta) = \frac{e^{Da_i(\theta - b_i)}}{1 + e^{Da_i(\theta - b_i)}} \qquad (i = 1, 2, \ldots, n). \qquad (3.2)$$

Appendix A was prepared to provide readers with some familiarity with logistic distribution functions. Values of $e^x/1 + e^x$ for $x = -4$ to $+4$ in increments of .10 are reported.

There is an alternative way to write $P_i(\theta)$ above. If the numerator and denominator of equation (3.2) are multiplied by $e^{-Da_i(\theta - b_i)}$, then $P_i(\theta)$ becomes

$$P_i(\theta) = \frac{1}{1 + e^{-Da_i(\theta - b_i)}},$$

which can be written as

$$P_i(\theta) = [1 + e^{-Da_i(\theta - b_i)}]^{-1}.$$

A final alternative is to write

$$P_i(\theta) = \{1 + \exp[-Da_i(\theta - b_i)]\}^{-1}$$

This latter format will be adopted in subsequent chapters of the book.

Birnbaum substituted the two-parameter logistic cumulative distribution function for the two-parameter normal ogive function as the form of the item characteristic curve. Logistic curves have the important advantage of being more convenient to work with than normal ogive curves. Statisticians would say that the logistic model is more "mathematically tractable" than the normal ogive model because the latter involves an integration while the former is an explicit function of item and ability parameters. $P_i(\theta)$, b_i, a_i, and θ have essentially the same interpretation as in the normal ogive model. The constant D is a scaling factor. It has been shown that when $D = 1.7$, values of $P_i(\theta)$ for the two-parameter normal ogive and the two-parameter logistic models differ absolutely by less than .01 for all values of θ (Haley, 1952).

An inspection of the two-parameter normal ogive and logistic test models reveals an implicit assumption that is characteristic of most item response models: Guessing does not occur. This must be so since for all items with $a_i > 0$ (that is, items for which there is a positive relationship between performance on the test item and the ability measured by the test), the probability of a correct response to the item decreases to zero as ability decreases.

3.3.3 Three-Parameter Logistic Model

The three-parameter logistic model can be obtained from the two-parameter model by adding a third parameter, denoted c_i. The mathematical form of the three-parameter logistic curve is written

$$P_i(\theta) = c_i + (1 - c_i)\frac{e^{Da_i(\theta - b_i)}}{1 + e^{Da_i(\theta - b_i)}} \qquad (i = 1, 2, \ldots, n),$$

$$(3.3)$$

where:

$P_i(\theta)$ = the probability that an examinee with ability level θ answers item i correctly;

b_i = the item difficulty parameter;

a_i = the item discrimination parameter;

$D = 1.7$ (a scaling factor).

The parameter c_i is the lower asymptote of the item characteristic curve and represents the probability of examinees with low ability correctly answering an item. The parameter c_i is included in the model to account for item response data from low-ability examinees, where, among other things, guessing is a factor in test performance. It is now common to refer to the parameter c_i as the *pseudo-chance level* parameter in the model.

Typically, c_i assumes values that are smaller than the value that would result if examinees of low ability were to guess randomly to the item. As Lord (1974a) has noted, this phenomenon can probably be attributed to the ingenuity of item writers in developing "attractive" but incorrect choices. Low ability examinees are attracted to these incorrect answer choices. They would score higher by randomly guessing the correct answers. For this reason, avoidance of the label "guessing parameter" to describe the parameter c_i seems desirable.

Figure 3–2 provides an example of a typical three-parameter model item characteristic curve. The b-value for the test item is located at the point on the ability scale where the slope of the ICC is a maximum. The slope of the curve at b equals $.425\ a(1 - c)$, where a is the discriminating power of the item. High values of a result in steeper ICCs. This point is easily seen from a review of figures 3-3 to 3-12. The lower asymptote, which is measured on the probability scale, is c, which indicates the probability of a correct answer from low-ability examinees. Notice that when the c parameter $= 0$, the probability associated with a correct response at b on the ability scale is $(1 + c)/2$. When $c = 0$, that probability is 50 percent. At other times that $c > 0$, the probability exceeds 50 percent.

To obtain the two-parameter logistic model from the three-parameter logistic model, it must be assumed that the pseudo-chance level parameters have zero-values. This assumption is most plausible with free response items but it can often be approximately met when a test is not too difficult for the examinees. For example, the assumption of minimal guessing is likely to be met when competency tests are administered to students following effective instruction.

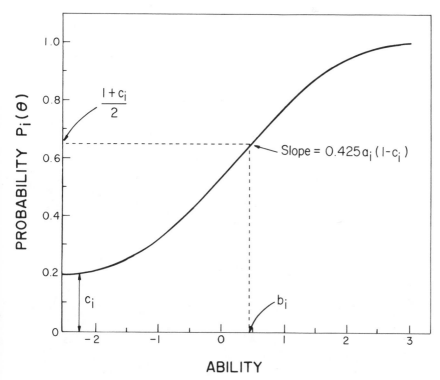

Figure 3-2. A Typical Three-Parameter Model Item Characteristic Curve

Table 3–1 provides the item parameters for 10 sets of items. For the first five sets, $c = 0$; for the second five sets, $c = .25$. Within each set, the items are located at five levels of difficulty. Also, from sets 1 to 5, and sets 6 to 10, the items have increasing levels of discriminating power. The corresponding item characteristic curves are represented in figures 3-3 to 3-12.

3.3.4 One-Parameter Logistic Model (Rasch Model)

In the last decade especially, many researchers have become aware of the work in the area of item response models by Georg Rasch, a Danish mathematician (Rasch, 1966), both through his own publications and the papers of others advancing his work (Anderson, Kearney, & Everett, 1968; Wright, 1968, 1977a, 1977b; Wright & Panchapakesan, 1969; Wright &

Table 3-1.   Three-Parameter Item Statistics

| Figure | Item | Item Statistics | | |
		b	a	c
3–3	1	−2.00	.19	.00
	2	−1.00	.19	.00
	3	0.00	.19	.00
	4	1.00	.19	.00
	5	2.00	.19	.00
3–4	1	−2.00	.59	.00
	2	−1.00	.59	.00
	3	0.00	.59	.00
	4	1.00	.59	.00
	5	2.00	.59	.00
3–5	1	−2.00	.99	.00
	2	−1.00	.99	.00
	3	0.00	.99	.00
	4	1.00	.99	.00
	5	2.00	.99	.00
3–6	1	−2.00	1.39	.00
	2	−1.00	1.39	.00
	3	0.00	1.39	.00
	4	1.00	1.39	.00
	5	2.00	1.39	.00
3–7	1	−2.00	1.79	.00
	2	−1.00	1.79	.00
	3	0.00	1.79	.00
	4	1.00	1.79	.00
	5	2.00	1.79	.00
3–8	1	−2.00	.19	.25
	2	−1.00	.19	.25
	3	0.00	.19	.25
	4	1.00	.19	.25
	5	2.00	.19	.25
3–9	1	−2.00	.59	.25
	2	−1.00	.59	.25
	3	0.00	.59	.25
	4	1.00	.59	.25
	5	2.00	.59	.25

(Continued next page)

Table 3-1   *(continued)*

| Figure | Item | *Item Statistics* | | |
		b	*a*	*c*
3–10	1	−2.00	.99	.25
	2	−1.00	.99	.25
	3	0.00	.99	.25
	4	1.00	.99	.25
	5	2.00	.99	.25
3–11	1	−2.00	1.39	.25
	2	−1.00	1.39	.25
	3	0.00	1.39	.25
	4	1.00	1.39	.25
	5	2.00	1.39	.25
3–12	1	−2.00	1.79	.25
	2	−1.00	1.79	.25
	3	0.00	1.79	.25
	4	1.00	1.79	.25
	5	2.00	1.79	.25

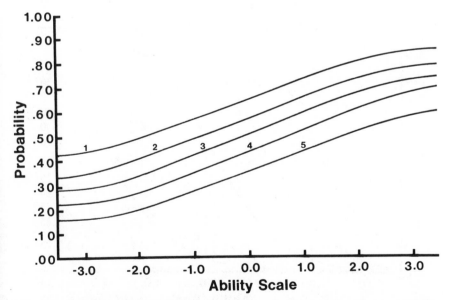

Figure 3-3. Graphical Representation of Five Item Characteristic Curves (b = −2.0, −1.0, 0.0, 1.0, 2.0; a = .19, c = 0.0)

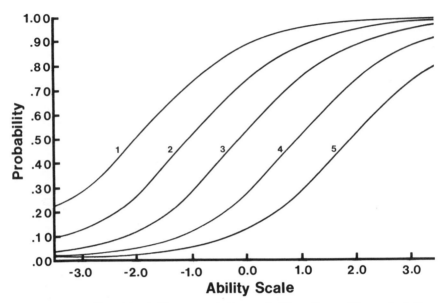

Figure 3-4. Graphical Representation of Five Item Characteristic Curves (b = −2.0, −1.0, 0.0, 1.0, 2.0; a = .59, c = .00)

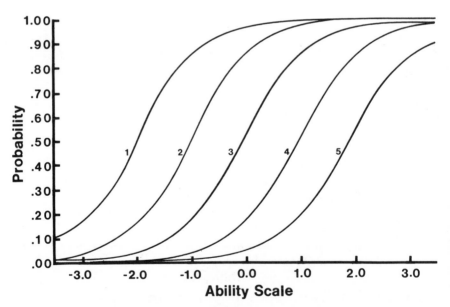

Figure 3-5. Graphical Representation of Five Item Characteristic Curves (b = −2.0, −1.0, 0.0, 1.0, 2.0; a = .99, c = .00)

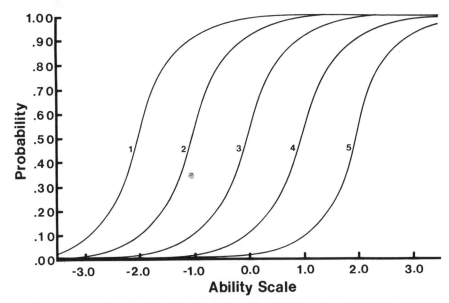

Figure 3-6. Graphical Representation of Five Item Characteristic Curves (b = −2.0, −1.0, 0.0, 1.0, 2.0; a = 1.39, c = .00)

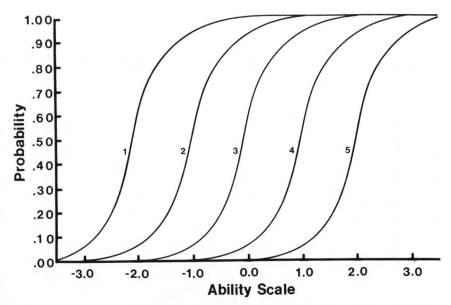

Figure 3-7. Graphical Representation of Five Item Characteristic Curves (b = −2.0, −1.0, 0.0, 1.0, 2.0; a = 1.79, c = .00)

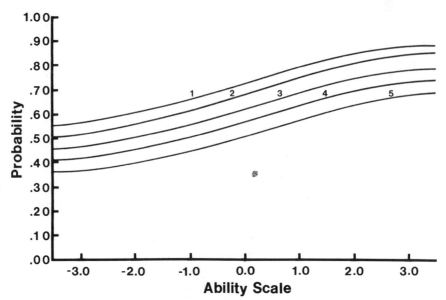

Figure 3-8. Graphical Representation of Five Item Characteristic
Curves (b = −2.0, −1.0, 0.0, 1.0, 2.0; a = .19, c = .25)

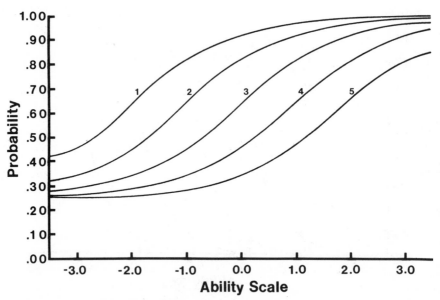

Figure 3-9. Graphical Representation of Five Item Characteristic
Curves (b = −2.0, −1.0, 0.0, 1.0, 2.0; a = .59, c = .25)

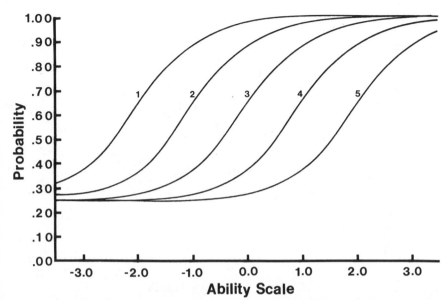

Figure 3-10. Graphical Representation of Five Item Characteristic
Curves (b = −2.0, −1.0, 0.0, 1.0, 2.0; a = .99, c = .25)

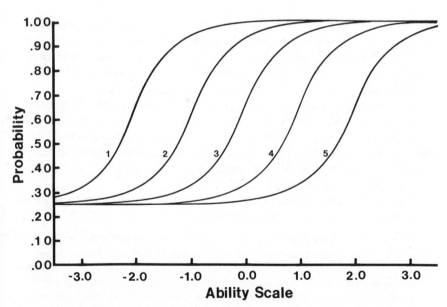

Figure 3-11. Graphical Representation of Five Item Characteristic
Curves (b = −2.0, −1.0, 0.0, 1.0, 2.0; a = 1.39, c = .25)

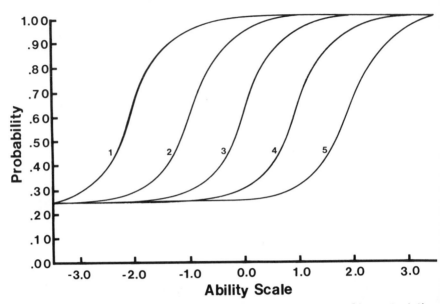

Figure 3-12. Graphical Representation of Five Item Characteristic Curves (b = −2.0, −1.0, 0.0, 1.0, 2.0; a = 1.79, c = .25)

Stone, 1979). Although the Rasch model was developed independently of other item response models and along quite different lines, Rasch's model can be viewed as an item response model in which the item characteristic curve is a one-parameter logistic function. Consequently, Rasch's model is a special case of Birnbaum's three-parameter logistic model, in which (1) all items are assumed to have equal discriminating power and (2) guessing is assumed to be minimal. The assumption that all item discrimination parameters are equal is restrictive, and substantial evidence is available to suggest that unless test items are specifically chosen to have this characteristic, the assumption will be violated (e.g., Birnbaum, 1968; Hambleton & Traub, 1973; Lord, 1968; Ross, 1966).

Traub (1983) was especially doubtful about the appropriateness of the two assumptions for achievement test data:

> These assumptions about items fly in the face of common sense and a wealth of empirical evidence accumulated over the last 80 years. Common sense rules against the supposition that guessing plays no part in the process for answering multiple-choice items. This supposition is false, and no amount of pretense will make it true. The wealth of empirical evidence that has been accumulated concerns item discrimination. The fact that otherwise acceptable achievement

items differ in the degree to which they correlate with the underlying trait has been observed so very often that we should expect this kind of variation for any set of achievement items we choose to study. (p. 64)

One possibility is that the Rasch model may be robust with respect to departures of model assumptions normally observed in actual test data. Model robustness will be addressed in chapter 8.

The equation of the item characteristic curve for the one-parameter logistic model can be written as

$$P_i(\theta) = \frac{e^{D\bar{a}(\theta - b_i)}}{1 + e^{D\bar{a}(\theta - b_i)}} \qquad (i = 1, 2, \ldots, n), \qquad (3.4)$$

in which $\bar{a}$, the only term not previously defined, is the common level of discrimination for all the items. Wright (1977a) and others prefer to write the model with $D\bar{a}$ incorporated into the θ scale. Thus, the right-hand side of the probability statement becomes $e^{\theta' - b_i'}/1 + e^{\theta' - b_i'}$, where $\theta' = D\bar{a}\theta$ and $b_i' = D\bar{a}b_i$.

While the Rasch or one-parameter logistic model is a special case of the two- and three-parameter logistic test models, the model does have some special properties that make it especially attractive to users. For one, since the model involves fewer item parameters, it is easier to work with. Second, the problems with parameter estimation are considerably fewer in number than for the more general models. This point will be discussed in Chapters 5 and 7.

There appears to be some misunderstanding of the ability scale for the Rasch model. Wright (1968) originally introduced the model this way: The odds in favor of success on an item i, by an examinee with ability level θ_a^*, denoted 0_{ia} are given by the product of an examinee's ability θ_a^* and by the reciprocal of the difficulty of the item, denoted b_i^*, where $0 \le \theta_a^* \le \infty$ and $0 \le b_i^* \le \infty$. Odds for success will be higher for brigher students and/or easier items. The odds of success are defined as the ratio of P_{ia} to $1 - P_{ia}$ where P_{ia} is the probability of success by examinee a on item i. Therefore,

$$\frac{\theta_a^*}{b_i^*} = \frac{P_{ia}}{1 - P_{ia}} \qquad (3.5)$$

and, it is easily shown that

$$P_{ia} = \frac{\theta_a^*}{\theta_a^* + b_i^*}. \qquad (3.6)$$

Equation (3.4) can be obtained from equation (3.6) by setting $\theta_a^* = e^{D\bar{a}\theta_a}$ and $b_i^* = e^{D\bar{a}b_i}$. In equation (3.6), both θ^* and b_i^* are defined on the interval (0,

$+\infty$). If log ability and log difficulties are considered, then θ and b_i and $\log \theta^*$ and $\log b_i^*$ are measured on the same scale $(-\infty, +\infty)$, differing only by an expansion transformation.

We return again to the point above regarding the odds for success on an item. Clearly, there is an indeterminancy in the product of θ_a^* and $1/b_i^*$ as there always is when locating test items and ability scores on the same scale. This point will be discussed in more detail in the next chapter. When odds for success are changed, we could attribute the change to either θ_a^* or $1/b_i^*$. For example, if odds for success are doubled, it could be because ability is doubled or because the item is half as difficult. There are several ways to remedy the problem. For one we could choose a special set or "standard set" of test items and scale the b_i's, $i = 1, 2, \ldots, n$ so that $\bar{b}_i = 1$. Alternatively, we could do the same sort of scaling for a "standard" set of examinees such that the average of θ_a, $a = 1, 2, \ldots, N$ is set to one or any other constant value. The final point is clear. When one item is twice as easy as another on the θ^* scale, a person's odds for success on the easier item are twice what they are on the harder item. If one person's ability is twice as high as another person's ability, the first person's odds for success are twice those of the second person (Wright, 1968). In what sense are item and ability parameters measured on a ratio scale? An examinee with twice the ability (as measured on the θ^* ability scale) of another examinee has twice the odds of successfully answering a test item. Also, when one item is twice as easy as another item (again, as measured on the θ^* ability scale), a person has twice the odds of successfully answering the easier one. Other item response models do not permit this particular kind of interpretation of item and ability parameters.

3.3.5 Four-Parameter Logistic Model

High-ability examinees do not always answer test items correctly. Sometimes these examinees may be a little careless, other times they may have information beyond that assumed by the test item writer; so they may choose answers that are not "keyed" as correct. To handle this problem, McDonald (1967) and more recently Barton and Lord (1981) have thus described a four-parameter logistic model:

$$P_i(\theta) = c_i + (\gamma_i - c_i) \frac{e^{Da_i(\theta - b_i)}}{1 + e^{Da_i(\theta - b_i)}}.$$

This model differs from the three-parameter model in that γ_i assumes a value slightly below "1." This model may be of theoretical interest only because

Figure 3-13. Mathematical Forms of the Logistic Item Characteristic Curves.

Models	Mathematical Forms
One-Parameter Logistic	$P_i(\theta) = \dfrac{e^{D(\theta - b_i)}}{1 + e^{D(\theta - b_i)}}$ or $[1 + e^{-D(\theta - b_i)}]^{-1}$
Two-Parameter Logistic	$P_i(\theta) = \dfrac{e^{Da_i(\theta - b_i)}}{1 + e^{Da_i(\theta - b_i)}}$ or $[1 + e^{-Da_i(\theta - b_i)}]^{-1}$
Three-Parameter Logistic	$P_i(\theta) = c_i + (1 - c_i)\dfrac{e^{Da_i(\theta - b_i)}}{1 + e^{Da_i(\theta - b_i)}}$ or $c_i + (1 - c_i)[1 + e^{-Da_i(\theta - b_i)}]^{-1}$
Four-Parameter Logistic	$P_i(\theta) = c_i + (\gamma_i - c_i)\dfrac{e^{Da_i(\theta - b_i)}}{1 + e^{Da_i(\theta - b_i)}}$ or $c_i + (\gamma_i - c_i)[1 + e^{-Da_i(\theta - b_i)}]^{-1}$

Barton and Lord (1981) were unable to find any practical gains that accrued from the model's use. A summary of the mathematical forms for the four logistic models is found in figure 3–13.

3.3.6 One-, Three-, and Four-Parameter Normal Ogive Models

Although Lord (1952) based his important work on the two-parameter normal ogive model, there is no theoretical reason at least for not considering normal ogive models with more or less than two item parameters. The mathematical forms of these models are given in figure 3–14. But given the similarity of these models to the logistic models, and the mathematical convenience associated with the logistic models, the normal ogive models are apt to be of theoretical interest only.

3.3.7 Nominal Response Model

The one-, two-, three-, and four-parameter logistic and normal ogive test models can be applied only to test items that are scored dichotomously. The nominal response model, introduced by Bock (1972) and Samejima (1972),

Figure 3-14. Mathematical Forms of the Normal Ogive Item Characteristic Curves.

Models	Mathematical Forms
One-Parameter Normal Ogive	$P_i(\theta) = \displaystyle\int_{-\infty}^{\theta - b_i} \frac{1}{\sqrt{2\pi}} e^{-z^2/2} dz$
Two-Parameter Normal Ogive	$P_i(\theta) = \displaystyle\int_{-\infty}^{a_i(\theta - b_i)} \frac{1}{\sqrt{2\pi}} e^{-z^2/2} dz$
Three-Parameter Normal Ogive	$P_i(\theta) = c_i + (1 - c_i) \displaystyle\int_{-\infty}^{a_i(\theta - b_i)} \frac{1}{\sqrt{2\pi}} e^{-z^2/2} dz$
Four-Parameter Normal Ogive	$P_i(\theta) = c_i + (\gamma_i - c_i) \displaystyle\int_{-\infty}^{a_i(\theta - b_i)} \frac{1}{\sqrt{2\pi}} e^{-z^2/2} dz$

is applicable when items are multichotomously scored. The purpose of the model is to maximize the precision of obtained ability estimates by utilizing the information contained in each response to an item or point on a rating scale. This multichotomously-scored response model represents another approach in the search for differential scoring weights that improve the reliability and validity of mental test scores (Wand & Stanley, 1970). *Each item option is described by an* item option characteristic curve—*even the* "omit" response can be represented by a curve. For the correct response, the curve should be monotonically increasing as a function of ability. For the incorrect options, the shapes of the curves depend on how the options are perceived by examinees at different ability levels.

There are, of course, many choices for the mathematical form of the item option characteristic curves (Samejima, 1972). For one, Bock (1972) assumed that the probability that an examinee with ability level θ will select a particular item option k (from m available options per item) to item i is given by

$$P_{ik}(\theta) = \frac{e^{b_{ik}^* + a_{ik}^* \theta}}{\displaystyle\sum_{h=1}^{m} e^{b_{ih}^* + a_{ih}^* \theta}} \quad (i = 1, 2, \ldots, n; \, k = 1, 2, \ldots, m). \quad (3.7)$$

For any ability level θ, the sum of the probabilities of selecting each of the m item options is equal to one. The quantities b_{ik}^* and a_{ik}^* are item parameters related to the kth item option. When $m = 2$, the items are dichotomously scored, and the two-parameter logistic model and the nominal response model are identical.

3.3.8 Graded Response Model

This model was introduced by Samejima (1969) to handle the testing situation where item responses are contained in two or more ordered categories. For example, with test items like those on the Raven's Progressive Matrices, one may desire to score examinees on the basis of the correctness (for example, incorrect, partially correct, correct) of their answers. Samejima (1969) assumed any response to an item i can be classified into $m_i + 1$ categories, scored $x_i = 0, 1, \ldots, m_i$, respectively. Samejima (1969) introduced the *operating characteristic* of a graded response category. She defines it as

$$P_{x_i}(\theta) = P_{x_i}^*(\theta) - P_{(x_i+1)}^*(\theta). \qquad (3.8)$$

$P_{x_i}^*(\theta)$ is the regression of the binary item score on latent ability, when all the response categories less than x_i are scored 0, and those equal to or greater than x_i are scored 1. $P_{x_i}^*(\theta)$ represents the probability with which an examinee of ability level θ receives a score of x_i. The mathematical form of $P_{x_i}^*$ is specified by the user. Samejima (1969) has considered both the two-parameter logistic and two-parameter normal ogive curves in her work. In several applications of the graded response model, it has been common to assume that discrimination parameters are equal for $P_{x_i}^*(\theta)$, $x_i = 0, 1, \ldots, m_i$. This model is referred to as the *homogeneous case* of the graded response model. Further, Samejima defines $P_0^*(\theta)$ and $P_{(m_i+1)}^*(\theta)$ so that

$$P_0^*(\theta) = 1 \qquad (3.9)$$

and

$$P_{(m_i+1)}^*(\theta) = 0. \qquad (3.10)$$

Also, for any response category x_i,

$$P_{x_i}(\theta) = P_{x_i}^*(\theta) - P_{(x_i+1)}^*(\theta) > 0.$$

The shape of $P_{x_i}(\theta)$, $x_i = 0, 1, \ldots, m_i$ will in general be non-monotonic except when $x_i = m_i$, and $x_i = 0$. (This is true as long as $P_{x_i}^*(\theta)$ is monotonically increasing, for all $x_i = 0, 1, \ldots, m_i$.)

3.3.9 Continuous Response Model

The continuous response model can be considered as a limiting case of the graded response model. This model was introduced by Samejima (1973b) to handle the situation where examinee item responses are marked on a continuous scale. The model is likely to be useful, for example, to social psychologists and other researchers interested in studying attitudes.

3.4 Summary

There is no limit to the number of IRT models that can be generated (see, for example, McDonald, 1982). In this chapter we have introduced some of the most commonly used models but many others are being developed and applied to educational and psychological test data. For example, we considered several generalizations of the Rasch model in this chapter by including up to three additional item parameters (a_i, c_i, γ_i) in the model. Masters (1982) recently described another generalization of the Rasch model to handle responses that can be classified into ordered categories. Such a model can be fitted to attitudinal data collected from Likert or semantic differential scales, for example. Other models have been considered by Andrich (1978a, 1978b, 1978c). Fischer and his colleagues in Europe have generalized the Rasch model by describing the item difficulty parameter in the model in terms of cognitive factors that influence item difficulty (Fischer, 1974; Fischer & Formann, 1982; Fischer & Pendl, 1980). This generalized Rasch model, referred to as the linear logistic model, is presently being used successfully by psychologists to understand the cognitive processes that serve to define item difficulty. In their work,

$$b_i = \sum_{j=1}^{m} w_{ij} n_j + \varepsilon,$$

where n_j, $j = 1, 2, \ldots, m$ are the cognitive operations that influence item difficulty and w_{ij}, $j = 1, 2, \ldots, m$ are the weights that reflect the importance of each factor or operation with item i. The value ε is a scaling factor.

In the remainder of this text our attention will be focused on logistic test models. Presently these models are receiving the most attention and use from psychometricians in the United States. In addition, an understanding of these logistic models will help newcomers to the IRT field grasp more quickly the nature, significance, and usefulness of the new models that are now appearing in the psychometric literature.

4 ABILITY SCALES

4.1 Introduction

The purpose of item response theory, as with any test theory, is to provide a basis for making predictions, estimates, or inferences about *abilities* or *traits* measured by a test. In this chapter, several characteristics of ability scores will be considered: definitions, legitimate transformations, relationship to true scores and observed scores, and validity of interpretations.

A common paradigm for obtaining ability scores is illustrated in figure 4-1. The researcher begins with an observed set of item responses from a relatively large group of examinees. Next, after conducting several pre-liminary checks of model data fit, a model for use is selected. As was seen in chapter 3 there are many promising models that can be used for the analysis of data and the ultimate estimation of ability scores. Then, the chosen model is fitted to the test data. Ability scores are assigned to examinees and parameter estimates to items so that there is maximum agreement between the chosen model and the data. This type of analysis is described in chapter 7 and usually carried out with the aid of one of two widely used computer programs, BICAL, described by Wright and Stone (1979), and LOGIST, described by Wingersky (1983). Once the parameter estimates are obtained,

1) Data Collection   2) Model Selection

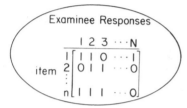

Figure 4-1.   Steps for Obtaining Ability Scores

the fit of the model to the data is examined. Steps for carrying out model-data fit studies are described in chapters 8 and 9. In most cases, the one-, the two-, and the three-parameter item response models are fitted to the data and the model that best fits the data is chosen.

The alternative to the above paradigm is the situation where the item parameter values for the test are assumed to be known for a chosen model. What remains is to obtain ability scores from the item response data. This case is considered in chapter 5.

4.2 Definition of Ability and Transformation of the Ability Scale

It is axiomatic in item response theory that underlying an examinee's performance on a set of test items is an ability (or abilities). The term "ability" (or latent ability, as it is sometimes called) is a label which is used to designate the trait or characteristic that a test measures. The trait measured may be broadly defined to include cognitive abilities, achievement, basic

Figure 4-2. Ability Scores in Item Response Theory

What is the underlying latent trait or ability that is described in item response theory?

- Ability, e.g., "numerical ability," is the label that is used to describe what it is that the set of test items measures.
- The ability or trait can be a broadly defined aptitude or achievement variable (e.g., reading comprehension), a narrowly defined achievement variable (e.g., ability to multiply whole numbers), or a personality variable (e.g., self concept or motivation).
- Construct validation studies are required to validate the desired interpretations of the ability scores.
- There is no reason to think of the "ability" as innate. Ability scores can change over time and they can often be changed through instruction.

competencies, personality characteristics, etc. Rentz and Bashaw (1977) have noted, "The term 'ability' should not be mysterious; it should not be entrusted with any surplus meaning nor should it be regarded as a personal characteristic that is innate, inevitable or immutable. Use of the word 'ability' is merely a convenience." Several important points about ability scores are highlighted in figure 4-2.

The scale on which ability is defined is arbitrary to some extent. This can be seen from the form of the item response model. For the one-parameter logistic model, a form of the item response function for item i is given by:

$$P_i(\theta) = \{1 + \exp[-D(\theta - b_i)]\}^{-1}. \qquad (4.1)$$

If θ and b_i are transformed into θ^* and b_i^* where

$$\theta^* = \theta + k \qquad (4.2a)$$
$$b_i^* = b_i + k, \qquad (4.2b)$$

then

$$P_i(\theta) = P_i(\theta^*).$$

Thus a simple linear transformation can be made on the ability scale (with the corresponding transformation on the item difficulty parameter) without altering the mathematical form of the item response function. This in turn implies that the probability with which an examinee with ability θ responds correctly to an item is unaffected by changing the scale of θ, if the item parameter scale is also changed appropriately.

With the three-parameter model (equation 3.3) or the two-parameter model (equation 3.2), it is possible to transform θ into θ^*, b_i into b_i^*, a_i into a_i^* such that

$$\theta^* = \ell\theta + k \qquad\qquad\qquad (4.3a)$$

$$b_i^* = \ell b_i + k \qquad\qquad\qquad (4.3b)$$

$$a_i^* = a_i/\ell. \qquad\qquad\qquad (4.3c)$$

Then, for the three-parameter model, with $c_i^* = c_i$,

$$
\begin{aligned}
P_i(\theta^*) &= c_i^* + (1 - c_i^*)\{1 + \exp[-Da_i^*(\theta^* - b_i^*)]\}^{-1}\\
&= c_i + (1 - c_i)\{1 + \exp[-D(a_i/\ell)(\ell\theta + k - eb_i - k)]\}^{-1}\\
&= c_i + (1 - c_i)\{1 + \exp[-Da_i(\theta - b_i)]\}^{-1}\\
&= P_i(\theta).
\end{aligned}
$$

Thus the item response function is invariant with respect to a linear transformation. The same result is obtained for the two-parameter model.

To summarize, in the one-parameter model where the discrimination parameter a_i is one, the ability and the item difficulty parameter can be transformed by adding a constant. In the two- and three-parameter models linear transformations of the type indicated in equation 4.3a–4.3c are permissible. It should be pointed out that if the one-parameter model is specified with an average discrimination parameter, i.e.

$$P_i(\theta) = \{1 + \exp[-D\bar{a}(\theta - b_i)]\}^{-1},$$

then the transformations given by equation 4.3a–4.3c apply.

This arbitrariness of the θ-scale has several implications. In the estimation of parameters, this arbitrariness or "indeterminacy" must be eliminated. The simplest way to remove the indeterminacy is to choose ℓ and k in equation 4.3a such that the mean and the standard deviation of θ are zero and one respectively (similar scaling can be done with the difficulty parameters).

It is common to obtain ability estimates from LOGIST which have mean zero and standard deviation one. Hence, ability estimates in this case are defined in the interval $(-\infty, \infty)$. But ability estimates or scores on such a scale are not always convenient. For example, as sometimes happens with z scores, negative signs are mistakenly dropped, and it is not convenient to work with decimals. To avoid this, the ability scores may be transformed, for example, into a scale that has a mean of 200 and standard deviation equal to 10. This is done by setting $\ell = 10$ and $k = 200$. However, care must be taken to similarly adjust the item parameter values.

This scaling of ability, with mean 200 and standard deviation 10, was used by Rentz and Bashaw (1977) in the development of the National Reference Scale (NRS) for reading. However, these authors found the ability scale, albeit transformed, not directly interpretable. They recommend transforming the probability of correct response $P_i(\theta)$ to "log-odds". If $P_i(\theta)$ is the probability of a correct response to item i, then $Q_i(\theta) = 1 - P_i(\theta)$ is the probability of an incorrect response. The ratio $O_i = P_i(\theta)/Q_i(\theta)$ is the odds for a correct response or success. For the Rasch model,

$$P_i(\theta) = \exp(\theta - b_i)/[1 + \exp(\theta - b_i)],$$

and

$$Q_i(\theta) = 1/[1 + \exp(\theta - b_i)].$$

Hence

$$O_i = P_i(\theta)/Q_i(\theta) = \exp(\theta - b_i). \qquad (4.4)$$

Taking natural logarithms (to the base $e = 2.718$), denoted as ln, we have

$$\ln O_i = \theta - b_i.$$

This represents the log-odds scale and the units on this scale are "logits" (Wright, 1977). To see its usefulness, suppose that two examinees have ability scores θ_1 and θ_2. Then for item i, the log-odds are

$$\ln O_{i1} = \theta_1 - b_i$$

and

$$\ln O_{i2} = \theta_2 - b_i$$

for the two examinees, respectively. On subtracting, we obtain

$$\ln O_{i1} - \ln O_{i2} = \theta_1 - \theta_2,$$

or,

$$\ln(O_{i1}/O_{i2}) = \theta_1 - \theta_2.$$

If the abilities differ by one point, i.e., $\theta_1 - \theta_2 = 1$, then

$$\ln(O_{i1}/O_{i2}) = 1,$$

or alternatively,

$$O_{i1}/O_{i2} = \exp(1)$$
$$= 2.718.$$

Thus a difference of one point on the ability scale, or equivalently, the log-odds scale, corresponds approximately to a factor of 2.72 in odds for success. A difference in the log-odds scale of .7 (more accurately, .693) corresponds to a doubling of the odds for success while a difference of 1.4 corresponds to quadrupling the odds. Thus, the log-odds transformation provides a direct way to compare different examinees.

Different items may also be compared using this transformation. Suppose that an examinee with ability θ has odds, O_i for success on item i and odds O_j for success on item j. Then

$$\ln(O_i/O_j) = b_i - b_j.$$

If the item difficulties differ by seven-tenths of a point, i.e., $b_i - b_j = .7$, then item j is easier than item i, and an examinee's odds for success on item j is twice that for item i.

Clearly, the base of the logarithm in the log-odds scale is arbitrary and can be chosen to facilitate interpretation. For example, if it is decided that a difference of one unit for abilities (or item difficulties) should correspond to an odds ratio of 2, then the scale of θ can be chosen to reflect this. One way to accomplish this is to express the odds for success O_i using logarithms to the base two, i.e., define

$$\log_2 O_i = \theta - b_i.$$

When two examinees differ one unit in ability,

$$\log_2 (O_i/O_j) = 1$$

and hence the ratio of odds for success is two.

Although the definition of the log-odds scale with reference to any logarithmic base is valid, it may not be consistent with the definition of probability of success in terms of the logistic model. The definition of log-odds as

$$\log_2 O_i = \theta - b_i$$

implies that

$$P_i(\theta) = 2^{(\theta - b_i)}/[1 + 2^{(\theta - b_i)}]$$

which is not the logistic model given in equation (4.1). Taking logarithms to the base e, we have

$$\ln O_i = (\theta - b_i)(\ln 2)$$

or, approximately,

$$\ln O_i = .7(\theta - b_i).$$

Thus, scaling the ability scale by a multiplicative factor of .7 and using log-odds units to the base e is tantamount to employing a log-odds scale to the base two.

Woodcock (1978) recommends transforming the ability scale to the W scale (for the Woodcock-Johnson Psycho-educational Battery) using a logarithmic base of nine. The scale is defined as

$$W_\theta = C_1 \log_9 Z + C_2$$

where $Z = \exp(\theta)$. Thus the W scale requires an exponential transformation of θ followed by a logarithmic transformation. Since

$$\log_9[\exp(\theta)] = \theta \log_9(e)$$
$$= \theta/\ln 9$$
$$= .455\theta,$$
$$W_\theta = .455 C_1 \theta + C_2.$$

Furthermore C_1 is set at 20 and C_2 is chosen so that a value of 500 on the scale corresponds to the average performance level of beginning fifth-graders on a particular subtest. Assuming $C_2 = 500$, the W scale reduced to

$$W_\theta = 9.1\theta + 500.$$

The item difficulties are also scaled in the same manner, i.e.,

$$W_b = 9.1b + 500.$$

The advantage of the W scale is that the differences $(W_\theta - W_b) = 20, 10, 0, -10, -20$ correspond to the following probabilities of correct responses: .90, .75, .50, .25, .10. Wright (1977) has recommended a slight modification of the W scale. Noting that $\ln 9 = 2 \ln 3$, Wright (1977) has modified the W scale as

$$W_\theta = 10 \log_3 Z + 100$$
$$= 9.1\theta + 100,$$

and has termed it the "WITs" scale. The two scales provide identical information.

The above non-linear transformations of the ability scale are also applicable to the two- and three-parameter logistic model. For the two-parameter logistic model, the log-odds for success becomes

$$\ln O_i = 1.7 a_i(\theta - b_i).$$

Two examinees with ability θ_1 and θ_2 can be compared by obtaining the log-odds ratio:

$$\ln{(O_{i1}/O_{i2})} = 1.7a_i(\theta_1 - b_i) - 1.7a_i(\theta_2 - b_i)$$
$$= 1.7a_i(\theta_1 - \theta_2).$$

Unlike in the Rasch model, the log-odds ratio involves the discrimination parameter a_i and hence comparisons must take this into account.

For the three-parameter logistic model, the log-odds ratio is defined differently. In this case

$$P_i(\theta) = c_i + (1 - c_i)\{1 + \exp[-1.7a_i(\theta - b_i)]\}^{-1},$$

and hence

$$\frac{P_i(\theta) - c_i}{Q_i(\theta)} = \exp[1.7a_i(\theta - b_i)]$$

or,

$$\ln(P_i - c_i)/Q_i = 1.7a_i(\theta - b_i).$$

Thus the "log-odds" ratio O_i is defined by taking into account the pseudo-chance level parameter c_i. Alternately, defining

$$\theta^* = k \exp(\ell\theta)$$
$$b_i^* = k \exp(\ell b_i)$$

and

$$a_i^* = 1.7a_i/\ell,$$

we have

$$\frac{P_i - c_i}{Q_i} = \left(\frac{\theta^*}{b_i^*}\right)^{a_i^*}.$$

According to Lord (1980a), "this last equation relates probability of success on an item to the simple ratio of examinee ability θ^* to item difficulty b^*. The relation is so simple and direct as to suggest that the θ^*-scale may be as good or better for measuring ability then the θ-scale (p. 84)."

To summarize, the ability scale should be scaled to aid the interpretation. A linear transformation of the scale is the simplest. However, a non-linear transformation of the scale should be considered if it aids interpretation. While some simple non-linear transformations have been discussed, other transformations converting ability scores to domain scores are considered in the following sections. Beyond these transformations, empirical transformations of the ability scale that will result in reduced correlations among estimates of item parameters should also be considered (Lord, 1980a) since these will greatly aid in the construction of tests.

4.3 Relation of Ability Scores to Domain Scores

If one were to administer two tests measuring the same ability to the same group of examinees and the tests were not strictly parallel, two different test score distributions would result. The extent of the differences between the two distributions would depend, among other things, on the difference between the difficulties of the two tests. Since, there is no basis for preferring one distribution over the other, the test score distribution provides no information about the distribution of ability scores. This situation occurs because the raw-score units from each test are unequal and different. On the other hand, the ability scale is one on which examinees will have the same ability score across non-parallel tests measuring a common ability. Thus, even though an examinee's test scores will vary across non-parallel forms of a test measuring an ability, the ability score for an examinee will be the same on each form.

The concept of *true score* (or *domain score*), is of primary importance in classical test theory. It is defined as the expected test score (on a set of test items) for an examinee. For an examinee with observed score x and true score t, it follows that $t = E(x)$ where E is the expected value operator (Lord & Novick, 1968, p. 30).

The true score or the domain score has an interesting relation to the ability score θ of an examinee. If the observed total score of an examinee is defined as r, based on an n item test, then

$$r = \sum_{i=1}^{n} U_i \qquad (4.5)$$

where U_i, the response to item i, is either one or zero. A more useful quantity is the examinee's proportion correct score, $\hat{\pi}$, which can be taken as the estimate of the examinee's domain score, π. It follows then that

$$\hat{\pi} = \frac{1}{n} \sum_{i=1}^{n} U_i. \qquad (4.6)$$

By the definition of true scores, $E(\hat{\pi}) = \pi$, i.e.,

$$E(\hat{\pi}) = \pi = \frac{1}{n} \sum_{i=1}^{n} E(U_i). \qquad (4.7)$$

For an examinee with ability θ, the above expressions are conditional on θ and should be so expressed. Thus the expressions should become:

$$\hat{\pi}\,|\,\theta = \frac{1}{n}\sum_{i=1}^{n}(U_i\,|\,\theta);\qquad\qquad (4.8)$$

and

$$E(\hat{\pi}\,|\,\theta) = \pi\,|\,\theta \qquad\qquad (4.9)$$

$$= \frac{1}{n}\sum_{i=1}^{n}E(U_i\,|\,\theta). \qquad\qquad (4.10)$$

Since U_i is a random variable with value one or zero, it follows that

$$E(U_i\,|\,\theta) = (U_i = 1)P_i(U_i = 1\,|\,\theta) + (U_i = 0)P_i(U_i = 0\,|\,\theta)$$
$$= 1\cdot P_i(U_i = 1\,|\,\theta) + 0\cdot P_i(U_i = 0\,|\,\theta)$$
$$= P_i(U_i = 1\,|\,\theta)$$
$$= P_i(\theta), \qquad\qquad (4.11)$$

the item response function. Hence,

$$\pi\,|\,\theta = \frac{1}{n}\sum_{i=1}^{n}P_i(\theta). \qquad\qquad (4.12)$$

To simplify the notation, $\pi\,|\,\theta$ will be denoted as π when no confusion arises. This function which is the average of the item response functions for the n items is known as the *Test Characteristic Function*.[1] The curve $n^{-1}\Sigma P_i(\theta)$ is also referred to as the *Test Characteristic Curve*. These terms are used interchangeably.

The domain score, π, and θ are monotonically related, the relation being given by the test characteristic function. Clearly then, the two concepts π and θ are the same, except for the scale of measurement used to describe each. One difference is that the domain score is defined on the interval $[0, 1]$ whereas ability scores are usually defined in the interval $(-\infty, \infty)$. The most important difference is that while the scale for ability is independent of the items, the scale for domain score is dependent on the items that are used.

4.4 Relationship between Ability Distribution and Domain Score Distribution

When ability θ is mapped onto domain score π through the test characteristic function, as a result of the non-linear transformation, the distribution of θ will not be similar to the distribution of π. To illustrate this, suppose that the test is made up of parallel items (with the same item characteristic curve). Then the test characteristic curve coincides with the item characteristic curve. Further suppose that the ability distribution is uniform on the interval $[-4, 4]$, and that the test characteristic curve has the three-parameter logistic form. To obtain the distribution of the domain scores, it is first necessary to transform the end points of the intervals of the ability distribution according to the logistic item characteristic curve, i.e.,

$$\pi(\theta) = c + (1 - c)\{1 + \exp[-1.7a(\theta - b)]\}^{-1}.$$

Suppose that the ability scale is divided into 16 intervals of width 0.5 from $\theta = -4$ to $\theta = +4$. The end points of the first interval are $[-4.0, -3.5]$. With $c = .05$, $b = 0$, $a = .5$, and $\theta = -4$,

$$\pi(-4) = .08,$$

and

$$\pi(-3.5) = .10.$$

The end points of the intervals of the ability distribution and the corresponding intervals for $a = 0.5$ and $a = 2.5$ (with $c = .05$ and $b = 0$) are given in table 4-1.

Since the distribution of θ is uniform, 6.25% of the cases fall in each interval. When $a = 0.5$, the distribution of the domain scores has a slight concentration of observations at the ends with almost a uniform distribution in the middle range. On the other hand, when $a = 2.5$, the domain score distribution is highly concentrated in the two tails, with 37.5% of the observations falling in the interval $[.05, .15]$ and 43.75% of the observations falling in the interval $[.90, 1.00]$. The steep test characteristic curve (with $a = 2.5$) results in a platykurtic domain score distribution with the distribution being almost U-shaped.

In general, if the test is not very discriminating, the test characteristic curve will be almost straight in the middle ability range. If the majority of the examinees fall in the middle of the ability scale, little distortion will take place. However, if there is a wide range in the ability distribution, the domain scores will be typically squeezed into the middle range. A highly discriminating test, on the other hand, will result in a stretching of the domain score distribution when the difficulty is at a medium level.

The effects of the discrimination and difficulty parameters on the domain score distribution are illustrated in figure 4-3 for two ability distributions.

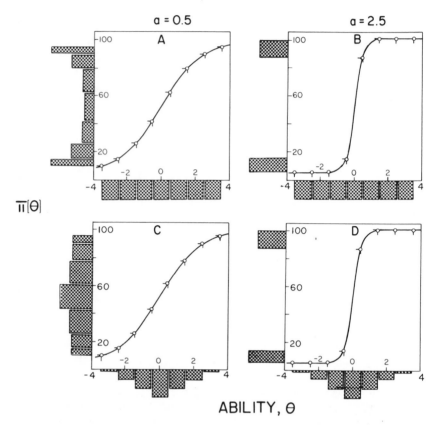

Figure 4-3. Effect of Item Parameter Values on the Relationship between Ability Score Distributions and Domain Score Distributions

These illustrate that if the purpose of the test is to make decisions about examinees at various domain score levels, the test characteristic curve can be chosen to facilitate this decision making. To spread the domain scores as much as possible, a test characteristic curve that is as steep as possible in the middle should be used. Such a test can be made up of items with high discriminations and medium difficulties. To spread out the domain scores only at the high range, the test must be composed of highly difficult and highly discriminating items. We shall return to this important topic of test development using item characteristic curve methods in chapter 11.

The procedures illustrated here are valid when the true domain score π is known. Unfortunately, π is never known and only $\hat{\pi}$ can be determined. As is shown in the next section, as the test is lengthened $\hat{\pi}$ can be taken as π, and there will be a close resemblance between the true domain score distribution and the observed domain score distribution.

Table 4-1. Relationship between Ability Distribution and Domain Score Distribution for Various Values of the Discrimination Parameter ($b = 0.0$; $c = .05$)

Relative Frequency (%)	θ	Class Intervals	
		$\pi(\theta)$ $(a = .5)$	$\pi(\theta)$ $(a = 2.5)$
6.25	$-4.0 - -3.5$	$.08 - .10$	$.05 - .05$
6.25	$-3.5 - -3.0$	$.10 - .12$	$.05 - .05$
6.25	$-3.0 - -2.5$	$.12 - .15$	$.05 - .05$
6.25	$-2.5 - -2.0$	$.15 - .20$	$.05 - .05$
6.25	$-2.0 - -1.5$	$.20 - .26$	$.05 - .05$
6.25	$-1.5 - -1.0$	$.26 - .33$	$.05 - .06$
6.25	$-1.0 - -0.5$	$.33 - .43$	$.06 - .15$
6.25	$-.05 - 0.0$	$.43 - .53$	$.15 - .53$
6.25	$0.0 - 0.5$	$.53 - .62$	$.53 - .90$
6.25	$0.5 - 1.0$	$.62 - .72$	$.90 - .99$
6.25	$1.0 - 1.5$	$.72 - .79$	$.99 - 1.00$
6.25	$1.5 - 2.0$	$.79 - .85$	$1.00 - 1.00$
6.25	$2.0 - 2.5$	$.85 - .90$	$1.00 - 1.00$
6.25	$2.5 - 3.0$	$.90 - .93$	$1.00 - 1.00$
6.25	$3.0 - 3.5$	$.93 - .95$	$1.00 - 1.00$
6.25	$3.5 - 4.0$	$.95 - .97$	$1.00 - 1.00$

4.5 Relationship Between Observed Domain Score and Ability

The observed domain score $\hat{\pi}$ is defined as

$$\hat{\pi} \mid \theta = \frac{1}{n} \sum_{i=1}^{n} (U_i \mid \theta).$$

Clearly $E(\hat{\pi} \mid \theta) = \pi$. Since, as demonstrated

$$\pi = \frac{1}{n} \sum_{i=1}^{n} P_i(\theta),$$

the regression of $\hat{\pi}$ on θ is non-linear with the conditional means lying on the test characteristic curve.

At a given ability level θ, the conditional variance, $\mathrm{Var}(\hat{\pi} \mid \theta)$, is given by

$$\mathrm{Var}(\hat{\pi}\,|\,\theta) = \mathrm{Var}\{\tfrac{1}{n}\sum_{i=1}^{n}(U_i\,|\,\theta)\} \qquad (4.13)$$

By the assumption of local independence,

$$\mathrm{Var}\,\tfrac{1}{n}\sum_{i=1}^{n}(U_i\,|\,\theta) = \tfrac{1}{n^2}\sum_{i=1}^{n}\mathrm{Var}(U_i\,|\,\theta). \qquad (4.14)$$

Since $U_i\,|\,\theta$ is a binomial variable,

$$\mathrm{Var}(U_i\,|\,\theta) = P_i(\theta)Q_i(\theta). \qquad (4.15)$$

Thus

$$\mathrm{Var}\,\tfrac{1}{n}(U_i\,|\,\theta) = \tfrac{1}{n^2}P_i(\theta)Q_i(\theta) \qquad (4.16)$$

and it follows that

$$\mathrm{Var}(\hat{\pi}\,|\,\theta) = \tfrac{1}{n^2}\sum_{i=1}^{n}P_i(\theta)Q_i(\theta) \qquad (4.17)$$

The above derivation shows that the conditional means of $\hat{\pi}\,|\,\theta$ lie on the test characteristic curve. However, there will not be a one-to-one correspondence between $\hat{\pi}\,|\,\theta$ and θ because of the scatter at each ability level. The amount of scatter is determined by the conditional variance, $\mathrm{Var}(\hat{\pi}\,|\,\theta)$ given in equation (4.17). As the test is lengthened by adding an infinite number of parallel items, i.e., $n \to \infty$, $\hat{\pi}\,|\,\theta \to \pi$ and $\mathrm{Var}(\hat{\pi}\,|\,\theta) \to 0$. Thus $\hat{\pi}$ is a consistent estimator of π, the domain score.

The expressions for the mean and variance of $\hat{\pi}$ given θ are derived with the assumption that the value of θ is known. This is however never realized in practice. Usually an estimate $\hat{\theta}$ of θ is available and from this an estimate of the test characteristic function (or curve) is obtained. The value of the test characteristic curve at the given value of $\hat{\theta}$ is taken as the estimate of the domain score, $\hat{\pi}\,|\,\hat{\theta}$. Thus, we could define the estimate $\hat{\pi}\,|\,\hat{\theta}$ as

$$\hat{\pi}\,|\,\hat{\theta} = \frac{1}{n}\sum_{i=1}^{n}P_i(\hat{\theta}) \qquad (4.18)$$

These expressions are notationally confusing. Recall that $\hat{\pi}\,|\,\theta$ as defined in equation (4.8) is a linear combination of observed scores. It is an unbiased estimate of π, the population domain score defined in equation (4.12). However, the estimate defined in the previous paragraph in terms of the test characteristic curve (equation 4.18) is not an unbiased estimate of π. The mean and variance of $\hat{\pi}\,|\,\hat{\theta}$ are not easily determined since $P_i(\hat{\theta})$ is a non-linear transformation of θ. However, as the test is lengthened, $\hat{\theta}$ approaches θ

asymptotically (see Chapter 5). Thus, $\pi|\hat\theta$ is an unbiased estimate of π asymptotically.

The natural question that arises then is that of the advantage of $\hat\pi|\hat\theta$ over $\hat\pi|\theta$. Since $\hat\pi|\theta$ is defined as the observed proportion correct score, it is clearly dependent on the items administered to the individual. The estimated ability $\hat\theta$ is independent of the sample of items and the sample of examinees, and is therefore preferred. As pointed out earlier, the non-linear transformation of $\hat\theta$, $n^{-1}\Sigma_i P_i(\hat\theta)$, is also item dependent. However, $\hat\pi|\hat\theta$ need not be based on the items actually administered to the examinee. Ability, $\hat\theta$, can be determined from one set of items, and $\hat\pi|\hat\theta$ can be determined from another set of items (not administered to the examinee) as long as the item parameter values are known. Thus $\hat\pi|\hat\theta$ is not item dependent in the same sense as $\hat\pi|\theta$. While we have established the advantage of $\hat\pi|\hat\theta$ over $\hat\pi|\theta$, the advantage of using $\hat\pi|\hat\theta$ over $\hat\theta$ may not be obvious.

Ability estimates have the definite advantage of being "item-free." However, ability scores are measured on a scale which appears to be far less useful to test users than the domain score scale. After all, what does it mean to say, $\hat\theta = 1.5$? Domain scores are usually defined on the interval $[0, 1]$ and provide information about, for example, examinee levels of performance (proportions of content mastered) in relation to the objectives measured by a test. It is on the test score metric and hence is easy to interpret.

When the test items included in the test are a representative sample of test items from the domain of items measuring the ability, the associated test characteristic function transforms the ability score estimates into meaningful domain score estimates. A problem arises, however, if a non-representative sample of test items is drawn from a pool of test items measuring an ability of interest. Such a sample may be drawn to, for example, improve decision making accuracy in some region of interest on the ability scale. The test characteristic function derived from such a non-representative sample of test items does provide a way for converting ability score estimates to domain score estimates. While ability estimates do not depend upon the choice of items, the domain score estimates will be biased due to the non-representative selection of test items. However, if the test characteristic function for the *total pool* of items is available (and it will be if all items which serve to define the relevant domain of content have been calibrated), this curve can be used to obtain unbiased domain score estimates from non-representatively selected test items. It is therefore possible to select test items to achieve one purpose (see chapters 11 and 12 for further discussion) and at the same time, obtain unbiased domain score estimates. Figure 4-4 provides a graphical representation of the situation which was just described. Although examinee

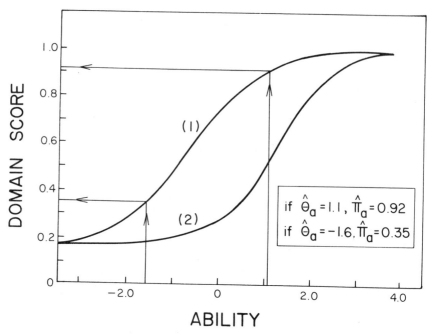

Figure 4–4.   Test Characteristic Curves for (1) the Total Pool of Items in a Content Domain of Interest, and (2) a Selected Sample of the Easier Items

ability is estimated from the test represented by curve (2) in the figure, unbiased domain score estimates are obtained by utilizing the test characteristic function based on the total pool of items measuring the ability of interest. Thus, ability scores provide a basis for *content-referenced interpretations* of examinee test scores. This interpretation will have meaning regardless of the performance of other examinees. Needless to say, ability scores provide a basis for *norm-referenced interpretations* as well.

4.6 Relationship Between Predicted Observed Score Distribution and Ability Distribution

The relationship between observed score $r = \Sigma_i U_i$ and ability was discussed in the above section to some extent. In some instances it may be of importance to construct a predicted observed score distribution given the ability level. An important application of this arises with respect to equating two tests (chapter 10). We present a brief discussion of this issue in this section and return to it in chapter 10.

The basic problem is to construct the frequency distribution $f(r|\theta)$, where r is the number right score given an ability. If all the items in an n-item test were equivalent, then the probability of correct response to an item will be $P(\theta)$ and will be the same for all items. In this case $f(r|\theta)$ is given by the familiar binominal distribution, i.e.

$$f(r|\theta) = \binom{n}{r}P(\theta)^r Q(\theta)^{n-r}$$

where $Q(\theta) = 1 - P(\theta)$. Thus the relative frequency of a particular score r can be obtained from the above equation. It is well known that the term on the right side of this equation is the rth term in the expansion $(P+Q)^n$.

When the items have different item characteristic curves, the probability of a correct response will vary from item to item. If P_i is the probability of a correct response to item i, then the distribution $f(r|\theta)$ has the compound binomial form. The relative frequency of a particular score r can be obtained from the expansion of

$$(P_1 + Q_1)(P_2 + Q_2) \ldots (P_n + Q_n) = \prod_{i=1}^{n} (P_i + Q_i) \quad (4.19)$$

For example, in a four item test, the score $r=4$ occurs with relative frequency $P_1P_2P_3P_4$, while the score $r=0$ occurs with relative frequency $Q_1Q_2Q_3Q_4$. The score $r=3$ occurs with relative frequency

$$P_1P_2P_3Q_4 + P_1P_2Q_3P_4 + P_1Q_2P_3P_4 + Q_1P_2P_3P_4.$$

Similarly the relative frequencies for the scores $r=2$ and $r=1$ can be determined.

These relative frequencies are dependent on ability level θ. Once the form of the item characteristic curve is known, the relative frequencies can be determined and an observed score distribution can be computed. It is worth noting that there is one major difference between the predicted observed score and the true score (or domain score) distributions. The true score distribution is bounded below by $\Sigma_i c_i$ for the three-parameter model (the domain score distribution is bounded below by $n^{-1}\Sigma c_i$). This is not so for the observed score distribution since the score $r=0$ occurs with relative frequency $Q_1Q_2Q_3Q_4$.

4.7 Perfect Scores

The nature of ability scores and scales has been discussed in the above sections. However, procedures for obtaining ability scores once the item response data are obtained have not been described. Detailed treatment of this topic will be found in chapters 5 and 7.

It is worth noting here that, in general, problems arise when assigning ability scores to individuals who have a zero score or a perfect score. The maximum likelihood estimation procedure (see chapter 5) will yield an ability score of $-\infty$ for the zero score and $+\infty$ for the perfect score. No linear transformation of these ability scores will yield finite scores. Clearly this is not desirable in applied testing situations since every examinee must receive a finite score and be included in the statistical analyses of scores.

The most direct solution in this case is to convert ability scores into proportion correct scores (or domain scores). Equation (4.18) is appropriate in this case. When $\hat{\theta} = +\infty$, $P_i(\hat{\theta}) = 1$ and hence $\hat{\pi}|\hat{\theta} = 1$. When $\hat{\theta} = -\infty$, for the one- and two-parameter models, $\hat{\pi}|\theta = 0$. However, for the three-parameter model, corresponding to $\hat{\theta} = -\infty$, $\hat{\pi}|\hat{\theta} = \Sigma c_i/n$. The ability scores can also be converted to the total score T instead of the domain score π. In this case the estimate of T is simply $n\hat{\pi}|\hat{\theta}$.

In some instances, it may be necessary to assign finite ability scores to examinees who receive perfect or zero scores. This would be the case when such scales as NRS, W, or WITs are used. One possible solution in this case is to construct the test characteristic curve, and read off the value of θ corresponding to $n - \frac{1}{2}$ for an examinee who receives a perfect score, and $\frac{1}{2}$ for an examinee who receives a zero score (for the three-parameter model the lower value is set at $\Sigma c_i + \frac{1}{2}$). If the test characteristic curve relates θ to $\hat{\pi}|\hat{\theta}$, then for a perfect score, $\hat{\pi}|\hat{\theta}$ is set at $(n - \frac{1}{2})/n$ while for a zero score it is set at $(\Sigma c_i + \frac{1}{2})/n$. Clearly, there are other solutions to this problem. A linear extrapolation of the test characteristic curve may be employed to yield ability scores. A more attractive solution is to employ a Bayesian estimation procedure. We shall return to these issues in the next chapter.

4.8 Need for Validity Studies

Many researchers have concentrated their evaluative activities of IRT on various goodness-of-fit studies. Goodness of fit studies which are described in Chapters 8 and 9 are important because of their implications for ability score interpretations. However, a good fit between the chosen model and the test data does not reveal what the test measures. The fact that a set of test items fits one of the item response models indicates that the items measure a common trait and nothing more. What is needed is a construct validity study to determine the characteristic(s) or trait measured by the test. In this respect the problem of validating ability score interpretations is no different from the problem associated with validating any set of test scores.

Wood (1978) highlights the problem of model-data fit and what a test measures. He demonstrated that coin-flipping data could be fitted to an item response model. In the example provided by Wood (1978), a candidate's score was the number of heads coming up in ten tosses of a coin. For this example, Wood (1978) was able to obtain both item parameter and ability estimates. The fit between the data and the one-parameter model was very good even though the underlying trait was both invalid and unreliably measured! Therefore, when ability scores are obtained, and before they are used, some evidence that the scores serve their intended purpose is needed. Obviously content validity evidence is important but this type of evidence is not usually sufficient to justify fully the use of a set of ability scores in ranking or describing examinees (Hambleton, 1982; Popham, 1980).

It may be tempting to substitute validity studies associated with raw scores but validity studies associated with raw scores are not totally acceptable as replacement validity studies for ability scores. In general, the relationship between test scores and ability scores is non-linear and non-monotonic. Even with the one-parameter model where there is a perfect monotonic relationship between test scores and ability scores, the validity coefficients for the two sets of scores with a common criterion will be somewhat different.

Essentially, evidence must be accumulated to enable a judgmental determination of whether or not the ability scores serve their intended purpose. For example, when a test is constructed to measure reading comprehension, a series of studies needs to be designed and carried out to determine if the ability scores are reliably determined, if the scores correlate with variables they should correlate with (called convergent validity evidence) and if the scores are uncorrelated with variables that they should *not* in fact correlate with (called divergent validity evidence). Basically, test developers should proceed in the following manner to validate the desired interpretations from the test scores:

- A theory that incorporates the trait measured by the test is formulated.
- Hypotheses derived from the theory about how the ability scores should function (i.e., what should the ability scores correlate with? What factors affect ability scores?) are stated. These hypotheses may relate to evidence that comes in the form of (1) analyses of test content, (2) reliability studies, (3) correlations of ability scores with other measures, (4) experimental studies, (5) prediction studies, (6) multi-trait multi-method investigations.

● The necessary data for the investigation of the hypotheses are collected and the results analyzed. The results are interpreted in relation to the hypotheses.

When the results are consistent with the predictions, that is, when the ability scores behave as they should if the test measured the trait it was designed to measure, the test developers and test score users can have confidence in the validity of their ability score interpretations. When the results are inconsistent, the following possibilities may be entertained: (1) the ability scores do not measure the trait of interest, (2) parts of the theory and/or the hypotheses are incorrect, or (3) both these possibilities.

Validity investigations are on-going activities. There is always a need to carry out additional investigations. While no single investigation can prove the validity of the desired interpretations, a single investigation can demonstrate the invalidity of a set of ability scores or provide corroborating evidence to strengthen the validity of the desired interpretations.

A final point bearing on validity considerations involves the treatment of misfitting test items. It is not unusual for test developers using item response models to define a domain of content: write, edit, and pilot their test items; and, finally, discard test items that fail to fit the selected model. It is with respect to this last point that a problem is created. In deleting test items because of misfit, the characteristics of the item domain are changed (perhaps) in subtle or unknown ways. For example, if items "tapping" minor topics or processes within the domain are deleted, the types of items (content and format) being discarded must be carefully scrutinized since it is necessary to redefine the domain to which ability scores are referenced.

4.9 Summary

It is axiomatic in item response theory that an examinee's performance on a set of items is related to his/her ability θ. The ability θ is unobserved, but based on an examinee's response to a set of items, an ability score can be assigned. The most important property of ability θ is that it is neither dependent on the set of items to which an examinee responds nor on the performance of other examinees. This property enables direct comparisons of items, tests, or the performance of different groups of examinees.

The metric on which ability θ is defined is not unique. Linear transformations of the θ-scale can be made to result in scales that are more meaningful. The advantage of linear transformations is that the statistical properties of the θ-scale are preserved. Non-linear transformations of the θ-scale can also aid in the interpretation of ability scores. One important transformation is through the test characteristic function. The test characteristic function (defined in section 4.3) transforms ability into domain score or proportion correct score. The relationship that exists between ability and domain score permits optimal choice of items to achieve certain decision goals (section 4.4). It should be noted, however, that the domain score scale is dependent on the items used.

From the observed performance of a group of examinees on a set of items, an observed score distribution can be generated. This distribution is useful in describing the performance of a particular group of examinees on a particular set of items, but it does not permit comparisons of distributions. However, once the ability scores and item parameter values are available, a predicted observed score distribution can be generated (section 4.6). While this distribution depends on the items used, it is not group specific and hence comparison of the performance of groups of examinees possible (see Chapter 10 for applications).

The availability of a θ-scale does not ensure its interpretability. Validation studies must be carried out to determine whether or not the ability scores serve their intended purpose (section 4.8). The validity of interpretation may be affected when items that do not "fit" the item response model under consideration are deleted. Thus care must be exercised in interpreting the ability scores even when the model-data fit appears to be good.

Note

1. The test characteristic function may also be defined as $\Sigma P_i(\theta)$. However the average of the item response functions is more convenient and is used as the definition of the test characteristic function here.

5 ESTIMATION
OF ABILITY

5.1 Introduction

Once an appropriate item response model is chosen, it is necessary to determine the values of the item and ability parameters that characterize each item and examinee. Since in the sequel we assume that the latent space is unidimensional, only one parameter, θ, characterizes an examinee. However, several parameters may characterize an item, and the number of item parameters is usually implied by the name of the item response model chosen. The item and ability parameters are usually unknown at some stage of model specification. Typically, a random sample (or calibration sample) from a target population is selected, and the responses to a set of items are obtained. Given the item responses, ability and item parameters are estimated. The item parameters estimated from the sample may be treated as known, and with this assumption item banks may be constructed. In subsequent applications, these items, which have known item parameter values, are administered to examinees and their abilities estimated. The basic problem is then that of determining the item and ability parameters from a knowledge of the responses of a group of examinees. In this chapter, we shall assume that item parameters are known from previous calibration and consider the problem of estimation of ability.

The observable quantities—the responses of examinees to items—are usually obtained for a sample, and hence, the determination of ability parameters must be treated as a problem in statistical estimation. While several estimation procedures are currently available, in this chapter only the maximum likelihood procedure (MLE) will be described in detail while other procedures will be discussed briefly.

5.2 The Likelihood Function

The probability that an examinee with ability θ obtains a response U_i on item i, where

$$U_i = \begin{cases} 1 & \text{for a correct response} \\ 0 & \text{for an incorrect response} \end{cases}$$

is denoted as $P(U_i | \theta)$. For a correct response, the probability $P(U_i = 1 | \theta)$ is the item response function and is customarily denoted as $P_i(\theta)$ or simply as P_i. As described earlier, the item response function is a function of an examinee's ability, θ, and the parameters that characterize the item. Since U_i is a binomial variable, the probability of a response, U_i, can be expressed as

$$P(U_i | \theta) = P(U_i = 1 | \theta) P(U_i = 0 | \theta)$$
$$= P_i^{U_i}(1 - P_i)^{1 - U_i}$$
$$= P_i^{U_i} Q_i^{1 - U_i}, \tag{5.1}$$

where $Q_i = 1 - P_i$. If an examinee with ability θ responds to n items, the joint probability of the responses $U_1, U_2, \ldots, U_n$ can be denoted as $P(U_1, U_2, \ldots, U_n | \theta)$. If the latent space is complete (in this case, unidimensional), then local independence obtains; i.e., for given ability θ, the responses to n items are independent. This implies that

$$P(U_1, U_2, \ldots, U_n | \theta) = P(U_1 | \theta) P(U_2 | \theta), \ldots, P(U_n | \theta)$$

$$= \prod_{i=1}^{n} P(U_i | \theta) \tag{5.2}$$

$$= \prod_{i=1}^{n} P_i^{U_i} Q_i^{(1 - U_i)}. \tag{5.3}$$

The above expression is the joint probability of responses to n items. However, when the responses are observed, i.e., when the random variables $U_1, U_2, \ldots, U_n$ take on specific values $u_1, u_2, \ldots, u_n$ where u_i is either one or zero, the above expression ceases to be a probability statement. On the other hand, it is a mathematical function of θ known as the *likelihood function* denoted as

$$L(u_1, u_2, \ldots, u_n \mid \theta) = \prod_{i=1}^{n} P_i^{U_i} Q_i^{1-u_i}. \tag{5.4}$$

When $u_i = 1$, the term with Q_i drops out, and when $u_i = 0$, the term with P_i drops out.

Example 1

Suppose that an examinee has the following response vector on five items:

$$u = (u_1 u_2 u_3 u_4 u_5) = (1 \ 0 \ 1 \ 1 \ 0).$$

The likelihood function is then given by

$$L(u \mid \theta) = P_1 Q_2 P_3 P_4 Q_5.$$

If we assume that the item response model is the one-parameter model,

$$P_i = \exp D(\theta - b_i)/[1 + \exp D(\theta - b_i)]$$

and

$$Q_i = 1/[1 + \exp D(\theta - b_i)].$$

The likelihood function given by equation (5.4) and illustrated above may be viewed a criterion function. The value of θ that maximizes the likelihood function can be taken as the estimator of θ. This is the maximum likelihood estimator of θ. In a loose sense, the maximum likelihood estimator of θ can be interpreted as that value of the examinees' ability that generates the greatest "probability" for the observed response pattern.

The likelihood function given by equation (5.4) can be plotted, and from the graph the maximum likelihood estimator of θ can be determined. However, instead of graphing the function $L(u \mid \theta)$, the function $\ln L(u \mid \theta)$ may be graphed. Here ln denotes the natural logarithm. Since $\ln L$ and L are monotonically related, the value of θ that maximizes $L(u \mid \theta)$ is the same as the value of θ that maximizes $\ln L(u \mid \theta)$. Moreover, since P_i and Q_i are

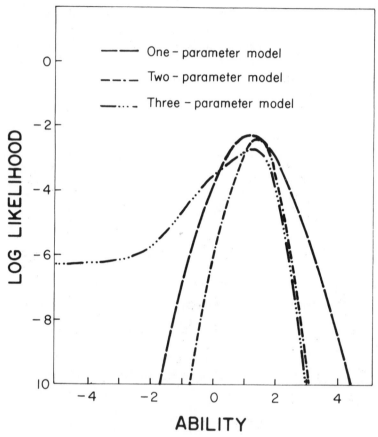

Figure 5-1. Log-Likelihood Functions for Three Item Response Models

probabilities, $L(u|\theta)$ is bounded between zero and one. Hence, the range of $\ln L$ is $(-\infty, 0)$. The main advantage of working with $\ln L(u|\theta)$ instead of $L(u|\theta)$ is that products can be expressed as the sum of logarithms. Thus, the logarithm of the likelihood function given in the example becomes

$$\ln L(u|\theta) = \ln P_1 + \ln Q_2 + \ln P_3 + \ln P_4 + \ln Q_5.$$

Three graphs of $\ln L(u|\theta)$ are displayed in figure 5-1 for the likelihood function given by equation 5.4. These graphs are based on the following values of item parameters:

$$a = [\quad 1.0 \quad 1.5 \quad 1.0 \quad 2.0 \quad 2.5]$$
$$b = [-1.0 \quad 1.0 \quad 0.0 \quad 1.5 \quad 2.0]$$
$$c = [\quad .30 \quad .10 \quad .10 \quad .10 \quad .30].$$

Clearly for the Rasch model, only the item difficulties given in b are used; for the two-parameter model, item difficulty and discriminations given in b and a are used; for the three-parameter model, item difficulties, discriminations and pseudo-chance level parameters given in b, a, and c, respectively, are used. The three functions have maximum values near $\theta = 1.18$, and hence this value is taken as the maximum likelihood estimate $\hat{\theta}$ of θ for each of the three item response models.

The maximum likelihood estimate of θ when the likelihood function is given by equation (5.4) can be determined by graphical methods as demonstrated above. However, this procedure may not be feasible in general. The maximum of the likelihood function $L(u|\theta)$ or, equivalently, $\ln L(u|\theta)$, where

$$\ln L(u|\theta) = \sum_{i=1}^{n} [u_i \ln P_i + (1 - u_i) \ln Q_i] \qquad (5.5)$$

is attained when θ satisfies the equation[1]

$$\frac{d}{d\theta} \ln L(u|\theta) = 0 \qquad (5.6)$$

and, hence, the MLE of θ can be obtained as that value that satisfies this equation. This equation, known as the *likelihood equation*, is, in general, nonlinear and cannot be solved explicitly. Hence, numerical procedures have to be employed. A well-known procedure is the Newton-Raphson procedure, which can be illustrated as follows: Suppose that the equation to be solved is

$$f(x) = 0,$$

and an approximate solution to the equation is x_o. Then a more accurate solution, x_1, is given as

$$x_1 = x_o - h.$$

From figure 5–2, it follows that

$$h = \frac{f(x_o)}{\tan \alpha}.$$

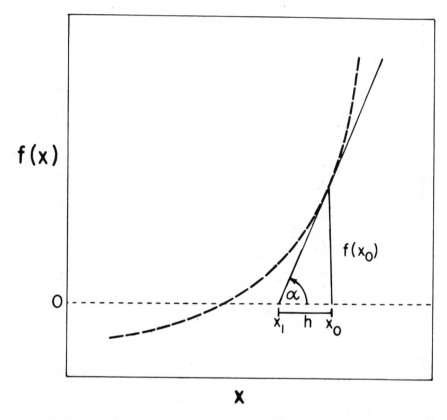

Figure 5-2.   Illustration of the Newton-Raphson Method

Since $\tan \alpha$ is slope of the function $f(x)$ at x_o, $\tan \alpha = f'(x_o)$, where $f'(x_o)$ is the derivative of the function evaluated at x_o. Thus,

$$h = \frac{f(x_o)}{f'(x_o)},$$

whence it follows that a more accurate solution to the equation is

$$x_1 = x_o - \frac{f(x_o)}{f'(x_o)}, \qquad (5.7)$$

Once x_1 is obtained, an improvement on x_1 may be obtained in the same manner.

This process is repeated. In general, if x_m is the approximate solution at the mth stage, then an improved solution x_{m+1} is given by

$$x_{m+1} = x_m - \frac{f(x_m)}{f'(x_m)} . \qquad (5.8)$$

This procedure is iterated until the difference between the mth approximation and the $(m + 1)$th approximation, $(x_{m+1} - x_m)$, is below a pre-established small value. When this happens, the process is said to have converged, and the solution to the equation $f(x) = 0$ is taken as x_m. It can be shown (we shall not attempt it here) that the Newton-Raphson procedure converges rapidly as long as $f'(x)$ is not zero (for details, the reader is referred to Isaacson and Keller, 1966).

In the current situation,

$$f(x) \equiv \frac{d}{d\theta} \ln L(u \,|\, \theta),$$

and hence

$$f'(x) \equiv \frac{d^2}{d\theta^2} \ln L(u \,|\, \theta).$$

Thus, if θ_m is the mth approximation to the maximum likelihood estimator θ, then by virtue of equation (5.8) the $(m + 1)$th approximation is given by

$$\theta_{m+1} \equiv \theta_m - \left[\frac{d}{d\theta} \ln L(u \,|\, \theta) \right]_m \Big/ \left[\frac{d^2}{d\theta^2} \ln L(u \,|\, \theta) \right]_m . \qquad (5.9)$$

This process is repeated until convergence takes place. The converged value is taken as the maximum likelihood estimate of θ and denoted as $\hat{\theta}$.

5.3 Conditional Maximum Likelihood Estimation of Ability

Suppose that a group of N examinees are administered n items with known item parameter values and it is necessary to estimate the abilities θ_a $(a = 1, \ldots, N)$. Since item parameter values are known, this is referred to as *conditional estimation* of θ.

Let

$$\boldsymbol{u}_a = [u_{1a}, u_{2a}, \ldots, u_{na}] \qquad (a = 1, \ldots, N)$$

be the response vector of the ath examinee on n items, and $[\theta_1, \theta_2, \ldots, \theta_N]$ denote the vector of abilities for the N examinees. The likelihood function for the $(Nn \times 1)$ vector $\boldsymbol{u}$ of the responses of N examinees on n items where

$$\boldsymbol{u} = [\boldsymbol{u}_1, \boldsymbol{u}_2, \ldots, \boldsymbol{u}_a, \ldots, \boldsymbol{u}_N]$$

is

$$L(\boldsymbol{u} \,|\, \boldsymbol{\theta}) \equiv L(\boldsymbol{u}_1, \boldsymbol{u}_2, \ldots, \boldsymbol{u}_a, \ldots, \boldsymbol{u}_N \,|\, \theta_1, \theta_2, \ldots, \theta_N) = \prod_{a=1}^{N} L(\boldsymbol{u}_a \,|\, \theta_a)$$

$$= \prod_{a=1}^{N} \prod_{i=1}^{n} L(u_{ia} \,|\, \theta) = \prod_{a=1}^{N} \prod_{i=1}^{n} P_{ia}^{u_{ia}} Q_{ia}^{1-u_{ia}}, \tag{5.10}$$

where $P_{ia} \equiv P_i(\theta_a)$. The logarithm of the likelihood function is then given by

$$\ln L(\boldsymbol{u}_1, \boldsymbol{u}_2, \ldots, \boldsymbol{u}_N \,|\, \boldsymbol{\theta}) = \sum_{a=1}^{N} \sum_{i=1}^{n} [u_{ia} \ln P_{ia} + (1 - u_{ia}) \ln (1 - P_{ia})]. \tag{5.11}$$

The maximum likelihood estimators of $\theta_1, \theta_2, \ldots, \theta_N$ are obtained by solving the set of likelihood equations for $\theta_1, \theta_2, \ldots, \theta_N$:

$$\frac{\partial}{\partial \theta_a} \ln L(\boldsymbol{u}_1, \boldsymbol{u}_2, \ldots, \boldsymbol{u}_N \,|\, \boldsymbol{\theta}) = 0 \qquad (a = 1, \ldots, N). \tag{5.12}$$

These equations can be expressed as

$$\frac{\partial \ln L}{\partial \theta_a} = \sum_{i=1}^{n} \frac{\partial \ln L}{\partial P_{ia}} \frac{\partial P_{ia}}{\partial \theta_a}$$

$$= \sum_{i=1}^{n} \left(\frac{U_{ia}}{P_{ia}} - \frac{1 - U_{ia}}{1 - P_{ia}} \right) \frac{\partial P_{ia}}{\partial \theta_a}$$

$$= \sum_{i=1}^{n} \left(\frac{U_{ia} - P_{ia}}{P_{ia} Q_{ia}} \right) \frac{\partial P_{ia}}{\partial \theta_a} = 0. \tag{5.13}$$

Each of these equations is in terms of a single θ_a, and, hence, these equations can be solved separately once the form of the item response function is specified. These expressions and the expressions for the second derivatives are summarized in table 5-1.

For the one-parameter model, the likelihood equation becomes

$$\frac{\partial \ln L}{\partial \theta_a} \equiv D \sum_{i=1}^{n} (u_{ia} - P_{ia}) = 0, \tag{5.14}$$

or

$$D(r_a - \sum_{i=1}^{n} P_{ia}) = 0, \tag{5.15}$$

where $r_a = \Sigma u_{ia}$ is the number correct score for examinee a. The second derivative is

$$\frac{\partial^2 \ln L}{\partial \theta_a^2} = D^2 \sum_{i=1}^{n} P_i Q_i. \tag{5.16}$$

An initial value for θ_a, θ_{oa} for examinee a is given by

$$\theta_{oa} = \ln[r_a/(n - r_a)],$$
$$\equiv \theta_o. \tag{5.17}$$

(The subscript for examinee a has been dropped since no confusion arises in this case.)

The value of θ at the $(m + 1)$th iteration can be obtained using the recurrence relation

$$\theta_{m+1} = \theta_m - h_m.$$

Here the correction factor h_m, is given by

$$h_m = D \left[r - \sum_{i=1}^{n} P_i(\theta_m) \right] / \left[-D^2 \sum_{i=1}^{n} P_i(\theta_m) Q_i(\theta_m) \right]. \tag{5.18}$$

When $|h_m|$ given above is less than a prescribed small value, ε (commonly chosen to be .001), the iterative procedure is terminated.

In this case,

$$|h_m| = |\theta_{m+1} - \theta_m| < \varepsilon.$$

When this occurs, the value θ_{m+1} is taken as the maximum likelihood estimate of θ and denoted as $\hat{\theta}$.

Table 5-1. First and Second Derivatives of the Log-Likelihood Function for Three Logistic Item Response Models

Derivative	One-Parameter Model	Two-Parameter Model	Three-Parameter Model
First $\left(\dfrac{\partial \ln L}{\partial \theta_a} \right)$	$D \displaystyle\sum_{i=1}^{n} (u_{ia} - P_{ia})$	$D \displaystyle\sum_{i=1}^{n} a_i(u_{ia} - P_{ia})$	$D \displaystyle\sum_{i=1}^{n} a_i(u_{ia} - P_{ia})(P_{ia} - c_i)/P_{ia}(1 - c_i)$
Second $\left(\dfrac{\partial^2 \ln L}{\partial \theta_a^2} \right)$	$-D^2 \displaystyle\sum_{i=1}^{n} P_{ia}(1 - P_{ia})$	$-D^2 \displaystyle\sum_{i=1}^{n} a_i^2 P_{ia}(1 - P_{ia})$	$D^2 \displaystyle\sum_{i=1}^{n} a_i^2(P_{ia} - c_i)(u_{ia}c_i - P_{ia}^2)Q_{ia}/P_{ia}^2(1 - c_i)^2$

Example 2

Suppose that the one-parameter item response model is appropriate with item difficulties and response pattern given in example 1. To obtain the maximum likelihood estimate of θ, we implement the Newton-Raphson procedure.

Step 1

Since the examinee has a number right score of 3, the starting value θ_o is

$$\theta_o = \ln[3/(5-3)] = .4054.$$

Step 2

1. With this starting value, ΣP_i and $\Sigma P_i Q_i$ are computed.
2. The correction factor h_o is computed using equation (5.18).
3. The new value $\theta_1 = \theta_o - h_o$ is computed.
4. The computations in (1), (2), and (3) are repeated until the correction h is negligible.

The computations are summarized in table 5–2.

The procedure for estimating ability parameters in the two- and three-parameter logistic models when item parameters are known proceed in the same manner. In general, the likelihood equation can be expressed as (from table 5–1)

$$\frac{\partial \ln L}{\partial \theta_a} \equiv \sum_{i=1}^{n} k_i u_{ia} - \sum_{i=1}^{n} k_i P_{ia} = 0 \qquad (a = 1, \ldots, N).$$

$$(5.19)$$

The values of k_i for the one-, two-, and the three-parameter logistic models are, respectively,

$$k_i = D \qquad (5.20)$$
$$k_i = Da_i \qquad (5.21)$$

and

$$k_i = Da_i(P_{ia} - c_i)/P_{ia}(1 - c_i). \qquad (5.22)$$

Table 5-2. Summary of Computations for Estimation of Ability

		Probability $P_i(\theta_m)$ *for Iteration* m		
Item		$m = 0$	$m = 1$	$m = 2$
i	*difficulty*	$P_i(\theta_0)$	$P_i(\theta_1)$	$P_i(\theta_2)$
1	−1.0	.9159	.9784	.9760
2	1.0	.2667	.6020	.5761
3	0.0	.6656	.8922	.8815
4	1.5	.1345	.3926	.3675
5	2.0	.0623	.2165	.1989
$\Sigma P_i(\theta_m)$		2.0451	3.0818	3.0000
$\Sigma P_i(\theta_m)Q_i(\theta_m)$		.6699	.7649	−.7638
h_m		−.8384	.0629	−.0000
$\theta_{m+1} = \theta_m - h_m$		1.2438	1.1808	1.1808

The maximum likelihood estimate of $\theta = 1.18$.

Since the item discrimination parameters, a_i, are usually positive and since in the three-parameter model $P_{ia} - c_i$ is nonnegative (c_i being the lower asymptote), k_i is a positive quantity for the three models. It is evident that when an examinee responds incorrectly to all the items, $u_i = 0$ for $i = 1, \ldots , n$. Thus, the likelihood equation (5.19) reduces to

$$\sum_{i=1}^{n} k_i P_{ia} = 0. \qquad (5.23)$$

Since each k_i is positive and P_{ia} is the probability of a correct response, this equation is satisfied only when $\theta_a = -\infty$. Similarly, when an examinee responds correctly to all the items, $u_{ia} = 1$ for all i, and the likelihood equation reduces to

$$\sum_{i-1}^{n} k_i = \sum_{i=1}^{n} k_i P_{ia} \qquad (5.24)$$

and is satisfied only when $\theta_a = +\infty$. It is evident then that maximum likelihood estimators do not exist for these cases. Examinees who obtain perfect scores or zero-correct scores are eliminated from the estimation procedure. The effect of deletion of examinees on the likelihood function is currently not known. It can be surmised that the properties of the maximum likelihood estimator do not obtain under these circumstances. We shall return to the problem of assigning $\theta-$ values to examinees when they obtain perfect or zero scores.

A further problem that may be encountered in obtaining the maximum likelihood estimator is that the likelihood function may possess several maxima in the interval $-\infty < \theta < \infty$. In this case, the value determined by solving the equation $\partial \ln L/\partial \theta = 0$ may not correspond to the true maximum. This may also happen if the value of the likelihood function at $\theta = \pm\infty$ is larger than the maximum value found in the interval $-\infty < \theta < \infty$. The maximum likelihood estimator does not exist in this case. These problems arise in the case of the three-parameter model and was first noted by Samejima (1973a).

To demonstrate, consider a three-parameter model and a response vector for an examinee;

$$u = [1 \ 0 \ 1 \ 0 \ 0].$$

Further, assume that the item parameters are:

$$a = [2.0 \quad 1.0 \quad 2.5 \quad 1.5 \quad 2.5],$$
$$b = [0.0 \quad -.5 \quad 0.0 \quad -.5 \quad 0.5],$$

and

$$c = [.25 \quad 0.0 \quad .25 \quad 0.0 \quad 0.1].$$

As $\theta \to \infty$, $P_{ia} \to c_i$ and $Q_{ia} \to (1 - c_i)$. Thus,

$$\lim_{\theta \to -\infty} \ln L(u_1, u_2, \ldots, u_n \mid \theta) = \sum_{i=1}^{n} [u_i \ln c_i + (1 - u_i) \ln(1 - c_i)]$$

$$= \ln .25 + \ln 1.0 + \ln .25 + \ln 1.0$$
$$+ \ln .9$$
$$= -2.88.$$

The function, illustrated in figure 5–3 attains a local maximum value lower than this value at $\theta = -.03$. If a numerical procedure such as the Newton-Raphson procedure is employed to locate the maximum value, and if the starting value is close to the false maximum value, the iterations will converge to this value. An erroneous value for the maximum likelihood estimate will be obtained.

The problem of several maxima is indeed a formidable problem to solve. However, it should be pointed out that in the illustration the response pattern is abnormal, and the number of items is small. Lord (1980a, p. 51) notes that

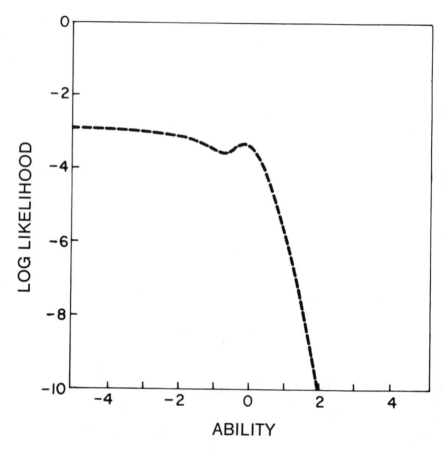

Figure 5-3. Log-Likelihood Function Illustrating a Local Maximum

this problem does not arise when working with large number items ($n > 20$) as is usually the case in practice.

5.4 Properties of Maximum Likelihood Estimators

Maximum likelihood estimators possess several useful and important properties. Under general conditions, maximum likelihood estimators are:

1. Consistent; i.e., as the sample size and number of items increase, the estimators converge to the true values;

2. Functions of sufficient statistics when sufficient statistics exist; i.e., the sufficient statistic contains all the information about the parameter. No further data are necessary;
3. Efficient; i.e., asymptotically the maximum likelihood estimators have the smallest variance;
4. Asymptotically normally distributed.

In the one-parameter logistic model, the number-correct score is a sufficient statistic for ability θ. For the two-parameter logistic model, the score r_a for the ath examinee defined as

$$r_a = \sum_{i=1}^{n} a_i u_{ia}, \qquad (5.25)$$

where u_{ia} is the response to item i, is a sufficient statistic for θ (see Lord, 1980a, p. 57). No sufficient statistic exists for the three-parameter logistic model, or in the case of any of the normal ogive models.

The property of asymptotic normality is particularly useful in practice. The maximum likelihood estimator of θ, $\hat{\theta}$, is asymptotically normal with mean θ and variance $[I(\theta)]^{-1}$, where $I(\theta)$ is the information function given by the expression (see appendix to this chapter)

$$I(\theta) = -E[\partial^2 \ln L/\partial \theta^2] = \sum_{i=1}^{n} P_i'^2 /P_i Q_i. \qquad (5.26)$$

Here, E denotes expected value, and P_i' is the derivative of the item response function with respect to θ. While this is a useful form, the information function can also be obtained directly from the second derivatives.

The reciprocal of the information function evaluated at ability θ is the asymptotic variance of the maximum likelihood estimator $\hat{\theta}$. This should be expressed as

$$V(\hat{\theta}\,|\,\theta) = [I(\theta)]^{-1}, \qquad (5.27)$$

where V denotes variance. This is true only if $\hat{\theta}$ is a consistent estimator of θ, a condition that is met in the current situation. To evaluate the variance of $\hat{\theta}$, it is necessary to know the value of the unknown parameter θ. This presents a problem in constructing a confidence band for θ. Fortunately $\hat{\theta}$ can be substituted for θ in (5.26), and an "estimate" of $V(\hat{\theta}\,|\,\theta)$, denoted usually as $I(\hat{\theta})$, results in this situation. Birnbaum (1968, p. 457) has pointed out that this procedure yields a *maximum likelihood confidence limit estimator*.

The $(1 - \alpha)$th percentile confidence interval for θ is given by

$$\theta - z_{\frac{\alpha}{2}} [I(\theta)]^{-\frac{1}{2}} \le \theta \le \theta + z_{\frac{\alpha}{2}} [I(\theta)]^{-\frac{1}{2}}, \qquad (5.28)$$

where $z_{\frac{\alpha}{2}}$ is the upper $\frac{1}{2}\alpha$ percentile point of the standard normal curve. Clearly, $[I(\theta)]^{-\frac{1}{2}}$ is the standard error of the maximum likelihood estimator.

Example 3

For the Rasch model with item difficulties as specified in example 2, the maximum likelihood estimate of θ is 1.18. The computation of the value of the information function at $\hat{\theta} = 1.18$ is given in table 5–3. Since $\hat{\theta}$ is correct to two decimals, the rounded-off information function is 2.21, and it follows that the standard error of $\hat{\theta}$ is .67. The 95 percent asymptotic confidence interval for θ is

$$1.18 - (1.96)(.67) \le \theta \le 1.18 + (1.96)(.67),$$

i.e.

$$-.13 \le \theta \le 2.49.$$

It follows from equation (5.28) that the width, ω, of the confidence interval for θ is given by

$$\omega = 2z_{\frac{\alpha}{2}} [I(\theta)]^{-\frac{1}{2}}, \qquad (5.29)$$

Table 5–3. Computation of Item Information

Item i	b_i	$P_i(\theta)$	$Q_i(\theta)$	$D^2 P_i(\theta)Q_i(\theta)$
1	−1.0	.9760	.0234	.0659
2	1.0	.5761	.4239	.7057
3	0.0	.8815	.1185	.3020
4	1.5	.3674	.6326	.6716
5	2.0	.1989	.8011	.4604

$$I(\theta) = D^2 \sum_{i=1}^{n} P_i(\theta)Q_i(\theta)$$

$$= 2.2056.$$

Table 5-4. Information Function for Three Logistic Item Response Models

Model	$P_i'(\theta)$	$\Sigma P_i'^2/P_i Q_i$
One-parameter	$DP_i Q_i$	$\sum_i D^2 P_i Q_i$
Two-Parameter	$Da_i P_i Q_i$	$\sum_i D^2 a_i^2 P_i Q_i$
Three-parameter	$Da_i Q_i (P_i - c_i)/(1 - c_i)$	$\sum_i D^2 a_i^2 Q_i (P_i - c_i)^2/(1 - c_i)^2 P_i$

or, equivalently,

$$I(\theta) \propto 1/\omega^2. \qquad (5.30)$$

This demonstrates that the information function is inversely proportional to the square of the width of the asymptotic confidence interval for θ. Thus, the larger the value of the information function, the smaller the width of the confidence interval, and, in turn, the more precise the measurement of ability. Furthermore, since the information function is a function of the ability, it will have different values at different ability levels; hence, the precision of measurement can be evaluated at a specified ability level.

The expression for the information function given by equation (5.26) can be evaluated once the form of the item response function is specified. The derivative $P_i'(\theta)$ and the information function for the three logistic item response models are given in table 5–4.

The maximum likelihood estimator of θ asymptotically attains the minimum variance attainable, with the minimum variance being $[I(\theta)]^{-1}$. No other estimator of θ can therefore have a smaller variance, asymptotically.

It should be pointed out that the properties of the maximum likelihood estimator of θ discussed in this section obtain asymptotically and may not be valid for any sample size. Since we are concerned with the estimation of θ when item parameters are known, asymptotic results are valid when the *number of items* (not the number of examinees) becomes large.

5.5 Bayesian Estimation

As indicated in section 5.3, when examinees obtain perfect scores or zero scores, maximum likelihood estimation fails unless these examinees are removed prior to estimation. The effect of this procedure on the properties of the maximum likelihood estimator is not well understood.

When prior information on the distribution of abilities of a group of examinees is available, a Bayesian procedure may provide meaningful estimates of ability. Suppose that prior to estimating the abilities of examinees in a group, we are willing to make the assumption that the information regarding the ability of any one examinee is no different from that of any other examinee; i.e., the information on examinees is *exchangeable*. This assumption implies that the abilities $\theta_a(a = 1, \ldots, N)$ may be considered as a random sample from a population (Novick, Lewis, & Jackson, 1973). To complete the specification of prior information, it is necessary to specify the distribution of θ_a. For example, if it is believed that a small proportion of examinees have abilities outside a given range, a sizable proportion of examinees have ability levels around an unspecified mean, and so on, then this belief can be indicated by specifying that the ability distribution is, say, normal, i.e.

$$\theta_a \sim N(\mu, \phi),$$

where $N(\mu, \phi)$ denotes a normal distribution with mean μ and variance ϕ. The values of μ and ϕ need to be specified, or these parameters may be specified via further distributions. Owen (1975) assumed, in the context of adaptive testing, that $\mu = 0$ and $\phi = 1$.

The normal prior distribution is a convenient one. Other forms are also possible. Birnbaum (1969) assumed the prior distribution of θ_a to be a logistic density function, $f(\theta)$, where

$$f(\theta) = \exp(\theta)/[1 + \exp(\theta)]^2.$$

Empirical specification of prior distributions may be appropriate in some instances. From a distribution of raw scores or transformed raw scores as indicated in equation (5.17), it may be possible to estimate a prior distribution.

At the heart of the Bayesian procedure is Bayes's theorem, which relates conditional and marginal probabilities:

$$P(B \mid A) = P(A \mid B)P(B)/P(A). \tag{5.31}$$

In the context of estimation of ability, A may be considered as θ_a, and B as the set of observed responses on n items, u. Then equation (5.31) can be re-expressed as

$$P(\theta_a \mid u) = P(u \mid \theta_a)P(\theta_a)/P(u). \tag{5.32a}$$

Since θ_a is a continuous variable, the above should be interpreted as density functions. The notation $P(\theta_a)$ for the prior distribution of θ_a may be confused with that for the item response function. Hence, we shall indicate these as density fucntions with $f(\ )$ denoting their forms. Thus,

$$f(\theta_a \mid u) = f(u \mid \theta_a)f(\theta_a)/f(u). \tag{5.32b}$$

Clearly, for a given set of responses, $f(u)$ is a constant, the density function $f(\theta_a \mid u)$ is the *posterior density* of θ_a, and $f(\theta_a)$ is the *prior* of θ_a. From section 5.2, $f(u \mid \theta_a)$ can be identified as the likelihood function of the observations. Thus, equation (5.32b) may be written as

$$f(\theta_a \mid u) \propto L(u \mid \theta_a)f(\theta_a), \tag{5.33}$$

where $L(u \mid \theta_a)$ is the likelihood function, given by equation (5.4). Alternatively, the above relationship can be stated as

$$\text{posterior} \propto \text{likelihood} \times \text{prior.} \tag{5.34}$$

When N examinees are involved, the posterior and prior densities are joint densities of $\theta_1, \theta_2, \ldots, \theta_N$. Thus, equation (5.33) can be expanded as

$$f(\theta_1, \theta_2, \ldots, \theta_N \mid u_1, \ldots, u_N)$$
$$\propto L(u_1, u_2, \ldots, u_N \mid \theta_1, \theta_2, \ldots, \theta_N)f(\theta_1, \theta_2, \theta_N). \tag{5.35}$$

The likelihood function in this case is given by equation (5.10).

Once the form of the prior density is specified, and an appropriate item response model is chosen, the posterior density function of the abilities is determined. This joint posterior density contains all the information necessary about the group of examinees. It may be of interest to note that when a "noninformative" or uniform prior distribution for $f(\theta_a)$ is specified, i.e.,

$$f(\theta_a) = \text{constant,}$$

then equation (5.33) for the posterior distribution reduces to

$$f(\theta_a \mid u) \propto L(u \mid \theta_a),$$

or the likelihood function. In this case the Bayesian estimator is numerically equivalent to maximum likelihood estimator.

The Bayesian procedure can be illustrated by assuming that the prior distribution for θ_a is normal with zero mean and unit variance, i.e.,

$$\theta_a \sim N(0, 1)$$

or

$$f(\theta_a) \propto \exp(-\tfrac{1}{2}\theta_a^2). \tag{5.36}$$

If we assume a priori that the ability parameters are independently distributed, a reasonable assumption, then the posterior distribution

$$f(\theta_1, \theta_2, \ldots, \theta_N \mid u) \propto L(u \mid \theta_1, \theta_2, \ldots, \theta_N) f(\theta_1, \theta_2, \ldots \theta_{2N}). \tag{5.37}$$

Since

$$f(\theta_1, \theta_2, \ldots, \theta_N) = f(\theta_1)f(\theta_2), \ldots , f(\theta_N)$$

$$\propto \prod_{a=1}^{N} \exp(-\tfrac{1}{2}\theta_a^2)$$

$$= \exp(-\tfrac{1}{2} \sum_{a=1}^{N} \theta_a^2), \tag{5.38}$$

the posterior distribution is

$$f(\theta_1, \theta_2, \ldots, \theta_N \mid u) \propto L(u \mid \theta_1, \theta_2, \ldots, \theta_N)[\exp(-\tfrac{1}{2}\Sigma\theta_a^2)]. \tag{5.39}$$

While the posterior density contains all the information about the abilities, it is not in a readily usable form. Point estimates of the ability parameters are useful in such situations. The joint modal estimates of the parameters may be taken as appropriate, as suggested by Lindley and Smith (1972), Novick, Lewis, and Jackson (1973), and Swaminathan and Gifford (1982).

The joint modal estimates are those values of the parameters that correspond to the maximum of the posterior density function. These may be more conveniently obtained as those values that maximize the natural logarithm of the posterior distribution, i.e.,

$$\ln f(\theta \mid u) = \text{constant} + \ln L(u \mid \theta) - \tfrac{1}{2} \sum_{a=1}^{N} \theta_a^2. \tag{5.40}$$

The solution of the set of equations

$$\frac{\partial}{\partial \theta_a} \ln f(\theta \mid u) = 0 \quad a = 1, \ldots, N \tag{5.41}$$

are Bayes's modal estimators of $\theta_1, \theta_2, \ldots, \theta_N$.

Utilizing equation (5.19), the above equations may be expressed as

$$\sum_{i=1}^{n} k_i(u_{ia} - P_{ia}) - \theta_a = 0, \qquad (5.42)$$

where $k_i(>0)$ are given by equations 5–20 through 5–22.

Equation (5.42) explains the primary difference between maximum likelihood estimation and Bayesian estimation. Writing this in the form

$$\sum_{i=1}^{n} k_i P_{ia} = \sum_{i=1}^{n} k_i u_{ia} - \theta_a, \qquad (5.43)$$

we see that estimates of θ_a exist for zero scores and perfect scores. For a zero score,

$$\sum k_i P_{ia} = -\theta_a. \qquad (5.44)$$

Since the mean of θ is specified as zero, θ_a that corresponds to a zero score is negative, and hence equation (5.44) will possess a solution. Similar consideration applies to a perfect score.

The modal equations (equation 5.42) can be solved using the Newton-Raphson procedure described in section 5.2. We shall not provide the details of this here.

Swaminathan and Gifford (1982) and Swaminathan (in press) have provided a more general Bayesian framework for obtaining Bayes estimators. Their procedure, based on the hierarchical scheme advocated by Lindley and Smith (1972) and Novick, Lewis, and Jackson (1973) is applicable in a variety of situations. These methods are beyond the scope of this presentation; interested readers are referred to chapter 7 and the sources listed for complete discussions.

5.6 Estimation of θ for Perfect and Zero Scores

It was pointed out in section 5.3 that maximum likelihood estimators of ability corresponding to perfect scores and zero scores are $+\infty$ and $-\infty$, respectively. While this may not be a problem in theory, it presents a problem when reporting of ability scores is necessary. One possible solution to this problem is to employ a Bayes estimator of ability. With an informative prior specification such as specifying a normal prior distribution for θ, Bayes estimators of θ corresponding to perfect or zero scores are possible.

However appealing the Bayes estimator may be, it may not be acceptable to those who are philosophically opposed to the notion of specifying prior beliefs. A simple solution to the problem in this case is to report scores on the true score metric. The true score ξ is given by

$$\xi = \sum_{i=1}^{n} P_i(\theta). \tag{5.45}$$

When $\theta = +\infty$, $P_i(\theta) = 1$, and hence $\xi = n$. Similarly, when $\theta = -\infty$, $P_i(\theta) = c_i$ (for the three-parameter model). In this case,

$$\xi = \sum_{i=1}^{n} c_i. \tag{5.46}$$

The problem with this is that an examinee with a zero observed score may obtain an estimated true score greater than zero. However, when $c_i = 0$, as for the one- and two-parameter models, $\xi = 0$.

Alternatively, estimates of θ corresponding to perfect and zero scores can be obtained by modifying the likelihood equations. For a zero score, the likelihood equation is (equation 5.23)

$$\sum_{i=1}^{n} k_i P_{ia} = 0.$$

This equation may be modified as follows:

$$\sum_{i=1}^{n} k_i P_{ia} = \varepsilon, \tag{5.47}$$

where ε is a small positive quantity. Similarly, the likelihood equation (equation 5.24) corresponding to a perfect score may be modified as

$$\sum_{i=1}^{n} k_i P_{ia} = \sum_{i=1}^{n} k_i - \varepsilon. \tag{5.48}$$

The choice of ε is arbitrary.

Another approach that may be employed exploits the relationship between true score and ability as described in section 4.7. In this case, the equation

$$\sum_{i=1}^{n} P_{ia}(\theta) = n - \varepsilon \tag{5.49}$$

is solved for a perfect score, while the equation

$$\sum_{i=1}^{n} P_{ia}(\theta) = \sum_{i=1}^{n} c_i + \varepsilon \tag{5.50}$$

is solved for a zero score. Again, ε is an arbitrarily chosen small positive number.

These two methods are similar to the Bayesian solution, albeit without the justification.

5.7 Summary

The estimation of ability parameters when item parameters are known is accomplished in a straightforward manner using the maximum likelihood estimation procedure. The maximum likelihood estimators enjoy several useful properties, particularly those of consistency and asymptotic normality. With sufficiently large numbers of items, the standard error of the ability estimate is obtained using the information function. With this, asymptotic confidence intervals may be established for θ.

Maximum likelihood estimation fails when a perfect score or a zero score is encountered. This problem can be solved using a Bayesian approach. The Bayes estimators have smaller standard errors than their maximum likelihood counterparts. However, the Bayesian approach requires specification of prior belief regarding an examinee's ability, and hence may not be appealing to all.

When it is necessary to report ability values corresponding to perfect or zero scores, maximum likelihood estimators are not appropriate since these are $+\infty$ or $-\infty$, respectively. Bayesian estimators may be used in this case. Alternatively, ability values may be transformed to the true score metric, and estimated true scores reported. Ability estimates may also be obtained by adjusting the likelihood equations, a procedure that may not be completely justified.

Note

1. For the value to correspond to a maximum value, $\partial^2 \{\ln L(\boldsymbol{u}|\theta)\}/\partial\theta^2 < 0$.

Appendix: Derivation of the Information Function

The information function $I(\theta)$ is defined as (Kendall & Stuart, 1973, p. 10)

$$I(\theta) = -E\{\partial^2 \ln L/\partial\theta^2\}. \tag{5.51}$$

Since

$$\ln L = \sum_{i=1}^{n} [U_i \ln P_i + (1 - U_i) \ln(1 - P_i)], \tag{5.52}$$

$$\frac{\partial \ln L}{\partial \theta} = \sum_{i=1}^{n} \frac{\partial \ln L}{\partial P_i} \frac{\partial P_i}{\partial \theta}, \tag{5.53}$$

and, by the product rule,

$$\frac{\partial^2 \ln L}{\partial \theta^2} = \sum_{i=1}^{n} \frac{\partial}{\partial \theta} \left\{ \frac{\partial \ln L}{\partial P_i} \right\} \frac{\partial P_i}{\partial \theta} + \frac{\partial \ln L}{\partial P_i} \frac{\partial^2 P_i}{\partial \theta^2} \tag{5.54}$$

$$= \sum_{i=1}^{n} \frac{\partial^2 \ln L}{\partial P_i^2} \left(\frac{\partial P_i}{\partial \theta} \right)^2 + \frac{\partial \ln L}{\partial P_i} \frac{\partial^2 P_i}{\partial \theta^2}. \tag{5.55}$$

Now,

$$\frac{\partial \ln L}{\partial P_i} = \frac{U_i}{P_i} - \frac{1 - U_i}{(1 - P_i)} \tag{5.56}$$

and

$$\frac{\partial^2 \ln L}{\partial P_i^2} = -\frac{U_i}{P_i^2} - \frac{(1 - U_i)}{(1 - P_i)^2}. \tag{5.57}$$

Taking expectations and noting that

$$E(U_i | \theta) = P_i, \tag{5.58}$$

we have

$$E \left(\frac{\partial \ln L}{\partial P_i} \right) = 0 \tag{5.59}$$

and

$$E\left(\frac{\partial^2 \ln L}{\partial P_i^2}\right) = -\frac{1}{P_i} - \frac{1}{(1-P_i)} = -\frac{1}{P_i Q_i}. \qquad (5.60)$$

Substituting (5.59), (5.60), (5.55), and, finally, (5.51), we have

$$I(\theta) = -E\left(\frac{\partial^2 \ln L}{\partial \theta^2}\right) = \sum_{i=1}^{n}\left(\frac{\partial P_i}{\partial \theta}\right)^2 / P_i Q_i = \sum_{i=1}^{n}(P_i')^2 / P_i Q_i.$$

6 THE INFORMATION FUNCTION AND ITS APPLICATIONS

6.1 Introduction

The notion of an information function, $I(\theta)$, was introduced in chapter 5 with reference to the standard error of the maximum likelihood estimator of ability θ. This fundamental notion gives rise to various applications that are central to the field of measurement.

The information function has applications in

1. Test construction;
2. Item selection;
3. Assessment of precision of measurement;
4. Comparison of tests;
5. Determination of scoring weights;
6. Comparison of scoring methods.

Some of these applications will be discussed in this chapter, while others will be described in detail in later chapters.

6.2 Score Information Function

As indicated in chapter 5, the information function $I(\theta)$ is defined as

$$I(\theta) = -E\left\{ \frac{\partial^2}{\partial\theta^2} [\ln L(u\,|\,\theta)] \right\}, \tag{6.1}$$

where $L(u\,|\,\theta)$ is the likelihood function. It was further shown in the appendix to chapter 5 that from the above definition, $I(\theta)$ can be expressed as

$$I(\theta) = \sum_{i=1}^{n} \{[P_i'(\theta)]^2 / P_i(\theta)Q_i(\theta)\}, \tag{6.2}$$

where $P_i'(\theta)$ is the derivative of $P_i(\theta)$.

While the above expression is extremely useful and important, it is useful to define the information function of a scoring formula $y(u)$, a function of the responses to the items. Such an information function has been defined by Lord (1952, 1980a, pp. 65–70) and Birnbaum (1968, pp. 417–418). Lord (1952) approached the problem by assessing the effectiveness of a test score in discriminating between two individuals with ability θ_1 and θ_2. He suggested (Lord, 1980a, p. 69) that an appropriate index is

$$(\mu_{y|\theta_2} - \mu_{y|\theta_1})/\sigma_{y|\theta}, \tag{6.3}$$

where $\mu_{y|\theta_i}$ is the mean of the distribution $f(y|\theta_i)$. The quantity $\sigma_{y|\theta}$ is an "average" standard deviation of $\sigma_{y|\theta_1}$ and $\sigma_{y|\theta_2}$. A more appropriate index that can be interpreted as providing per unit discrimination between ability level is

$$[(\mu_{y|\theta_2} - \mu_{y|\theta_1})/\sigma_{y|\theta}]/(\theta_2 - \theta_1). \tag{6.4}$$

As $\theta_2 \to \theta_1$, the index defined in equation (6.4) becomes, in the limit,

$$\left(\frac{d}{d\theta}\mu_{y|\theta} \right)/\sigma_{y|\theta}. \tag{6.5}$$

On squaring the quantity in equation (6.5), we obtain the following definition of information:

$$I(\theta, y) = \left[\frac{d}{d\theta}\mu_{y|\theta} \right]^2 / \sigma_{y|\theta}^2 \tag{6.6}$$

$$\equiv \left[\frac{d}{d\theta}E(y\,|\,\theta) \right]^2 / \sigma_{y|\theta}^2. \tag{6.7}$$

Birnbaum (1968) arrived at the same definition by considering the width of the asymptotic confidence interval estimate of the ability θ of an individual with score y.

The function defined by equation (6.7) is called the *score information function*. It is the *square of the ratio of the slope of the regression of y on θ to the standard error of measurement for a given θ*. The score information function is a function of θ and varies at different levels of θ. From equation (6.7), it follows:

1. The steeper the slope at a particular θ level, the greater the information.
2. The smaller the standard error of measurement, the greater the information provided by the score formula y.

Consider a scoring formula defined as

$$y = \sum_{i=1}^{n} w_i u_i. \tag{6.8}$$

Then,

$$E(y \mid \theta) = \sum_{i=1}^{n} w_i E(u_i \mid \theta) = \sum_{i=1}^{n} w_i P_i, \tag{6.9}$$

and

$$\frac{d}{d\theta} E(y \mid \theta) = \sum_{i=1}^{n} w_i P_i'. \tag{6.10}$$

Furthermore,

$$\sigma_{y \mid \theta}^2 = \sum_{i=1}^{n} w_i^2 \sigma^2(u_i \mid \theta) \tag{6.11}$$

$$= \sum_{i=1}^{n} w_i^2 P_i Q_i. \tag{6.12}$$

Thus,

$$I(\theta, y) = \left[\sum_{i=1}^{n} w_i P_i' \right]^2 \bigg/ \left[\sum_{i=1}^{n} w_i^2 P_i Q_i \right]. \tag{6.13}$$

This result has an important implication. In contrast to the test information function, defined in the next section, the contribution of individual items to the total information cannot be ascertained when a general scoring formula is used.

6.3 Test and Item Information Functions

The information function defined in chapter 5 (see Equation 6.2) as relating
to the asymptotic variance of the maximum likelihood estimator of

$$I(\theta, \hat{\theta}) = \sum_{i=1}^{n} \{(P_i')^2 / P_i Q_i\} \tag{6.14}$$

is called the *test information function*. The notation $I(\theta, \hat{\theta})$ is introduced
here to conform with the notation for the information function associated
with a score y. When no confusion arises, $I(\theta, \hat{\theta})$ may be replaced by
$I(\theta)$.

The features of the test information function are summarized in figure 6–1.
One of the most important features of the test information function is that the
contribution of each item to the total information is additive. Thus, the effect
of each item and its impact on the total test can be readily determined. Such a
feature is highly desirable in test development work. This property of
independent item contributions is not present in classical measurement
(Gulliksen, 1950). The contribution of each item to test score variability
(and subsequently, test score reliability and validity) depends to a substantial
degree on how highly each test item correlates with other items in the test.

Figure 6-1. Features of the Test Information Function

- Defined for a set of test items at each point on the ability scale.
- The amount of information is influenced by the *quality* and *number* of test
  items.

$$I(\theta) = \sum_{i=1}^{n} \frac{P_i'(\theta)^2}{P_i(\theta)Q_i(\theta)}$$

(I) The steeper the slope the greater the information
(II) The smaller the item variance the greater the information
- $I(\theta)$ does not depend upon the particular combination of test items. The
  contribution of *each* test item is independent of the other items in the test.
- The amount of information provided by a set of test items at an ability level is
  inversely related to the error associated with ability estimates at the ability
  level.

$$SE(\theta)^* = \frac{1}{\sqrt{I(\theta)}}$$

*$SE(\theta)$ = Standard error of the ability estimates at ability level θ

When new items are added to a test and other items dropped, the usefulness (or contribution) of each item to test quality will also change.

The individual terms under the summation in equation (6.14) are the contributions of each item. Hence, the quantity

$$I(\theta, u_i) = (P_i')^2 / P_i Q_i \qquad (6.15)$$

is termed the *item information function*. Since item information functions are the building blocks of the test information function, it is necessary to understand their behavior.

The item information function depends on the slope of the item response function and the conditional variance at each ability level, θ. The greater the slope and smaller the variance, the greater the information, and, hence, the smaller the standard error of measurement. Through this process of assessment, items with large standard errors of measurement may be discarded. A summary of the properties of the item information function is provided in table 6–1.

The item information functions are, in general, bell shaped. The maximum information is obtained at b_i on the ability scale for the one- and the two-parameter logistic models, while for the three-parameter model, the maximum is attained at

$$\theta_{max} = b_i + \frac{1}{Da_i} \ln[\tfrac{1}{2} + \tfrac{1}{2}\sqrt{1 + 8c_i}]. \qquad (6.16)$$

The maximum value of the information is constant for the one-parameter model, while in the two-parameter model, the maximum value is directly proportional to the square of the item discrimination parameter, a. The larger the value of a, the greater the information. For the three-parameter model, the maximum information is given by (Lord, 1980a, p. 152)

$$I(\theta, u_i)_{max} = \frac{D^2 a_i^2}{8(1 - c_i^2)} [1 - 20c_i - 8c_i^2 + (1 + 8c_i)^{3/2}].$$

$$(6.17)$$

As c_i decreases, the information increases, with maximum information obtained when $c_i = 0$. Table 6–2 contains the value of the information function for various ability levels: θ_{max} and $I(\theta, u_i)_{max}$. The 50 ICCs were given in table 3-1. Figures 6-2 through 6-11 graphically illustrate the various features and characteristics of these item information functions. The corresponding ICCs are shown in figures 3-3 to 3-12.

Since item parameter values have the effect of changing the maximum value of the item information function and the location where the maximum value is attained, items that contribute to measurement precision at the various parts of the ability continuum can be selected. Tests that have special purposes can be designed in this manner. We shall return to a more detailed discussion of this point in a later chapter.

To illustrate the points raised above and to demonstrate (1) the effects of item information on the test information function, and (2) the effect of lengthening a test, consider the following six item pools:

	Item Parameters		
Item Pool	b	a	c
1	−2.0 to 2.0	.6 to 2.0	.00
2	−1.0 to 1.0	.6 to 2.0	.00
3	0.0	.6 to 2.0	.00
4	−2.0 to 2.0	.6 to 2.0	.25
5	−1.0 to 1.0	.6 to 2.0	.25
6	0.0	.6 to 2.0	.25

In all six item pools, item discrimination parameters are in the range .6 to 2.0. In the first three item pools, the pseudo-chance level parameters are

Table 6-1. Description of Item Information Functions for Three Logistic Models

Model	P_i	P'_i
One-Parameter	$\{1 + \exp[-D(\theta - b_i)]\}^{-1}$	DP_iQ_i
Two-Parameter	$\{1 + \exp[-Da_i(\theta - b_i)]\}^{-1}$	$Da_iP_iQ_i$
Three-Parameter	$c_i + (1 - c_i)\{1 + \exp[-Da_i(\theta - b_i)]\}^{-1}$	$Da_iQ_i(P_i - c_i)/(1 - c_i)$

zero; in the second three item pools, the pseudo-chance level parameters have the value .25. The variability of item difficulty parameters ranges from wide (-2.0 to $+2.0$) in item pools 1 and 4, to moderately wide (-1.0 to $+1.0$) in item pools 2 and 5, to homogeneous (0.0 to 0.0) in item pools 3 and 6. In addition, for the purposes of studying the test information functions, tests of two lengths, 10 and 20 items, drawn from the six item pools will be considered here. The test information functions for the 12 tests considered are presented in table 6–3. Items for each test were drawn randomly from the appropriate pool.

The effect of test length on $I(\theta)$ is clear. Test information is considerably increased when test length increases. The test information functions have maximum values at different levels of ability. The effect of the pseudo-chance level parameter is also clear. The first three item pools have larger amounts of information than their counterparts in the last three item pools.

$I(\theta) = P_i'^2/P_i Q_i$	θ_{max}	$I(\theta, u_i)_{max}$
$D^2 P_i Q_i$	b_i	$\frac{1}{4}D^2$
$D^2 a_i^2 P_i Q_i$	b_i	$\frac{1}{4}D^2 a_i^2$
$D^2 a_i^2 Q_i (P_i - c_i)^2/(1 - c_i)^2$	$b_i + \dfrac{1}{Da_i}\left\{ \ln \dfrac{1 + (1 + c_i)^{\frac{1}{2}}}{2} \right\}$	$\dfrac{D^2 a_i^2}{8(1 - c_i^2)}[1 - 20c_i - 8c_i^2 \\ + (1 + 8c_i)^{3/2}]$

Table 6-2. Three-Parameter Model Item Information Functions

Item Statistics			Ability Scores								
b_g	a_g	c_g	−3.00	−2.00	−1.00	0.00	1.00	2.00	3.00	θ_{max}	$I(\theta, u_i)_{max}$
−2.00	.19	0.00	.03	.03	.03	.02	.02	.02	.01	−2.00	.03
−1.00	.19	0.00	.02	.03	.03	.03	.02	.02	.02	−1.00	.03
0.00	.19	0.00	.02	.02	.03	.03	.03	.02	.02	0.00	.03
1.00	.19	0.00	.02	.02	.02	.03	.03	.03	.03	1.00	.03
2.00	.19	0.00	.01	.02	.02	.02	.03	.03	.03	2.00	.03
−2.00	.59	0.00	.20	.25	.20	.11	.05	.02	.01	−2.00	.25
−1.00	.59	0.00	.11	.20	.25	.20	.11	.05	.02	−1.00	.25
0.00	.59	0.00	.05	.11	.20	.25	.20	.11	.05	0.00	.25
1.00	.59	0.00	.02	.05	.11	.20	.25	.20	.11	1.00	.25
2.00	.59	0.00	.01	.02	.05	.11	.20	.25	.20	2.00	.25
−2.00	.99	0.00	.37	.71	.37	.09	.02	.00	.00	−2.00	.71
−1.00	.99	0.00	.09	.37	.71	.37	.09	.02	.00	−1.00	.71
0.00	.99	0.00	.02	.09	.37	.71	.37	.09	.02	0.00	.71
1.00	.99	0.00	.00	.02	.09	.37	.71	.37	.09	1.00	.71
2.00	.99	0.00	.00	.00	.02	.09	.37	.71	.37	2.00	.71
−2.00	1.39	0.00	.44	1.40	.44	.05	.00	.00	.00	−2.00	1.40
−1.00	1.39	0.00	.05	.44	1.40	.44	.05	.00	.00	−1.00	1.40
0.00	1.39	0.00	.00	.05	.44	1.40	.44	.05	.02	0.00	1.40
1.00	1.39	0.00	.00	.00	.05	.44	1.40	.44	.05	1.00	1.40
2.00	1.39	0.00	.00	.00	.00	.05	.44	1.40	.44	2.00	1.40
−2.00	1.79	0.00	.40	2.31	.40	.02	.00	.00	.00	−2.00	2.31
−1.00	1.79	0.00	.02	.40	2.31	.40	.02	.00	.00	−1.00	2.31
0.00	1.79	0.00	.00	.02	.40	2.31	.40	.02	.00	0.00	2.31
1.00	1.79	0.00	.00	.00	.02	.40	2.31	.40	.02	1.00	2.31

0.00	.19	.25	.01	.01	.01	.02	.02	.02	.01	.97	.02
1.00	.19	.25	.01	.01	.01	.01	.02	.02	.02	1.97	.02
2.00	.19	.25	.00	.01	.01	.01	.01	.01	.02	2.97	.02
−2.00	.59	.25	.09	.15	.14	.08	.03	.01	.00	−1.69	.16
−1.00	.59	.25	.03	.09	.15	.14	.08	.03	.01	−0.69	.16
0.00	.59	.25	.01	.03	.09	.15	.14	.08	.03	.31	.16
1.00	.59	.25	.00	.01	.03	.09	.15	.14	.08	1.31	.16
2.00	.59	.25	.00	.00	.01	.03	.09	.15	.14	2.31	.16
−2.00	.99	.25	.12	.42	.27	.07	.01	.00	.00	−1.81	.44
−1.00	.99	.25	.01	.12	.42	.27	.07	.01	.01	−.81	.44
0.00	.99	.25	.00	.01	.12	.42	.27	.07	.01	.19	.44
1.00	.99	.25	.00	.00	.01	.12	.42	.27	.07	1.19	.44
2.00	.99	.25	.00	.00	.00	.01	.12	.42	.27	2.19	.44
−2.00	1.39	.25	.09	.84	.32	.04	.00	.00	.00	−1.87	.86
−1.00	1.39	.25	.00	.09	.84	.32	.04	.00	.00	−.87	.86
0.00	1.39	.25	.00	.00	.09	.84	.32	.04	.00	.13	.86
1.00	1.39	.25	.00	.00	.00	.09	.84	.32	.04	1.13	.86
2.00	1.39	.25	.00	.00	.00	.00	.09	.84	.32	2.13	.86
−2.00	1.79	.25	.05	1.39	.30	.02	.00	.00	.00	−1.90	1.43
−1.00	1.79	.25	.00	.05	1.39	.30	.02	.00	.00	−.90	1.43
0.00	1.79	.25	.00	.00	.05	1.39	.30	.02	.00	.10	1.43
1.00	1.79	.25	.00	.00	.00	.05	1.39	.30	.02	1.10	1.43
2.00	1.79	.25	.00	.00	.00	.00	.05	1.39	.30	2.10	1.43

Corresponding item information functions are shown in figures 6–2 to 6–11.

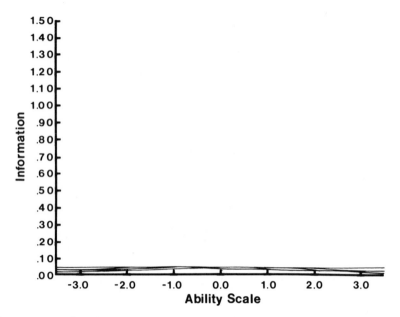

Figure 6-2. Graphical Representation of Five Item Information Curves
(b = −2.0, −1.0, 0.0, 1.0, 2.0; a = .19; c = .00)

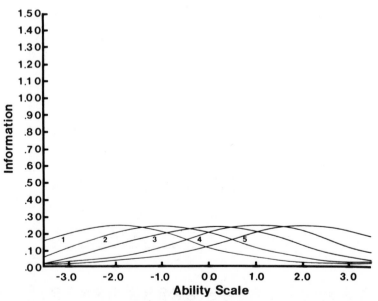

Figure 6-3. Graphical Representation of Five Item Information Curves
(b = −2.0, −1.0, 0.0, 1.0, 2.0; a = .59; c = .00)

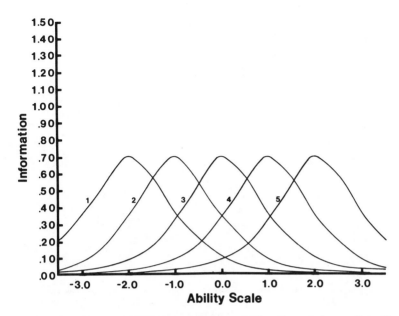

Figure 6-4. Graphical Representation of Five Item Information Curves
(b = −2.0, −1.0, 0.0, 1.0, 2.0; a = .99; c = .00)

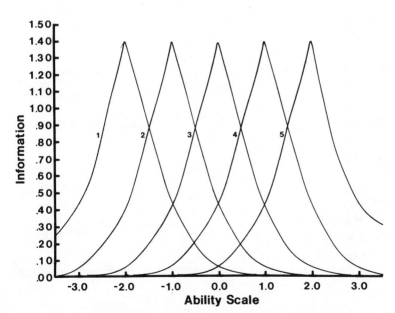

Figure 6-5. Graphical Representation of Five Item Information Curves
(b = −2.0, −1.0, 0.0, 1.0, 2.0; a = 1.39; c = .00)

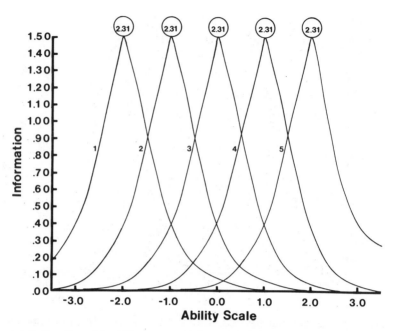

Figure 6-6. Graphical Representation of Five Item Information Curves
($b = -2.0, -1.0, 0.0, 1.0, 2.0$; $a = 1.79$; $c = .00$)

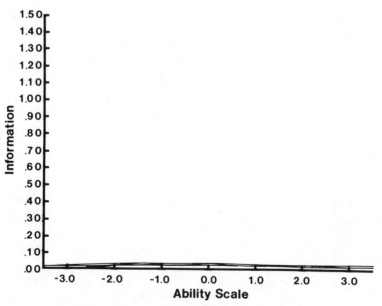

Figure 6-7. Graphical Representation of Five Item Information Curves
($b = -2.0, -1.0, 0.0, 1.0, 2.0$; $a = .19$; $c = .25$)

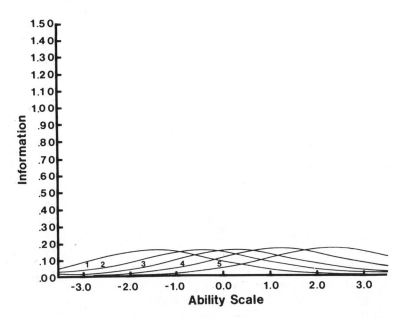

Figure 6-8. Graphical Representation of Five Item Information Curves
(b = −2.0, −1.0, 0.0, 1.0, 2.0; a = .59; c = .25)

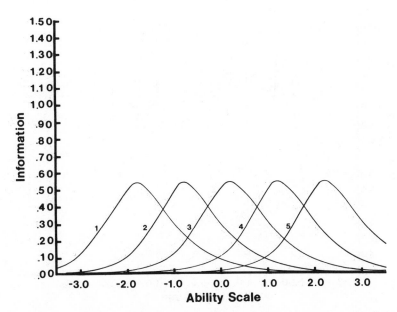

Figure 6-9. Graphical Representation of Five Item Information Curves
(b = −2.0, −1.0, 0.0, 1.0, 2.0; a = .99; c = .25)

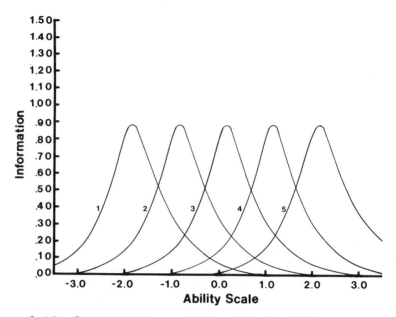

Figure 6-10. Graphical Representation of Five Item Information Curves
(b = −2.0, −1.0, 0.0, 1.0, 2.0; a = 1.39; c = .25)

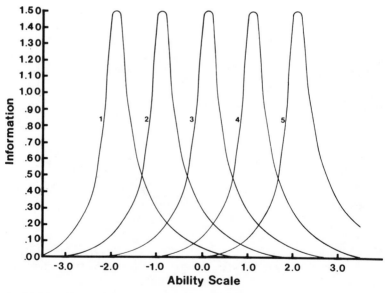

Figure 6-11. Graphical Representation of Five Item Information Curves
(b = −2.0, −1.0, 0.0, 1.0, 2.0; a = 1.79; c = .25)

Table 6-3. Test Information for Several Item Pools and Test Lengths at Several
Ability Levels

Item Pool	Test Length	Ability Level								
		−2.0	−1.5	−1.0	−0.5	0.0	0.5	1.0	1.5	2.0
1	10	5.84	7.34	5.75	3.53	2.02	1.69	2.30	2.98	2.68
	20	8.61	13.21	12.42	11.17	9.72	7.75	7.33	6.17	3.98
2	10	1.69	4.10	7.91	8.35	5.96	4.65	3.76	2.27	1.06
	20	2.63	6.67	14.45	19.51	17.50	13.41	8.11	3.62	1.50
3	10	.66	1.57	3.82	8.37	11.94	8.37	3.82	1.57	.66
	20	1.15	2.76	7.35	18.66	28.90	18.66	7.35	2.76	1.15
4	10	2.63	4.27	3.69	2.35	1.20	.74	1.04	1.68	1.77
	20	3.49	7.15	6.98	6.30	5.75	4.38	4.16	3.83	2.73
5	10	.34	1.27	3.91	5.05	3.60	2.77	2.47	1.61	.78
	20	.47	1.85	6.31	10.79	10.43	8.47	5.59	2.61	1.10
6	10	.07	.24	.93	3.46	7.16	5.81	2.77	1.16	.49
	20	.14	.42	1.59	7.22	17.34	13.08	5.35	2.03	.85

6.4 Scoring weights

Given that the score information function, $I(\theta, y)$, is

$$I(\theta, y) = \left[\sum_{i=1}^{n} w_i P_i' \right]^2 \bigg/ \sum_{i=1}^{n} w_i P_i Q_i,$$

the question that naturally arises is whether scoring weights, w_i, can be
chosen to maximize the information $I(\theta, y)$. Optimal weights for maximizing
information do exist. The result that relates optimal scoring weights to
maximum information is a consequence of a property of the maximum
likelihood estimator discussed in section 5.4. Recall the maximum likelihood
estimators (when they are consistent) have the smallest variance asymptotically, with the variance given by $[I(\theta)]^{-1}$, the reciprocal of the
information function or, in the present context, the test information function.
Thus it follows that the maximum information attainable for any scoring
system is $I(\theta)$.

This result can be seen more formally as a consequence of the Cauchy inequality (Birnbaum, 1968, p. 454). According to the well-known Cauchy inequality

$$\left[\sum_{i=1}^{n} k_i x_i \right]^2 \leq \left[\sum_{i=1}^{n} k_i^2 \right] \left[\sum_{i=1}^{n} x_i^2 \right], \qquad (6.18)$$

with equality holding when $k_i = mx_i$, where $m > 0$. Defining

$$k_i = w_i (P_i Q_i)^{1/2} \qquad (6.19)$$

and

$$x_i = P_i' / (P_i Q_i)^{1/2}, \qquad (6.20)$$

we have

$$\left[\sum_{i=1}^{n} w_i P_i' \right]^2 \leq \left[\sum_{i=1}^{n} w_i^2 P_i Q_i \right] \left[\sum_{i=1}^{n} P_i'^2 / P_i Q_i \right], \qquad (6.21)$$

or equivalently,

$$\left[\sum_{i=1}^{n} w_i P_i' \right]^2 / \left[\sum_{i=1}^{n} w_i^2 P_i Q_i \right] \leq \left[\sum_{i=1}^{n} P_i'^2 / P_i Q_i \right]. \qquad (6.22)$$

The left side of the inequality is clearly the score information function, $I(\theta, y)$, while the right side is $I(\theta)$. Thus,

$$I(\theta, y) \leq I(\theta). \qquad (6.23)$$

Alternatively, this result could be derived using the Cramer-Rao inequality (Kendall & Stuart, 1973, p. 9; Lord, 1980a, p. 71). The equality holds when $k_i = x_i$; i.e.

$$w_i (P_i Q_i)^{1/2} = P_i' / (P_i Q_i)^{1/2}. \qquad (6.24)$$

Solving for w_i, we obtain

$$w_i = P_i' / P_i Q_i. \qquad (6.25)$$

With these scoring weights,

Table 6-4. Optimal Scoring Weights w_i for Three Logistic Models

Model	$w_i = P_i'/P_iQ_i$	Remarks
One-Parameter	D	Independent of ability level
Two-Parameter	Da_i	
Three-Parameter	$\dfrac{Da_i}{(1 - c_i)}\dfrac{(P_i - c_i)}{P_i}$	Function of ability level

$$I(\theta, y^*) = I(\theta), \qquad (6.26)$$

where y^* denotes the scoring formula with optimal weights.

Once an item response model is specified, the optimal scoring weights can be determined from equation (6.25). These optimal weights are summarized in table 6–4.

The optimal scoring formula for the one-parameter model is

$$y^* = D \sum_{i=1}^{n} u_i, \qquad (6.27)$$

while for the two-parameter model,

$$y^* = D \sum_{i=1}^{n} a_i u_i. \qquad (6.28)$$

It is clear that the maximum information is obtained with the number-correct score for the one-parameter logistic model and with the "discrimination-weighted" score for the two-parameter model. These results could be anticipated since equations (6.27) and (6.28) correspond to sufficient statistics. An important distinction between the three-parameter model and the other two item response models emerges from a consideration of the optimal weights. While for the one- and the two-parameter models, the optimal weights are independent of ability, it is not so with the three-parameter model. The optimal weights are clearly functions of the ability level.

The optimal weights for the three-parameter model are

$$w_i = Da_i(P_i - c_i)/P_i(1 - c_i). \qquad (6.29)$$

At high-ability levels, $P_i \rightarrow 1$. Thus, the optimal weights are proportional to

a_i. At low-ability levels, $P_i \rightarrow c_i$, and, hence, the optimal weights are zeros. Lord (1980a) reasons that

> when low-ability examinees guess at random on difficult items, this produces a random result that would impair effective measurement if incorporated into the examinees' score; hence the need for a near-zero scoring weight. [P. 23]

The relationship between ability and optimal scoring weights is graphically depicted in figure 6–12. The graphs effectively demonstrate the points made above.

From the above discussion it is clear that when nonoptimal weights are used with particular logistic models, the score information obtained from equation (6.13) will be lower at all ability levels than one that would result from the use of optimal weights. The effect of nonoptimal weights on information was studied by Lord (1968) and by Hambleton and Traub (1971). These authors concluded that when a test is being used to estimate ability across a broad range of ability levels and when guessing is a factor, the scoring weights for the three-parameter model are to be preferred. Unit scoring weights lead to efficient estimates of ability only when there is little or no guessing and when the range of discrimination is not too wide.

Practical determination of optimal scoring weights for a particular examinee presents a problem in the three-parameter model since the weights depend on unknown ability. Lord (1977b; 1980a, p. 75–76) has recommended an approximation to the scoring weights. This involves substituting the conventional item difficulty p_i (proportion of correct answers to item i) for $P_i(\theta)$ in equation (6.29). The approximate weights

$$w_i = Da_i(p_i - c_i)/p_i(1 - c_i) \qquad (6.30)$$

are better than equal weights as demonstrated by Lord (1980a, p. 74) for the SCAT II–2A test. The discrimination weights (equation 6.28) provide similar improvement at high-ability levels but not at low-ability levels.

Given the above discussion, the advantage of scoring weights that do not depend on ability is clear. The expression for optimal scoring weights (equation 6.25),

$$w_i = P_i'/P_i Q_i,$$

can be expressed as

$$\frac{dP_i}{P_i(1 - P_i)} = w_i d\theta. \qquad (6.31)$$

This is a first-order differential equation. If w_i is to be a constant, then integrating both sides, it can be shown that (Lord, 1980a, p. 77)

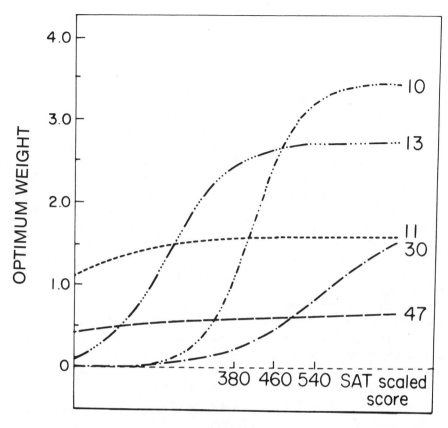

Figure 6-12.   Optimal (Logistic) Scoring Weights for Five Items as a
Function of Ability (From Lord, F. M. An analysis of Verbal Scholastic
Aptitude Test using Birnbaum's three-parameter logistic model. *Educational and Psychological Measurement*, 1968, *28*, 989–1020. Reprinted
with permission.)

$$\ln \frac{P_i}{1 - P_i} = (A_i\theta + B_i) \tag{6.32}$$

or, equivalently,

$$P_i = \exp(A_i\theta + B_i)/[1 + \exp(A_i\theta + B_i)]. \tag{6.33}$$

This is the form of a two-parameter logistic item response function. This result demonstrates that the most general item-response model that permits optimal scoring weights that are independent of ability is the two-parameter logistic model.

6.5 Effect of Ability Metric on Information

The score, test, and item information functions are dependent on ability levels. Since the ability metric is arbitrary, the information function cannot be interpreted in an absolute sense. For example, this problem arises when evaluating the item information function for the one-parameter model. The maximum value of the item information is the constant, D. This is because the common value of the discrimination parameter is set at 1.0. If, on the other hand, a value other than 1.0 is assumed for the common discrimination parameter, the maximum information will change. This change occurs because the metric of the ability level has been transformed. However, this effect cannot be noticed by examining the expression for the maximum information.

As Lord (1980a) has pointed out, $I(\theta, y)$ is an operator and not a function; i.e. $I(\theta^*, y)$ cannot be determined by substituting θ^* for θ in the expression given for $I(\theta, y)$. To study the effect of such changes in the metric of θ, the general expression given by equation (6.7) must be considered.

Using the notation employed by Lord (1980a, p. 85), the information function corresponding to the θ^* metric is expressed as

$$I(\theta^*, y) = \{dE(y|\theta^*)/d\theta^*\}^2/\sigma^2_{y|\theta^*}. \tag{6.34}$$

Now, if $\theta^* = \theta^*(\theta)$, a monotonic function, then

$$E(y|\theta^* = \theta^*_o) = E(y|\theta = \theta_o),$$

and

$$\sigma^2(y|\theta^* = \theta^*_o) = \sigma^2(y|\theta = \theta_o).$$

Furthermore, since by the chain rule, for any function $f(\theta)$,

$$(df/d\theta^*) = (df/d\theta)(d\theta/d\theta^*), \tag{6.35}$$

it follows that

$$dE(y|\theta^*)/d\theta^* = dE(y|\theta)/d\theta^* \tag{6.36}$$

$$= dE(y|\theta)/d\theta\{d\theta/d\theta^*\}. \tag{6.37}$$

Thus,

$$I(\theta^*, y) = \{dE(y \mid \theta^*)/d\theta^*\}^2/\sigma_{y \mid \theta^*}^2 \qquad (6.39)$$

$$= dE(y \mid \theta)/d\theta\}^2\{d\theta/d\theta^{*2}\}\sigma_{y \mid \theta}^2 \qquad (6.40)$$

$$= I(\theta, y)/(d\theta/d\theta^*)^2 \qquad (6.41)$$

$$= I(\theta, y)/(d\theta^*/d\theta)^2. \qquad (6.42)$$

Hence, when the θ-metric is transformed by a monotonic transformation, $\theta^* = \theta^*(\theta)$, the information function in the θ^*-metric is the original information function divided by the square of the derivative of the transformation (see section 4.5).

The above result indicates a potential problem with the information function. Unless a meaningful metric for θ is chosen, the information function cannot be used effectively to draw conclusions about the ability level at which the test or the item provides maximal information. Hence, item selection procedures that are based on the use of information functions must be applied cautiously. This important fact has been demonstrated effectively by Lord (1975a), who showed that information functions based on different transformations of the ability scale may have little resemblance to one another.

6.6 Relative Precision, Relative Efficiency, and Efficiency

While the score, test, and item information do not yield absolute interpretations, it is still possible to compare the relative merits of (1) score formulas, (2) tests, or (3) estimators.

In general, if $I_1(\theta, y_1)$ and $I_2(\theta, y_2)$ are information functions for any two test models and score formulas y_1 and y_2 for the same ability θ, then the ratio

$$RP(\theta) = I_1(\theta, y_1)/I_2(\theta, y_2) \qquad (6.43)$$

denotes the *relative precision* at (θ) of the two test models and score formulas. This notion was introduced by Birnbaum (1968, pp. 471–472). Since the information functions are functions of θ, the relative precision is also a function of θ.

A special case of the above notion arises in the case of a single test model. In this case, the ratio given above specializes to

$$RE\{y_1, y_2\} = I(\theta, y_1)/I(\theta, y_2). \qquad (6.44)$$

Here $RE\{y_1, y_2\}$ denotes *Relative Efficiency* of test score, y_1, with respect to y_2.

Finally, it may be of interest to compare the relative efficiency of a test score, y, with respect to optimally weighted test score, y_2. In this case

$$I(\theta_1, y_2) \equiv I(\theta, \hat{\theta}) \equiv I(\theta).$$

Hence, the expression given by equation (6.44) reduces to

$$\text{Eff} = I(\theta, y_1)/I(\theta) = RE\{y_1, \theta\}. \tag{6.45}$$

These three concepts play important roles in the choice of test models and scoring formulas. Numerous studies have been conducted to evaluate the relative merits of tests and those of scoring formulas. Birnbaum (1968) and Hambleton and Traub (1971) studied the loss in information due to the use of less-than-optimal scoring weights in the various item response models using equation (6.45). Lord (1968) demonstrated through this process that using unit scoring weights on the verbal section of the SAT resulted in the loss of information equivalent to discarding about 45 percent of the test items for low-ability examinees. At the same time, he noted that the loss in information was negligible at the higher-ability levels. Readers are referred to Lord (1974d, 1974e, 1975c) for additional discussion and applications of the points considered.

It was pointed out in section 6.5 that the information function cannot be interpreted in an absolute sense unless a valid θ-metric is defined. The effect of transformation was considered in this section. While the information function is affected by a transformation of the θ-metric, the quantities, relative precision, relative efficiency, and efficiency are unaffected by transformation of the θ-metric. To see this, consider the most general notion, relative precision, defined by the ratio

$$RP(\theta) = I_1(\theta, y_1)/I(\theta, y_2).$$

Now for a θ^*-metric, where $\theta^* = \theta^*(\theta)$ is a monotonic function of θ,

$$RP(\theta^*) = I(\theta^*, y_1)/I(\theta^*, y_2) \tag{6.46}$$

$$= \{I_1(\theta, y_1)(d\theta/d\theta^*)^2\}/\{I_2(\theta, y_2)(d\theta/d\theta^*)^2\} \tag{6.47}$$

by virtue of equation (6.41). It immediately follows that

$$RP(\theta^*) = RP(\theta). \tag{6.48}$$

The above result specializes to the concepts of relative efficiency and efficiency:

$$RE\{y_1, y_2\} = \frac{I(\theta^*, y_1)}{I(\theta^*, y_2)} = \frac{I(\theta, y_1)}{I(\theta, y_2)} \qquad (6.49)$$

and

$$Eff = \frac{I(\theta^*, y_1)}{I(\theta^*, \theta^*)} = \frac{I(\theta, y_1)}{I(\theta, \theta)} . \qquad (6.50)$$

This property of invariance of the measure of efficiency with respect to transformations of the θ-metric clearly has numerous advantages. Using these concepts, it is possible to evaluate tests, select items, determine scoring weights, and choose branching strategies as in adaptive testing. We shall return to more detailed applications of these concepts in later chapters.

6.7 Assessment of Precision of Measurement

The concept of reliability is one of the central concepts in classical test theory. Despite its wide use, it suffers from serious drawbacks, which have also received considerable attention. The main objection to the use of the reliability coefficient is that it is group dependent and, hence, of limited generalizability. The second major objection to the coefficient of reliability is that it suggests a rule for selecting test items that is contradictory to that provided by the validity coefficient. In addition to these, the standard error of estimation, σ_e, given by (Lord & Novick, 1968, pp. 66–68)

$$\sigma_e = \sigma_x[\rho_{xx'}(1 - \rho_{xx'})]^{1/2} \qquad (6.51)$$

and standard error of measurement, σ_E, given by

$$\sigma_e = \sigma_x[1 - \rho_{xx'}]^{1/2} \qquad (6.52)$$

are functions of the reliability coefficient, and, hence, suffer from the disadvantages of being group dependent. In addition, these two quantities are *average* standard errors, averaged over the ability levels, and hence introduce a further complication. This, together with the assumption of independence of true and error scores (Samejima, 1977a), makes these coefficients unpalatable.

The item and test information functions provide viable alternatives to the classical concepts of reliability and standard error. The information functions are defined independently of any specific group of examinees and, moreover, represent the standard error of measurement at any chosen ability level. Thus, the precision of measurement can be determined at any level of ability that is of interest. Furthermore, through the information function, the test constructor can precisely assess the contribution of each item to the precision of the total test and hence choose items in a manner that is not contradictory with other aspects of test construction.

6.8 Summary

The item and test information functions play key roles in item response theory. Through these, it is possible to ascertain the standard errors of measurement for each item at a given level of ability θ. In contrast, the standard error of measurement obtained through classical methods is an aggregate quantity over the entire range of ability.

A further important aspect of the use of item information functions is that the contribution of individual items to the precision of the total test can be determined. Consequently individual items can be added (or deleted) and the effect of this on the total test can be known in advance. Test development procedures are considerably improved as a result of this important property.

Item information functions are dependent on ability. This means that the precision of measurement is different at different ability levels. As a result, different items which maximize the precision of measurement at different levels of θ can be included in the test. Decision making at various levels of θ is enhanced through this procedure.

The weights that are attached to the observed scores on each item are known as scoring weights. The optimal scoring weights that maximize the information function for an item can be determined. These are different for the three item parameter models.

The concept of relative efficiency allows the comparison of several items, tests, and several scoring weight schemes in terms of the information function. The comparison can be depicted graphically and this facilitates making decisions regarding the relative merits of items, tests and scoring methods.

7 ESTIMATION OF ITEM AND ABILITY PARAMETERS

7.1 Introduction

The estimation of ability parameters when item parameters are known was considered in chapter 5 (see also, Swaminathan, 1983). While the problem of estimating ability parameters when item parameters are given is reasonably straightforward, the simultaneous estimation of ability and item parameters raises several problems. The estimators in such situations may not possess desirable properties. Despite some of the problems that exist, several estimation procedures are currently available. We shall discuss these procedures in this chapter.

7.2 Identification of Parameters

When N examinees take a test that has n items, the number of ability parameters, θ_a, that has to be estimated is N, one for each examinee. The number of item parameters depends on the item response model that is considered appropriate. For the one-parameter model, the number of item parameters is n, since the parameter b_i characterizes the "difficulty" of each item. Proceeding along similar lines, it can be readily seen that the number of item parameters for the two-parameter logistic model is $2n$, and $3n$ for the three-parameter logistic model. Thus, the total number of parameters to be estimated for the one-parameter model is $N + n$, $N + 2n$ for the two-parameter model, and $N + 3n$ for the three-parameter model.

A problem arises at this point. Since the item parameters and ability parameters are unobservable, there is a certain degree of indeterminacy in the model. This indeterminacy is formally termed the *identification problem*. In the one-parameter model, where the item-characteristic curve is given as

$$P_i(\theta \mid b_i) = \exp D(\theta - b_i)/[1 + \exp D(\theta - b_i)],$$

the transformations, $\theta^* = \theta + k$, and $b_i^* = b_i + k$, leave the item response function invariant, i.e.

$$P_i(\theta^* \mid b_i^*) = P_i(\theta \mid b_i).$$

Thus, there is an indeterminacy in the origin. To remove this indeterminacy, it is necessary to scale θs (or bs) so that their mean is fixed at a convenient value such as zero. Once the origin is fixed, there is one less parameter to estimate; i.e., $N + n - 1$ parameters have to be estimated in the one-parameter model.

In the two-parameter model, the transformations

$$\theta^* = (\theta + k)/\ell, \tag{7.1}$$

$$b_i^* = (b_i + k)/\ell, \tag{7.2}$$

and

$$a_i^* = \ell\, a_i \tag{7.3}$$

leave the item response function

$$P_i(\theta \mid a_i,\ b_i) = \exp Da_i(\theta - b_i)/[1 + \exp Da_i(\theta - b_i)]$$

invariant, i.e.

$$P_i(\theta^* \mid a_i^*,\ b_i^*) = P_i(\theta \mid a_i,\ b_i).$$

For the three-parameter model, since

$$P_i(\theta \mid a_i,\ b_i,\ c_i) = c_i + (1 - c_i)\{\exp Da_i(\theta - b_i)/$$
$$[1 + \exp Da_i(\theta - b_i)]\},$$

the above transformations (equations 7.1 through 7.3) with $c_i^* = c_i$ result in an invariant item response function, i.e.

$$P_i(\theta^* \mid a_i^*,\ b_i^*,\ c_i^*) = P_i(\theta \mid a_i,\ b_i,\ c_i).$$

Hence, for the two- and three-parameter models, it is convenient to fix the θs (or the bs) such that their mean is zero and standard deviation is one. With these restrictions, the total number of parameters to be estimated in the two-parameter model is $N + 2n - 2$, while it is $N + 3n - 2$ for the three-parameter model.

The total number of parameters to be estimated is generally large regardless of the item response model that is deemed appropriate. For example, if 200 examinees take a test that has 40 items, the total number of parameters that have to be estimated is 239 for the one-parameter model, 278 for the two-parameter model, and 318 for the three-parameter model. It is thus evident that as the number of examinees increases, the number of parameters to be estimated increases proportionately, unlike the familiar statistical models such as the regression model, where the number of parameters is usually independent of the number of observations.

7.3 Incidental and Structural Parameters

As pointed out above, as the number of examinees increases, the number of parameters increases, and this presents a potential estimation problem. To understand the nature of this problem, consider the problem discussed by Kendall and Stuart (1973, p. 61) and Zellner (1971, pp. 114–115). Suppose that n normal populations have differing means, $\mu_1, \mu_2, \ldots, \mu_n$, but the same variance, σ^2, and that n_{ij} is the jth observation in the ith population. Then

$$x_{ij} \sim N(\mu_i,\ \sigma^2) \qquad i = 1, \ldots, n; j = 1, \ldots, k. \tag{7.4}$$

Here $N(\mu,\ \sigma^2)$ indicates a normally distributed variable with mean μ and variance σ^2.

Since the density function of x_{ij}, given by $f(x_{ij} \mid \mu_i,\ \sigma^2)$, is

$$f(x_{ij} \mid \mu_i,\ \sigma^2) = (2\pi\sigma^2)^{-\frac{1}{2}} \exp - (x_{ij} - \mu_i)^2/\sigma^2, \tag{7.5}$$

the likelihood function of the observations $[x_1,\ x_2, \ldots, x_i, \ldots, x_n]$, where

$$x_i = [x_{i1}, x_{i2}, \ldots, x_{ik}]$$

is

$$L(x_1, x_2, \ldots x_n \mid \mu,\ \sigma^2) = \prod_{j=1}^{k} (2\pi\sigma^2)^{-n/2} \exp\left[-\tfrac{1}{2} \sum_{i=1}^{n} (x_{ij} - \mu_i)^2/\sigma^2\right] \tag{7.6}$$

$$= (2\pi\sigma^2)^{-nk/2} \exp[-\tfrac{1}{2}\sum_{j=1}^{k}\sum_{i=1}^{n} (x_{ij} - \mu_i)^2/\sigma^2]. \tag{7.7}$$

Taking logarithms, differentiating, and solving the resulting likelihood equations, we obtain the following estimators for μ_i and σ^2:

$$\hat{\mu}_i = \sum_{j=1}^{k} x_{ij}/k \tag{7.8}$$

$$\hat{\sigma}^2 = \sum_{j=1}^{k}\sum_{i=1}^{n} (x_{ij} - \hat{\mu}_i)^2/nk. \tag{7.9}$$

Clearly,

$$E(\hat{\mu}_i) = \mu_i, \tag{7.10}$$

but

$$E(\hat{\sigma}^2) = \sigma^2(kn - n)/kn \tag{7.11}$$

$$= \sigma^2(1 - \tfrac{1}{k}). \tag{7.12}$$

This result shows that while $\hat{\mu}_i$ is an unbiased estimator of μ_i, $\hat{\sigma}^2$ is not an unbiased estimator of σ^2. Moreover, $\hat{\sigma}^2$ is not a consistent estimator of σ^2 since the bias does not vanish as $n \to \infty$ with k *fixed*. The number of unknown parameters $(n + 1)$ increases as n increases, while the ratio of the number of parameters to the total number of observations, $(n + 1)/kn$, approaches $1/k$, which is appreciable when $k = 2$.

In this situation, the number of parameters, μ_i, increases with n and, hence, are called *incidental parameters*, while the parameter σ^2 is called the *structural parameter*. These names were given by Neyman and Scott (1948), who first studied this problem.

The problem discussed above has implications for the simultaneous estimation of item and ability parameters in item response models. As pointed out in chapter 5, with known item parameters the maximum likelihood estimator of θ converges to the true value when the number of items increases. Similarly when ability is known, maximum likelihood estimators of item parameters will converge to their true values when the number of examinees increases. However, when *simultaneous* estimation of item and ability parameters is attempted, the item parameters are the structural parameters and the ability parameters are the incidental parameters since their number increases with increasing numbers of examinees.[1] As illustrated with the problem of estimating the means and variance in n normal populations, the estimators of item parameters will not converge to their true values as the number of ability or incidental parameters increases.

This problem of the lack of consistent estimators of item (or ability) parameters in the presence of infinitely many examinees (or items) was first noted by Andersen (1973a), who demonstrated it for the one-parameter model.

When the number of items *and* the number of examinees increase, however, the maximum likelihood estimators of item and ability parameters may be unbiased. This has been shown formally for the one-parameter model by Haberman (1975) and suggested by Lord (1968). Empirical results obtained by Lord (1975b) and Swaminathan and Gifford (1983) provide support for the conjecture that as the number of items and the number of examinees increase, maximum likelihood estimators of the item and ability parameters converge to their true values.

7.4 Joint Maximum Likelihood Estimation

The likelihood function appropriate in this case is given by equation (5.10). The procedure outlined for the estimation of ability generalizes to this situation readily, and for the sake of generality, the three-parameter model is considered first.

The likelihood function for the three-parameter model should be indicated as $L(u\,|\,\theta, b, a, c)$ where u is an Nn dimensional vector of responses of the N examinees on n items. The vectors θ, b, a, c are the vectors containing the ability, difficulty, discrimination, and the chance-level parameters. The total number of parameters that have to be estimated is $N + 3n - 2$ since, as mentioned earlier, two constraints have to be imposed to eliminate indeterminacy in the model. The logarithm of the likelihood function is given by

$$\ln L(u\,|\,\theta, b, a, c) = \sum_{a=1}^{N} \sum_{i=1}^{n} [u_{ia} \ln P_{ia} + (1 - u_{ia}) \ln Q_{ia}].$$

To determine the maximum likelihood estimates of $\theta, a, b,$ and c, it is necessary to find the values of these parameters that jointly maximize the above function. This requires solving the likelihood equations

$$\partial \ln L/\partial t_k = 0, \qquad (k = 1, \ldots, N + 3n - 2), \qquad (7.13)$$

where t_k is an element of the parameter vector t, defined as

$$t' = [\theta' \; a' \; b' \; c'].$$

The Newton-Raphson procedure described in section 5.2 can be applied to solve the system of nonlinear equations (7.13). However, unlike the case of known item parameters where the estimation procedure required the solutions of independent equations, the system of equations given by equation (7.13) is not separable, and hence a multivariate version of the Newton-Raphson procedure is required.

In general, if $f(t)$ is a function of the p dimensional vector t, the value of t that maximizes $f(t)$ can be determined by applying the Newton-Raphson procedure. If $t^{(j)}$ is the jth approximation to the value of t that maximizes $f(t)$, then a better approximation is given by

$$t^{(j+1)} = t^{(j)} - \delta^{(j)}, \tag{7.14}$$

where

$$\delta^{(j)} = [f''(t^{(j)})]^{-1} f'(t^{(j)}). \tag{7.15}$$

Here f'' is the $(p \times p)$ matrix of second derivatives, and f' is the $(p \times 1)$ vector of first derivatives evaluated at $t^{(j)}$. Any convenient value may be taken as the starting value, $t^{(0)}$. The process is terminated when $t^{(j)}$ does not change appreciably from one iteration to another.

In the current situation, $t' = [\theta'\ a'\ b'\ c']$, and the function $f(t)$ is the logarithm of the likelihood function $\ln L(u|\theta,\ a,\ b,\ c)$. To obtain the maximum likelihood estimate of the parameters, the iterative procedure is carried out in two stages: Starting with initial values for a, b, c and treating the item parameters as known, θ_a is estimated as indicated in chapter 5; with the final values of $\theta_a(a = 1, \ldots, N)$ obtained from the above stage, and treating the ability parameters as known, the item parameters are estimated. This two-stage process is repeated until the ability and the item values converge, with the final values being taken as the maximum likelihood estimates.

In the first stage, where the ability parameters are estimated and the item parameters are treated as known, the matrix of second derivatives with respect to θ is diagonal. Hence, there is a single equation for each θ_a. In the second stage, when the abilities are held fixed, the matrix of second derivatives of the item parameters reduces to a diagonal block matrix as a consequence of the assumption of local independence, with each block being a (3×3) symmetric matrix of second derivatives. The upper diagonal entries of each of the (3×3) matrices, denoted as $H(a_i,\ b_i,\ c_i)$, are

$$\begin{bmatrix} \partial^2 \ln L/\partial a_i^2 & \partial^2 \ln L/\partial a_i b_i & \partial^2 \ln L/\partial a_i \partial c_i \\ & \partial^2 \ln L/\partial b_i^2 & \partial^2 \ln L/\partial b_i \partial c_i \\ & & \partial^2 \ln L/\partial c_i^2 \end{bmatrix}. \tag{7.16}$$

If we let $x_i' = [a_i \ b_i \ c_i]$, and if $x_i^{(0)}$ is the starting value for the triplet of item parameters for item i, then an improved estimate $x_i^{(1)}$ of the item parameters is given by

$$x_i^{(1)} = x_i^{(0)} - \{H[x_i^{(0)}]\}^{-1} f'[x_i^{(0)}], \qquad (7.17)$$

where $H[x_i^{(0)}]$ is the matrix of second derivatives and $f'[x_i^{(0)}]$ is the vector of first derivatives evaluated at $a_i^{(0)}$, $b_i^{(0)}$, and $c_i^{(0)}$. This iterative process is repeated to yield the $(j+1)$th improvement over the jth approximation:

$$x_i^{(j+1)} = x_i^{(j)} - \{H[x_i^{(j)}]\}^{-1} f'[x_i^{(j)}]. \qquad (7.18)$$

When the difference between the $(j+1)$th approximation and jth approximation is sufficiently small, the process is terminated.

The iterative scheme given by equation (7.18) is carried out for the n items. When convergence takes place, the item parameter values are treated as known, and the ability parameters are estimated. This two-stage procedure is repeated until the ability and item parameters converge.

It was pointed out earlier that as a result of indeterminacy in the model, restrictions have to be imposed. This may be done conveniently by specifying the mean of θ (or the bs) to be zero and the standard deviation of θ (or the bs) to be one. Strictly speaking, when the parameters θ, a, b, and c are estimated simultaneously by using equation (7.14), these restrictions have to be incorporated through the use of Lagrange multipliers. This procedure becomes rather complicated. Alternatively, when a two-stage procedure (that of estimating the ability parameters and then item parameters) is used, the abilities are scaled at each iteration to have mean zero and standard deviation one. Then item parameter estimates are scaled accordingly and estimated.

The relevant first and second derivatives for the parameters θ_a, a_i, b_i, and c_i are given in table 7–1. At the point of convergence, each of the N second derivatives of $\ln L(u \,|\, \theta, a, b, c)$ with respect to θ_a must be negative, and each of the n (3×3) second-derivative matrices of the item parameters must be negative definite. This ensures that at least a local maximum has been attained.

Although it cannot be established rigorously at this point that the estimators of item and ability parameters are consistent, empirical evidence (Swaminathan & Gifford, 1983) indicates that the estimators may be consistent. With this assumption, it is possible to obtain standard errors of the maximum likelihood estimators of item and ability parameters.

The properties of maximum likelihood estimators discussed in chapter 5 are applicable to the present situation. If consistent estimators of the vector of parameters t exist, then the *information matrix*, $I(t)$, is given as

Table 7-1.   First and Second Derivatives of Item and Ability Parameters for the Three-Parameter Logistic Model

Derivative	Expression
$\partial \ln L / \partial a_i$	$\dfrac{D}{(1-c_i)} \displaystyle\sum_{a=1}^{N} \dfrac{(\theta_a - b_i)(P_{ia} - c_i)(u_{ia} - P_{ia})}{P_{ia}}$
$\partial \ln L / \partial b_i$	$\dfrac{-Da_i}{(1-c_i)} \displaystyle\sum_{a=1}^{N} \dfrac{(P_{ia} - c_i)}{P_{ia}}(u_{ia} - P_{ia})$
$\partial \ln L / \partial c_i$	$\dfrac{1}{(1-c_i)} \displaystyle\sum_{a=1}^{N} \dfrac{(u_{ia} - P_{ia})}{P_{ia}}$
$\partial \ln L / \partial \theta_a$	$D \displaystyle\sum_{i=1}^{n} \dfrac{a_i(P_{ia} - c_i)}{(1-c_i)} \dfrac{(u_{ia} - P_{ia})}{P_{ia}}$
$\partial^2 \ln L / \partial a_i^2$	$\dfrac{D^2}{(1-c_i)^2} \displaystyle\sum_{a=1}^{N} \left\{ (\theta_a - b_i)^2 (P_{ia} - c_i) \dfrac{Q_{ia}}{P_{ia}} \left[\dfrac{u_{ia}}{P_{ia}} c_i - P_{ia} \right] \right\}$
$\partial^2 \ln L / \partial b_i^2$	$\dfrac{D^2 a_i^2}{(1-c_i)^2} \displaystyle\sum_{a=1}^{N} (P_{ia} - c_i) \dfrac{Q_{ia}}{P_{ia}} \left(\dfrac{u_{ia} c_i}{P_{ia}} - P_{ia} \right)$
$\partial^2 \ln L / \partial c_i^2$	$\dfrac{1}{(1-c_i)^2} \displaystyle\sum_{a=1}^{N} \left\{ \left(\dfrac{u_{ia}}{P_{ia}} - 1 \right) \dfrac{u_{ia} Q_{ia}}{P_{ia}^2} \right\}$
$\partial^2 \ln L / \partial a_i \partial b_i$	$\dfrac{-D}{(1-c_i)} \displaystyle\sum_{a=1}^{N} (P_{ia} - c_i) \left\{ \left(\dfrac{u_{ia}}{P_{ia}} - 1 \right) \right.$ $\left. + \dfrac{Da_i}{(1-c_i)} (\theta_a - b_i) \dfrac{Q_{ia}}{P_{ia}} \left(\dfrac{u_{ia} c_i}{P_{ia}} - P_{ia} \right) \right\}$
$\partial^2 \ln L / \partial a_i \partial c_i$	$\dfrac{-D}{(1-c_i)^2} \displaystyle\sum_{a=1}^{N} (\theta_a - b_i)(P_{ia} - c_i) \dfrac{Q_{ia}}{P_{ia}^2} u_{ia}$
$\partial^2 \ln L / \partial c_i \partial a_i$	$\dfrac{Da_i}{(1-c_i)^2} \displaystyle\sum_{a=1}^{N} (P_{ia} - c_i) \dfrac{Q_{ia}}{P_{ia}^2} u_{ia}$
$\partial^2 \ln L / \partial \theta_a^2$	$D^2 \displaystyle\sum_{i=1}^{n} a_i^2 \dfrac{(P_{ia} - c_i)}{(1-c_i)^2} \dfrac{Q_{ia}}{P_{ia}} \left\{ \dfrac{u_{ia} c_i}{P_{ia}} - P_{ia} \right\}$

$$I(t) = -E\{\partial^2 \ln L(u \mid t)/\partial t^2\}. \tag{7.19}$$

The matrix $I(t)$ is a square matrix of dimension $(N + 3n - 2)$.[2] The elements of the inverse of $I(t)$ correspond to the variances and covariances of the maximum likelihood estimators. If it can be assumed that at the last known iteration the ability parameters are known, then

$$I(x_i) = -E\{\partial^2 \ln L(u \mid \theta, x_i)/\partial x_i^2 \tag{7.20}$$

is the (3×3) information matrix corresponding to the estimators of the triplet of item parameters, (a_i, b_i, c_i). This (3×3) matrix can be inverted, and the asymptotic variances and covariances of the estimators of the item parameters obtained.

If we assume that the item parameters are given, then the standard error of the maximum likelihood estimator of θ_a is simply the reciprocal of $I(\theta_a)$ defined in chapter 5 and discussed extensively in chapter 6.

Recall that the information function for the estimator of θ is given by the expression

$$I(\theta) = \sum_{i=1}^{n} (\partial P_i/\partial\theta)^2/P_i Q_i. \tag{7.21}$$

As shown in the appendix to this chapter, the diagonal element of the information matrix $I(x_k)$, where x_k is one of the item parameters, a_i, b_i, c_i, is given by

$$I(x_k) = \sum_{a=1}^{N} (\partial P_{ia}/\partial x_k)^2/P_{ia} Q_{ia}, \tag{7.22}$$

while the off-diagonal element $I(x_k, x_j)$ is given by

$$I(x_k, x_j) = \sum_{a=1}^{N} (\partial P_{ia}/\partial x_k)(\partial P_{ia}/\partial x_j)/P_{ia} Q_{ia}. \tag{7.23}$$

Equations (7.22) and (7.23) provide an interesting parallel to the information function given for θ_a.

The elements of the information matrix for θ_a and the vector $x_i' = [a_i b_i c_i]$ are given in table 7–2. Once these elements are specified, standard errors can be determined as explained above. It should be pointed out that the elements of the information matrix are in terms of the unknown parameters. The values of the estimates may be substituted for the values of the parameters to obtain *estimates* of the standard errors. These in turn yield maximum likelihood confidence interval estimators for parameters of interest. Alterna-

Table 7-2 Information Matrix for Item and Ability Parameters in the Three-Parameter Logistic Model

Parameter	Information Matrix		
	a_i	b_i	c_i
a_i	$\dfrac{D^2}{(1-c_i)^2}\displaystyle\sum_{a=1}^{N}(\theta_a - b_i)^2(P_{ia}-c_i)^2 Q_{ia}/P_{ia}$		
b_i	$\dfrac{D^2 a_i^2}{(1-c_i)^2}\displaystyle\sum_{a=1}^{N}(\theta_a - b_i)(P_{ia}-c_i)^2 Q_{ia}/P_{ia}$	$\dfrac{D^2 a_i^2}{(1-c_i)^2}\displaystyle\sum_{a=1}^{N}(P_{ia}-c_i)^2 Q_{ia}/P_{ia}$	
c_i	$\dfrac{D}{(1-c_i)^2}\displaystyle\sum_{a=1}^{N}(\theta_a - b_i)(P_{ia}-c_i) Q_{ia}/P_{ia}$	$\dfrac{-Da_i}{(1-c_i)^2}\displaystyle\sum_{a=1}^{N}(P_{ia}-c_i) Q_{ia}/P_{ia}$	$\dfrac{1}{(1-c_i)^2}\displaystyle\sum_{a=1}^{N} Q_{ia}/P_{ia}$
θ_a		$D^2\displaystyle\sum_{i=1}^{n}a_i^2\, \dfrac{(P_{ia}-c_i)}{(1-c_i)^2}\, Q_{ia}\,(c_i - P_{ia})/P_{ia}$	

tively, when the number of examinees and the number of items are large, the matrix of second derivatives evaluated at the maximum of the likelihood function may be taken as an approximation to the information matrix.

The iterative scheme defined in equation (7.18) may not always converge rapidly. Problems may occur if at some point during the iteration, the matrix of second derivatives is indefinite. To avoid this problem, it may be judicious to replace the matrix of second derivatives by the information matrix. Since it can be shown that the information matrix is positive definite, this procedure has some clear advantages over the Newton-Raphson procedure. This procedure, known as Fisher's method of scoring (Rao, 1965, p. 302) is found to work efficiently in practice.

The joint maximum likelihood estimation procedure outlined above appears, in principle at least, straightforward. However, the fact that the item characteristic curves are nonlinear creates numerous problems that have hindered, until recently, the implementation of the maximum likelihood procedure. The item characteristic curves being nonlinear result in the likelihood equations being nonlinear. Solving a system of nonlinear equations is indeed a formidable problem, especially when there are as many as equations as there are in the case of the three-parameter model. Computers with large capacities are needed to implement the estimation procedure.

A second problem that arises is that solutions obtained through use of numerical procedures cannot always be guaranteed to be the true solutions of the equations. This is particularly a problem when an attempt is made to find the values of parameters that maximize a function. When the function is nonlinear, it may have several maxima, with one being the absolute maximum. The solution found may correspond to one of the "local" maxima and not the absolute maximum. The values of the parameter that correspond to a local maximum cannot be taken as maximum likelihood estimates of the parameters.

A third problem that arises is that the values of the parameters, or the estimates in this case, may take on values that fall outside the accepted range of values as a consequence of the numerical procedures employed. In this case, reasonable limits have to be imposed on the estimates to prevent them from going out of bounds, a practice that could raise concerns. Wright (1977a) has argued that this is an indication of the failure of the maximum likelihood estimation procedure in the two- and three-parameter models and hence has questioned the validity of the two- and three-parameter models.

As pointed out above, estimation in the three- and two-parameter models requires the estimation of the abilities of N examinees. When N is large, this may become cumbersome. However, in the one-parameter model, the estimation simplifies considerably. Since the number correct score is a sufficient statistic for ability when the one-parameter model is valid, examinees can be grouped into score categories, and the ability corresponding to each score category can be estimated. This was demonstrated in chapter 5. In the simultaneous estimation of parameters, the existence of a sufficient statistic for the ability parameters is clearly a great advantage. A sufficient statistic also exists for the difficulty parameters, and, hence, in theory at least, items that have the same conventional difficulty values can be grouped into categories. These results are evident on examination of the likelihood equations.

The first derivatives of the logarithm of the likelihood function given in table 7–1 can be readily specialized for the one-parameter model by setting $a_i = 1$ and $c_i = 0$. Setting these derivatives equal to zero, we obtain the likelihood equations. For estimating ability, θ_a, the equations are

$$D \sum_{i=1}^{n} (u_{ia} - P_{ia}) = 0 \qquad a = 1, \ldots, N, \tag{7.24}$$

and for estimating b_i, the corresponding equations are

$$-D \sum_{a=1}^{n} (u_{ia} - P_{ia}) = 0 \qquad i = 1, \ldots, n. \tag{7.25}$$

Denoting

$$\sum_{i=1}^{n} u_{ia} = r_a$$

and

$$\sum_{a=1}^{N} u_{ia} = s_i,$$

where r_a is the number right score for examinee a and s_i is the number of examinees who respond correctly to item i, the likelihood equations (7.24) and (7.25) can be re-expressed as

$$r_a - \sum_{i=1}^{n} P_{ia} = 0 \tag{7.26}$$

and

$$-s_i + \sum_{a=1}^{N} P_{ia} = 0. \tag{7.27}$$

These equations again demonstrate that r_a is a sufficient statistic for θ_a and s_i is a sufficient statistic for b_i. Thus only ability parameters for the $(n-1)$ score categories need be estimated (since ability corresponding to a zero right score or a perfect score cannot be estimated). Similarly, at the most, $n-1$ item parameters have to be estimated (since the mean of item difficulties may be set at zero). Thus, the total number of parameters that can be estimated in the one-parameter model is $2(n-1)$ as opposed to $n+N-1$.

The likelihood equations for the two-parameter model further reveal the primary advantage of the one-parameter model. The likelihood equations obtained by setting equal to zero the first derivatives with respect to θ_a, b_i, and a_i are

$$D \sum_{i=1}^{n} a_i(u_{ia} - P_{ia}) = 0, \qquad a = 1, \ldots, N; \qquad (7.28)$$

$$-D \sum_{a=1}^{N} a_i(u_{ia} - P_{ia}) = 0, \qquad i = 1, \ldots, n; \qquad (7.29)$$

and

$$D \sum_{a=1}^{N} (u_{ia} - P_{ia})(\theta_a - b_i) = 0 \qquad i = 1, \ldots, n. \qquad (7.30)$$

Equation (7.28) that corresponds to the estimation of θ_a, reduces to

$$\sum_{i=1}^{n} a_i u_{ia} - \sum_{i=1}^{n} a_i P_{ia} = 0. \qquad (7.31)$$

Clearly, if a_i were known, then the weighted score $\Sigma a_i u_{ia}$ is a sufficient statistic for θ_a. However, since the response pattern of an individual examinee is required to compute this weighted score, there will, in general, be as many such scores as there are examinees. Thus, no reduction in the number of ability parameters to be estimated results in this situation. Equation (7.29) reveals a similar fact about the estimation of difficulty parameters. Again no reduction in the number of parameters to be estimated is possible.

It is appropriate at this juncture to clarify the terminology that has been associated with the simultaneous estimation of item and ability parameters. Wright and Panchapakesan (1969) have termed the procedure for obtaining joint estimates of item and ability parameters in the Rasch model as the *unconditional maximum likelihood procedure (UCON)* (Wright & Douglas, 1977a, 1977b). They suggested this term to contrast with the conditional maximum likelihood estimation developed by Andersen (1972, 1973a). Since the term *unconditional estimation* can be interpreted as leading to marginal estimators, it should not be used. The term *joint maximum likelihood estimator* aptly describes the estimators considered in this section since the item and ability parameters are estimated jointly.

7.5 Conditional Maximum Likelihood Estimation

Andersen (1972, 1973a) argued that the maximum likelihood estimators of item parameters are not consistent since the bias in the estimator does not vanish when the number of examinees increases and showed that consistent maximum likelihood estimators of item parameters can be obtained by employing a conditional estimation procedure. The conditional procedure is predicated on the availability of sufficient statistics for the incidental ability parameters.

In the Rasch model, since the number correct score, r_a, is a sufficient statistic for θ_a, it is possible to express the likelihood function $L(u|\theta_a, b_i)$ in terms of r_a and not θ_a. This can be done by noting that for the Rasch model, dropping the subscript for r and θ,

$$P(U_i|\theta, b_i) = \exp DU_i(\theta - b_i)/[1 + \exp D(\theta - b_i)]. \quad (7.32)$$

Hence,

$$P[U_1, U_2, \ldots, U_n|\theta, b] = \prod_{i=1}^{n} P[U_i|\theta, b_i] \quad (7.33)$$

$$= [\exp(D\theta\Sigma U_i) \exp(-D\Sigma U_i b_i)]/ \prod_{i=1}^{n} [1 + \exp(\theta - b_i)] \quad (7.34)$$

$$= [\exp(D\theta r) \exp(-D\Sigma U_i b_i)]/g(\theta, b). \quad (7.35)$$

Now, the probability of obtaining a raw score r is given by

$$P[r|\theta, b] = [\exp(D\theta r)] \left[\sum_r \exp(-\Sigma U_i b_i) \right]/g(\theta, b), \quad (7.36)$$

where Σ_r denotes sum over the $\binom{n}{r}$ possible response patterns that yield the score r. It follows then that

$$P[U|r, b] = P[U|\theta, b]/P[r|\theta, b] \quad (7.37)$$

$$= \exp(-D\Sigma U_i b_i)/ \left[\sum_r \exp(-D\Sigma U_i b_i) \right] \quad (7.38)$$

$$= \exp(-D\Sigma U_i b_i)/\gamma_r, \quad (7.39)$$

where γ_r is defined as

$$\gamma_r = \sum_r \exp \left(-D \sum_{i=1}^{n} U_i b_i \right). \quad (7.40)$$

The above is a function of b and is known as an elementary symmetric function of order r. When the responses are observed, the probability $P(U|r, b)$ is interpreted as the likelihood function $L(u|r, b)$ which is independent of θ.

The maximum likelihood estimator of the item parameters can be obtained without any reference to the incidental ability parameters. As Andersen (1970) has pointed out, this conditional maximum likelihood estimator has the optimal properties listed in chapter 5.

The evaluation of the elementary symmetric functions and their first and second partial derivatives presents numerical problems. The algorithms currently available (Wainer, Morgan & Gustafsson, 1980) are effective with up to 40 items. The procedure is slow with 60 or more items. With 80 to 100 items, however, the numerical procedures break down, and the conditional estimation procedure is not viable in these cases.

7.6 Marginal Maximum Likelihood Estimation

As outlined in the previous section, the estimation of a fixed number of structural parameters in the presence of incidental parameters can be accomplished effectively via the conditional procedure when sufficient statistics are available for the incidental parameters. Unfortunately, sufficient statistics exist for the ability (incidental) parameters only in the Rasch model. While in the two-parameter logistic model the weighted response $r = \Sigma a_i u_i$ is a sufficient statistic for ability, it is dependent on the unknown item parameter a_i. Thus, it is not possible to extend the conditional approach to the two-parameter model.

Alternatively, the estimation of structural parameters can be carried out if the likelihood function can be expressed without any reference to the incidental parameters. This can be accomplished by integrating with respect to the incidental parameters if they are assumed to be continuous or summed over their values if they are discrete. The resulting likelihood function is the marginal likelihood function. The marginal maximum likelihood estimators of the structural parameters are those values that maximize the marginal likelihood function.

Bock and Lieberman (1970) determined the marginal maximum likelihood estimators of the item parameters for the normal ogive item response function. Originally, Bock and Lieberman (1970) termed the estimators of item parameters "conditional" estimators when they are estimated simultaneously with the ability parameters since in this case the examinees are treated as unknowns but *fixed*. In contrast, they suggested that when the examinees are considered a random sample and the likelihood function is integrated over the distribution of ability, the estimators of item parameters should be termed "unconditional" estimators. This terminology has caused some confusion in view of the usage of the terms *conditional* and *unconditional* by such writers as Andersen (1972) and Wright and Panchapakesan (1969). Andersen and Madsen (1977) pointed out this confusion and suggested the use of the more appropriate term *marginal estimators*.

Since the probability of examinee a obtaining the response vector, U, is

$$P[U|\theta, a, b, c] = \prod_{i=1}^{n} P_i^{U_i} Q_i^{1-U_i},$$

it follows that

$$P[U, \theta|a, b, c] = \prod_{i=1}^{n} P_i^{U_i} Q_i^{1-U_i} g(\theta) \tag{7.41}$$

and that

$$P[U|a, b, c] = \int_{-\infty}^{\infty} \prod_{i=1}^{n} P_i^{U_i} Q_i^{1-U_i} g(\theta) d\theta \equiv \pi_u. \tag{7.42}$$

The quantity πu is the unconditional or marginal probability of obtaining response pattern u. There are 2^n response patterns in all for n binary items. If r_u denotes the number of examinees obtaining response pattern u, the likelihood function is given by

$$L \propto \prod_{u=1}^{2^n} \pi_u^{r_u} \tag{7.43}$$

and

$$\ln L = c + r_u \sum_{u=1}^{2^n} \ln \pi_u, \qquad (7.44)$$

where c is a constant. The marginal maximum likelihood estimators are obtained by differentiating $\ln L$ with respect to the parameters a, b, and c, and solving the resulting likelihood equations.

Bock and Lieberman (1970) provided marginal maximum likelihood estimators of the parameters for the two-parameter model. They assumed that the ability distribution was normal with zero mean and unit variance and integrated over θ numerically. The resulting equations were solved iteratively. The basic problem with this approach was that the likelihood function had to be evaluated over the 2^n response patterns, a formidable task indeed. This restricted the application of the estimation procedure to the case where there were only 10 to 12 items.

More recently, Bock and Aitkin (1981) improved the procedure considerably by characterizing the distribution of ability empirically and employing a modification of the EM algorithm formulated by Dempster, Laird, and Rubin (1977). Thissen (1982) has adopted this procedure to obtain marginal maximum likelihood estimators in the Rasch model. For details of these procedures, the reader is referred to the above authors.

The marginal maximum likelihood procedure, in the Rasch model, yields comparable results to the conditional estimation procedure (Thissen, 1982). However, since the complex elementary symmetric functions are not required, the marginal procedure appears to be more effective than the conditional procedure.

Although the statistical properties of the marginal maximum likelihood estimators have not been conclusively established, it appears that these estimators have such desirable attributes as consistency and asymptotic normality. Further investigation is clearly needed in this area, as well as work in extending this procedure to the three-parameter model.

7.7 Bayesian Estimation

A Bayesian solution to the estimation problem may be appropriate when structural as well as incidental parameters have to be estimated (Zellner,

1971, pp. 114–119). The effectiveness of a Bayesian solution in such cases has been documented by Zellner (1971, pp. 114–161). As pointed out in chapter 5, Bayesian procedures for the estimation of ability parameters when item parameters are known have been provided by Birnbaum (1969) and Owen (1975). Bayesian procedures for the joint estimation of item and ability parameters have been provided only recently (see Swaminathan, in press; Swaminathan & Gifford, 1981, 1982). The estimation procedure developed by these authors parallels that described in chapter 5.

To illustrate the Bayesian procedure, we shall consider the three-parameter model, where

$$P_i(\theta \,|\, a,\, b,\, c) = c_i + (1 - c_i)\{1 + \exp[-Da_i(\theta - b_i)]\}^{-1}.$$

Let $f(\theta_a)$, $f(a_i)$, $f(b_i)$, and $f(c_i)$ denote the prior beliefs about the ability of examinee θ_a ($a = 1, \ldots, N$), the item discrimination parameter a_i ($i = 1, \ldots, n$), the item difficulty b_i ($i = 1, \ldots, n$), and the pseudo-chance level parameter c_i ($i = 1 \ldots, n$). Then the joint posterior density of the parameters θ, a, b, c is given by

$$f(\theta,\, a,\, b,\, c \,|\, u) \propto L(u \,|\, \theta,\, a,\, b,\, c) \left\{ \prod_{i=1}^{n} f(a_i) f(b_i) f(c_i) \right\} \prod_{a=1}^{N} f(\theta_a) \tag{7.45}$$

This is the first stage of the hierarchical Bayesian model.

In the second stage, it is necessary to specify the prior distribution for θ_a, a_i, b_i, and c_i. A priori, we may assume that

$$\theta_a \,|\, \mu_\theta,\, \phi_\theta \sim N(\mu_\theta,\, \phi_\theta), \tag{7.46}$$

where $N(\mu,\, \phi)$ denotes the normal density with mean μ and variance ϕ. Equivalently,

$$f(\theta_a \,|\, \mu_\theta,\, \phi_\theta) \propto \phi^{-\frac{1}{2}} \exp\{-(\theta_a - \mu_\theta)^2 / 2\phi_\theta\}, \tag{7.47}$$

where the constant $(2\pi)^{-\frac{1}{2}}$ has been omitted. A closer examination of equation (7.47) reveals that θ_a appears to be sampled from a normal population. This can be justified on the basis of *exchangeability* (Lindley and Smith, 1972). By this is meant that a priori the information about any θ is no different from any other θ.

The above procedure is repeated for the item difficulty, b_i. Again, we may assume a priori that the b_i are exchangeable and come from a normal population with mean μ_b and variance ϕ_b, i.e.

$$b_i \,|\, \mu_b,\, \phi_b \sim N(\mu_b,\, \phi_b). \tag{7.48}$$

Finally, priors have to be specified for a_i and c_i. Swaminathan (in press) has argued that since a_i is generally positive, being the slope of the item characteristic curve at the point of inflection, an appropriate prior for a_i is the chi-distribution defined as

$$f(a_i \,|\, v_i,\ \omega_i) \propto a_i^{v_i-1} \exp(-a_i^2/2\omega_i). \qquad (7.49)$$

The pseudo-chance level parameter, c_i, is bounded above by one and below by zero. The prior distribution for c_i can be taken as a Beta distribution with parameters s_i and t_i, i.e.

$$f(c_i \,|\, s_i,\ t_i) \propto c_i^{s_i}(1 - c_i)^{t_i}. \qquad (7.50)$$

Specification of these priors constitutes the second stage of the hierarchical model. In the third stage, it is necessary to specify prior distributions for the parameters, μ_θ, ϕ_θ, μ_b, ϕ_b, v_i, ω_i, s_i, and t_i.

Since the item response model is not identified (see section 7.2), identification conditions have to be imposed on the distribution of θ_a. And since it is convenient to fix the mean and the variance of the distribution, μ_θ and ϕ_θ are taken as zero and one, respectively, i.e.,

$$\theta_a \sim N(0,\ 1). \qquad (7.51)$$

Specification of prior belief for the parameters listed above is complex, and the reader is referred to the discussion provided by Swaminathan (in press), and Swaminathan and Gifford (1981, 1982). Once these prior distributions are specified, the values of the parameters $\boldsymbol{\theta}$, $\boldsymbol{a}$, $\boldsymbol{b}$, and $\boldsymbol{c}$ that maximize the joint posterior distribution given by equation (7.45) may be taken as Bayes' joint modal estimators. The procedure for obtaining these estimators parallels that for the maximum likelihood estimators.

The major advantage of the Bayesian procedure is that the estimation is direct. No constraints need to be imposed on the parameter space as with the maximum likelihood procedure since outward drifts of the estimates are naturally and effectively controlled by the priors. An illustration of this is seen in figure 7–1, where comparisons of the maximum likelihood and the Bayesian estimates of the discrimination parameters are provided with the aid of artificially generated data. The maximum likelihood estimates show tendency to drift out of bounds, while the Bayesian estimates display better behavior. In addition, the Bayesian estimates show a closer relationship to the true values. Despite these advantages, considerable further work needs to be done with the Bayesian procedure, especially with respect to the assessment of the posterior variance of the estimator, and the robustness of the procedure.

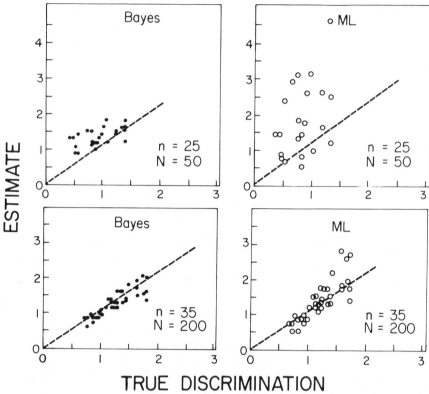

Figure 7-1. Bivariate Plot of True and Estimated Values of Item Discrimination (Two-Parameter Model)

7.8 Approximate Estimation Procedures

Although the estimation procedures that have been described have advantages as documented, obtaining the estimates may be time consuming and costly in some situations. This is particularly true when estimating the parameters in the three-parameter model. In these instances, with further assumptions it may be possible to obtain estimates that approximate maximum likelihood estimates. Although these estimates approximate maximum likelihood estimates, they may not possess the properties of maximum likelihood estimates. Despite this drawback, the approximate estimates are often useful and provide a considerable saving in computer costs.

Under the assumption that (1) the ability is normally distributed with zero mean and unit variance and (2) the appropriate item characteristic curve is the two-parameter normal ogive, Lord and Novick (1968, p. 377–378) have shown that the biserial correlation between θ and the response U_i to item i, $\rho'_{i\theta}$:

$$\rho'_{i\theta} = a_i/\{1 + a_i^2\}^{\frac{1}{2}}, \tag{7.52}$$

where a_i is the discrimination index of item i. Moreover, if γ_i is the normal deviate that cuts off an area π_i, where π_i is proportion of examinees who respond correctly to item i, to its right, (see figure 7–2), then,

$$\gamma_i = \rho'_{i\theta} b_i, \tag{7.53}$$

where b_i is the difficulty of item i. From these two expressions, once $\rho'_{i\theta}$ and γ_i are known, the item parameters a_i and b_i can be computed readily.

Unfortunately, $\rho'_{i\theta}$ cannot be obtained directly. However, it can be shown that the point biserial correlation between the binary scored response to item i and ability θ, $\rho'_{i\theta}$, and $\rho_{i\theta}$ are related according to

$$\rho_{i\theta} = \rho'_{i\theta}\phi(\gamma_i)/\{\pi_i(1 - \pi_i)\}^{\frac{1}{2}}, \tag{7.54}$$

where $\phi(\gamma_i)$ is the ordinate at γ_i. Thus once $\rho_{i\theta}$ is estimated, and π_i is determined, $\phi(\gamma_i)$ can be obtained, and finally, $\rho'_{i\theta}$ determined. From this, a_i and b_i can be computed from equations (7.52) and (7.53).

The point biserial correlation coefficient between the total test score (based on a long and homogeneous test) and the item score can be taken as an estimate of $\rho_{i\theta}$. In order for this to be a reliable estimate, there must be at least 80 items, and the KR–20 reliability must be at least .90 (Schmidt, 1977). The item difficulty for item i may be used as an estimator of π_i. With these estimates a_i and b_i can be estimated. Once a_i and b_i are obtained, they can be treated as known quantities, and the ability θ estimated using, say, the maximum likelihood procedure.

The procedure for estimating the parameters in the three-parameter model has been given by Urry (1974, 1976). In the three-parameter model, the probability of a correct response to an item is inflated by the presence of the pseudo-chance level parameter c_i. Hence, the item difficulty π'_i when the three-parameter model is used may be approximated using the expression

$$\pi'_i = c_i + (1 - c_i)\pi_i.$$

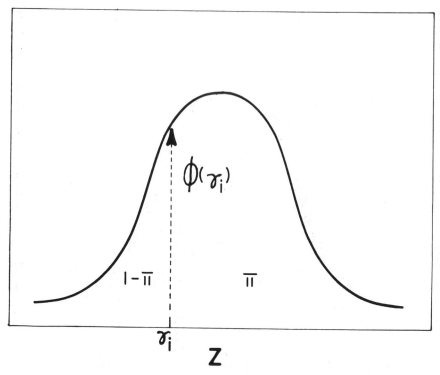

Figure 7-2.   Determination of γ_i

Thus, when $c_i \neq 0$, equation (7.54) becomes

$$\rho_{i\theta} = \rho'_{i\theta}\phi(\gamma_i)(1 - c_i)/\{\pi'_i - c_i)(1 - \pi'_i)\}^{\frac{1}{2}}. \qquad (7.55)$$

Once c_i is estimated, $\rho'_{i\theta}$ can be determined from a knowledge of $\rho_{i\theta}$, γ_i, and π'_i. From this, using equation (7.52) and (7.53), a_i and b_i can be computed. The simplest way to estimate c_i is to examine "the lower tail of a plot of the proportion of examinees responding correctly to an item at each item excluded test score" (Jensema, 1976).

A computer program for carrying out this estimation procedure is currently available. The program, called ANCILLES, basically implements the procedure described above with some refinements.

Swaminathan and Gifford (1983) and McKinley and Reckase (1980) have demonstrated that the procedure advocated by Urry (1976) does not compare favorably with the maximum likelihood procedure unless the number of examinees and items is very large. For small samples this procedure must be applied cautiously.

7.9 Computer Programs

Several computer programs that facilitate estimates of parameters are currently available. These programs can be grouped into the following categories:

1. Joint maximum likelihood estimation;
2. Conditional maximum likelihood estimation;
3. Marginal maximum likelihood estimation;
4. Approximate estimation in the three-parameter model.

The computer programs and their features are summarized in table 7–3 (see also, Wright & Mead, 1976; Wingersky, 1983). The most widely used of these computer programs are LOGIST and BICAL, two user-oriented programs, with LOGIST requiring a certain degree of understanding of item response theory. The procedures implemented follow closely with those outlined in this chapter.

7.10 Summary

The problem of estimating item and ability parameters in item response models is far more complex than that of estimating ability parameters when item parameters are known. The following procedures are currently available:

1. Joint maximum likelihood;
2. Conditional maximum likelihood (for the Rasch model);
3. Marginal maximum likelihood (for the Rasch and the two-parameter models);
4. Bayesian;
5. Approximate procedure (for the two- and three-parameter models).

The joint maximum likelihood estimation procedure is currently the most widely used. It is conceptually appealing, and as a result of the availability of

Table 7-3. Computer Programs with Brief Descriptions

Program	Characteristics	Reference
LOGIST5	1. Suitable for joint maximum likelihood estimation of parameters in the one-, two-, and three-parameter models.	Wingersky, Barton, & Lord (1982)
	2. Capable of dealing with omitted responses and not-reached items (in this case the likelihood function is modified).	
BICAL	1. Suitable for analysis with the one-parameter model.	Wright & Mead, (1976)
	2. Provides tests of fit for items and persons.	
ANCILLES; OGIVA	1. Suitable for joint estimation of item and ability parameters in the three-parameter model.	Urry (1976)
	2. Based partially on the minimum chi-square criterion.	
	3. Provides good estimates for large numbers of examinees and items.	
PML	1. Suitable for conditional maximum likelihood estimation in the one-parameter model.	Gustafsson (1980a)
	2. Provides estimation in the multi-category model.	
BILOG	1. Suitable for marginal maximum likelihood estimation in the one- and two-parameter models.	Mislevy & Bock (1982)

computer programs, it is readily implemented. However, in some instances, the joint maximum likelihood estimators of item parameters are not well behaved; hence, the values the estimators can take have to be restricted.

The conditional maximum likelihood procedure is valid only for the Rasch model. It exploits the existence of a sufficient statistic. However, for large numbers of items, the procedure is computationally tedious.

The marginal and Bayesian estimation procedures have the potential for solving some of the problems encountered with the joint maximum likelihood procedure. Still in the developmental stage, further work is required before these procedures can become user oriented.

The approximate procedure provides an alternative to the joint maximum likelihood procedure for the three-parameter model. Although it is cost effective, recent studies have indicated this procedure, as it is currently implemented, is not a viable alternative to the joint maximum likelihood procedure.

The maximum likelihood estimators have known asymptotic properties. The standard error of estimates can be computed once the estimators are available. The expression for standard errors are valid only for large numbers of item and examinees; hence, care must be taken when they are used with short tests and small sample of examinees.

Notes

1. Since the converse of this situation arises when the number of examinees is fixed while the number of items increases. In this case the ability parameters are the structural parameters, while the item parameters are incidental parameters. Again, the abilities will not converge to their true values when the number of items increases.

2. The dimension of $I(t)$ is assumed to be $(N + 3n - 2)$ rather than $(N + 3n)$ since otherwise the matrix $I(t)$ will be singular as a result of the indeterminacy in the model.

Appendix: Information Matrix for Item Parameter Estimates

The logarithm of the likelihood function is given by

$$\ln L(u \mid \theta, x_1, x_2, \ldots, x_i, \ldots, x_n) = \sum_{i=1}^{n} \sum_{a=1}^{N} [U_{ia} \ln P_{ia}$$
$$+ (1 - U_{ia}) \ln(1 - P_{ia})\}, \quad (7.56)$$

where $x_i = [a_i b_i c_i]$ is the triplet of item parameters for the ith item. When θ is known, the item parameter estimates are independent across the items. The (j, k) elements of the (3×3) Information matrix (for the three-parameter model) for item i (Kendall & Stuart, 1973, p. 57) is given as

$$I_i(x_j, x_k) = -E\{\partial^2 \ln L/\partial x_j \partial x_k\}, \quad j, k = 1, \ldots, 3. \quad (7.57)$$

Now from (7.55)

$$\frac{\partial \ln L}{\partial x_j} = \sum_{a=1}^{N} \left[\frac{U_{ia}}{P_{ia}} - \frac{(1 - U_{ia})}{(1 - P_{ia})} \right] \frac{\partial P_{ia}}{\partial x_j} \quad (7.58)$$

and, by the product and chain rules,

$$\frac{\partial^2 \ln L}{\partial x_j \partial x_k} = \sum_{a=1}^{N} \left\{ \frac{\partial}{\partial P_{ia}} \left[\frac{U_{ia}}{P_{ia}} - \frac{(1 - U_{ia})}{(1 - P_{ia})} \right] \frac{\partial P_{ia}}{\partial x_k} \frac{\partial P_{ia}}{\partial x_j} \right.$$
$$\left. + \left[\frac{U_{ia}}{P_{ia}} - \frac{(1 - U_{ia})}{(1 - P_{ia})} \right] \frac{\partial^2 P_{ia}}{\partial x_k \partial x_j} \right\}. \quad (7.59)$$

On taking expectations, the second term in (7.59) vanishes since $E(U_{ia} \mid \theta_a) = P_{ia}$. The first term, upon simplification, reduces to

$$\sum_{a=1}^{N} \left[-\frac{U_{ia}}{P_{ia}^2} - \frac{(1 - U_{ia})}{(1 - P_{ia})^2} \right] \left(\frac{\partial P_{ia}}{\partial x_j} \right) \left(\frac{\partial P_{ia}}{\partial x_k} \right).$$

Taking expectations and combining terms, it follows that

$$I_i(x_j, x_k) = \sum_{a=1}^{N} \left(\frac{\partial P_{ia}}{\partial x_j} \right) \left(\frac{\partial P_{ia}}{\partial x_k} \right) \Big/ P_{ia} Q_{ia}. \quad (7.60)$$

The diagonal term of the information matrix is

$$I_i(x_k) = \sum_{a=1}^{N} \left(\frac{\partial P_{ia}}{\partial x_k} \right)^2 \Big/ P_{ia} Q_{ia}. \quad (7.61)$$

8 APPROACHES
FOR ADDRESSING
MODEL-DATA FIT

8.1 Overview

Item response models offer a number of advantages for test score interpretations and reporting of test results, but the advantages will be obtained in
practice only when there is a close match between the model selected for use
and the test data.

From a review of the relevant literature, it appears that the determination
of how well a model accounts for a set of test data should be addressed in
three general ways:

1. Determine if the test data satisfy the assumptions of the test model of
   interest.
2. Determine if the expected advantages derived from the use of the item
   response model (for example, invariant item and ability estimates) are
   obtained.

Some material in this chapter has been adapted from Hambleton, Swaminathan, Cook,
Eignor, & Gifford (1978), Hambleton (1980), and Hambleton and Murray (1983).

3. Determine the closeness of the fit between predictions and observable outcomes (for example, test score distributions) utilizing model parameter estimates and the test data.

Although, strictly speaking, tests of model assumptions are not tests of goodness of fit, because of their central role in model selection and use in the interpretation of goodness-of-fit tests, we have included them first in a series of desirable goodness-of-fit investigations.

Promising practical approaches for addressing each category above will be addressed in subsequent sections. First, however, several statistical tests will be introduced, and the inappropriateness of placing substantial emphasis on results from statistical tests will be explained.

8.2 Statistical Tests of Significance

Statistical tests of goodness of fit of various item response models have been given by many authors (Andersen, 1973b; Bock, 1972; Gustafsson, 1980; Mead, 1976; Wright, Mead, & Draba, 1976; Wright & Panchapakesan, 1969; Wright & Stone, 1979). The procedure advocated by Wright and Panchapakesan (1969) for testing the fit of the one-parameter model has been one of the most commonly used statistical tests. It essentially involves examining the quantity f_{ij} where f_{ij} represents the frequency of examinees at the ith ability level answering the jth item correctly. Then, the quantity y_{ij} is calculated, where

$$y_{ij} = \{f_{ij} - E(f_{ij})\}/\{\mathrm{Var}\, f_{ij}\}^{\frac{1}{2}}$$

is distributed normally with zero mean and unit variance. Since f_{ij} has a binomial distribution with parameter p_{ij}, the probability of a correct response is given by $\theta_i^*/(\theta_i^* + b_j^*)$ for the one-parameter model, and r_i, the number of examinees in the score group. Hence, $E(f_{ij}) = r_i p_{ij}$, and $\mathrm{Var}(f_{ij}) = r_i p_{ij}(1 - p_{ij})$. Thus, a measure of the goodness of fit, χ^2, of the model can be defined as

$$\chi^2 = \sum_{i=1}^{n-1} \sum_{j=1}^{n} y_{ij}^2.$$

The quantity, χ^2, defined above has been assumed by Wright and his colleagues to have a χ^2 distribution with degrees of freedom $(n-1)(n-2)$, since the total number of observations in the matrix $F = \{f_{ij}\}$ is $n(n-1)$ and the number of parameters estimated is $2(n-1)$. Wright and Panchapakesan (1969) also defined a goodness-of-fit measure for individual items as

$$\chi_j^2 = \sum_{i=1}^{n-1} y_{ij}^2,$$

where χ_j^2 is assumed to be distributed as χ^2 with degrees of freedom, $(n-2)$. This method for determining the goodness of fit can also be extended to the two- and three-parameter item response models although it has not been extended to date.

Several problems are associated with the chi-square tests of fit discussed above. The χ^2 test has dubious validity when any one of the $E(f_{ij})$ terms— $i=1, 2, \ldots, n-1$; $j=1, 2, \ldots, n$—have values less than one. This follows from the fact that when any of the $E(f_{ij})$ terms is less than one, the deviates y_{ij}, $1-1, 2, \ldots, n-1$; $j=1, 2, \ldots, n$, are not normally distributed, and a χ^2 distribution is obtained only by summing the squares of normal deviates. Another problem encountered in using the χ^2 test is that it is sensitive to sample size. If enough observations are taken, the null hypothesis that the model fits the data will always be rejected using the χ^2 test. Divgi (1981a, 1981b) and Wollenberg (1980, 1982a, 1982b) have also demonstrated that the Wright-Panchapakesan goodness-of-fit statistic is not distributed as a χ^2 variable, and the associated degrees of freedom have been assumed to be higher than they actually are. Clearly, there are substantial reasons for not relying on the Wright-Panchapakesan statistic because of the role sample size plays in its interpretation and because of questions concerning the appropriate sampling distribution and degrees of freedom.

Alternatively, Wright, Mead, and Draba (1976) and Mead (1976) have suggested a method of test of fit for the one-parameter model, which involves conducting an analysis of variance on the variation remaining in the data after removing the effect of the fitted model. This procedure allows not only a determination of the general fit of the data to the model but also enables the investigator to pinpoint guessing as the major factor contributing to the misfit. This procedure for testing goodness of fit of the one-parameter model involves computing residuals in the data after removing the effect of the fitted model. These residuals are plotted against $(\theta_a - b_i)$. According to the model, the plot should be represented by a horizontal line through the origin. For guessing, the residuals (the discrepancy between actual and predicted performance) follow the horizontal line until the guessing becomes important. When this happens the residuals are positive since persons are doing better than expected and in that region have a negative trend. If practice or speed is involved, the affected items display negative residuals with a negative trend line over the entire range of ability. Bias for a particular group may be detected by plotting the residuals separately for the group of interest and the remaining examinees (sometimes called the "majority group"). It is generally found that the residuals have a negative trend for the unfavored group and a positive trend for the favored group.

When maximum likelihood estimates of the parameters are obtained, likelihood ratio tests can be obtained for hypotheses of interest (Waller, 1981). Likelihood ratio tests involve evaluating the ratio λ of the maximum values of the likelihood function under the hypothesis of interest to the maximum value of the likelihood function under the alternate hypothesis. If the number of observations is large, $-2 \log \lambda$ is known to have a chi-square distribution with degrees of freedom given by the difference in the number of parameters estimated under the alternative and null hypotheses. An advantage possessed by likelihood ratio tests over the other tests discussed earlier is apparent: Employing the likelihood ratio criterion, it is possible to assess the fit of a particular item response model against an alternative.

Andersen (1973b) and Bock and Liebermann (1970) have obtained likelihood ratio tests for assessing the fit of the Rasch model and the two-parameter normal ogive model, respectively. Andersen (1973b) obtains a conditional likelihood ratio test for the Rasch model based on the within-score group estimates and the overall estimates of item difficulties. He shows further that -2 times the logarithm of this ratio is distributed as χ^2 with degrees of freedom, $(n - 1)(n - 2)$. Based on the work of Bock and Liebermann (1970), likelihood ratio tests can be obtained for testing the fit of the two-parameter normal ogive model. This procedure can be extended to compare the fits of one model against another (Andersen, 1973b). The major problem with this approach is that the test criteria are distributed as chi-square only asymptotically. But, as was mentioned earlier, when large samples are used to accommodate this fact, the chi-square value may become significant owing to the large sample size!

The problem associated with examinee sample size and statistical tests of model-data fit was recently illustrated in a small simulation study by Hambleton and Murray (1983). A computer program, DATAGEN (Hambleton & Rovinelli, 1973), was used to simulate the item performance of 2400 examinees on a 50 item test. The items in the test were described by parameters in the three-parameter logistic model. Ability scores were assumed to be normally distributed ($\overline{\theta} = 0$, $SD_\theta = 1$). Next, the 1979 version of BICAL was used to conduct a one-parameter model analysis of the same test data and a summary of the misfitting items was tabulated. The test data deviated considerably from the assumptions of the one-parameter model

Table 8-1.   A Summary of Misfitting Items (50 Item Test)[1]

Examinee Sample Size	Misfitting Items	
	$p \leq .05$	$p \leq .01$
150	20	5
300	25	17
600	30	18
1200	38	28
2400	42	38

[1]From Hambleton and Murray (1983).

since the "a" parameters ranged from .40 to 2.00 and the "c" parameters ranged from .00 to .25. The study was carried out with five sample sizes: 150, 300, 600, 1200, and 2400 examinees. The first 150 examinees were selected for the first sample, the first 300 examinees for the second sample, and so on. In the 1979 version of BICAL a "t statistic" is used to summarize the misfit between the best fitting one-parameter item characteristic curve and the data.

The results in Table 8-1 show clearly the impact of sample size on the detection of misfitting items. Using the .01 significance level, the number of misfitting items ranged from 5 to 38 of the 50 items when sample size was increased from 150 to 2400! The number of misfitting items was of course substantially larger using the .05 significance level: The number ranged from 20 at a sample size of 150 to 42 at a sample size of 2400.

8.3 Checking Model Assumptions

Item response models are based on *strong* assumptions, which will not be completely met by any set of test data (Lord & Novick, 1968). There is evidence that the models are robust to some departures, but the extent of robustness of the models has not been firmly established (Hambleton, 1969; Hambleton et al., 1978; Hambleton & Traub, 1976; Panchapakesan, 1969). Given doubts of the robustness of the models, a practitioner might be tempted to simply fit the most general model since it will be based on the least restrictive assumptions. Unfortunately, the more general models are multidimensional (i.e., assume that more than one latent variable is required to account for examinee test performance) as well as complex and do not appear ready for wide-scale use. Alternatively, it has been suggested that the three-parameter logistic model, the most general of the unidimensional models in common use, be adopted. In theory, the three-parameter model should result in better fits than either the one- or two-parameter models. But there are three problems with this course of action: (1) More computer-time is required to conduct the analyses, (2) somewhat larger samples of examinees and longer tests are required to obtain satisfactory item and ability estimates, and (3) the additional item parameters (item discrimination and pseudo-chance levels) complicate the use of the model for practitioners. Of course, in spite of the problems, and with important testing programs, the three-parameter model may still be preferred.

Model selection can be aided by an investigation of four principal assumptions of several of the item response models: unidimensionality, equal discrimination indices, minimal guessing, and nonspeeded test administrations. Promising approaches for studying these assumptions are summarized in figure 8–1 and will be considered next. Readers are also referred to Traub and Wolfe (1981).

8.3.1 Unidimensionality

The assumption of a unidimensional latent space is a common one for test constructors since they usually desire to construct unidimensional tests so as to enhance the interpretability of a set of test scores (Lumsden, 1976). Factor analysis can also be used to check the reasonableness of the assumption of unidimensionality with a set of test items (Hambleton & Traub, 1973). However, the approach is not without problems. For example, much has been written about the merits of using tetrachoric correlations or phi correlations (McDonald & Ahlawat, 1974). The common belief is that using phi correlations will lead to a factor solution with too many factors, some of them "difficulty factors" found because of the range of item difficulties among the items in the pool. McDonald and Ahlawat (1974) concluded that "difficulty factors" are unlikely if the range of item difficulties is not extreme and the items are not too highly discriminating.

Tetrachoric correlations have one attractive feature: A sufficient condition for the unidimensionality of a set of items is that the matrix of tetrachoric item intercorrelations has only one common factor (Lord & Novick, 1968). On the negative side, the condition is not necessary. Tetrachoric correlations are awkward to calculate (the formula is complex and requires some numerical integration) and, in addition, do not necessarily yield a correlation matrix that is positive definite, a problem when factor analysis is attempted.

Kuder-Richardson Formula 20 has on occasion been recommended and/ or used to address the dimensionality of a set of test items. But Green,

Figure 8-1. Approaches for Conducting Goodness-of-Fit Investigations

---

Checking Model Assumptions

1. Unidimensionality (Applies to Nearly All Item Response Models)

   - Plot of Eigenvalues (from Largest to Smallest) of the Inter-Item Correlation Matrix—Look for a dominant first factor, and a high ratio of the first to the second eigenvalue (Reckase, 1979).
   - Comparison of Two Plots of Eigenvalues—The one described above and a plot of eigenvalues from an inter-item correlation matrix of random data (same sample size, and number of variables, random data normally distributed) (Horn, 1965).
   - Plot of Content-Based Versus Total-Test-Based Item Parameter Estimates (Bejar, 1980).
   - Analysis of Residuals After Fitting a One-Factor Model to the Inter-Item Covariance Matrix (McDonald, 1980a, 1980b).

2. Equal Discrimination Indices (Applies to the One-Parameter Logistic Model)

   - Analysis of Variability of Item-Test Score Correlations (for Example, Point-Biserial and Biserial Correlations).
   - Identification of Percent of Item-Test Score Correlations Falling Outside Some Acceptable Range (for Example, the Average Item-Test Score Correlation $\pm .15$).

3. Minimal Guessing (Applies to the One- and Two-Parameter Logistic Model)

   - Investigation of Item-Test Score Plots (Baker, 1964, 1965).
   - Consideration of the Performance of Low-Ability Examinees (Selected with the Use of Test Results, or Instructor Judgments) on the Most Difficult Test Items.
   - Consideration of Item Format and Test Time Limits (for Example, Consider the Number of Item Distractors, and Whether or Not the Test Was Speeded).

4. - Nonspeeded (Power) Test Administration (Applies to Nearly All Item Response Models).

   - Comparison of Variance of the Number of Items Omitted to the Variance of the Number of Items Answered Incorrectly (Gulliksen, 1950).
   - Investigation of the Relationship Between Scores on a Test with the Specified Time Limit and with an Unlimited Time Limit (Cronbach and Warrington, 1951).
   - Investigation of (1) Percent of Examinees Completing the Test, (2) Percent of Examinees Completing 75 Percent of the Test, and (3) Number of Items Completed by 80 Percent of the Examinees.

(continued on next page)

Figure 8-1 *(continued)*

Checking Expected Model Features

1. Invariance of Item Parameter Estimates (Applies to All Models)

   • Comparison of Item Parameter Estimates Obtained in Two or More Subgroups of the Population for Whom the Test is Intended (for Example, Males and Females; Blacks, Whites, and Hispanics; Instructional Groups; High and Low Performers on the Test or Other Criterion Measure, Geographic Regions). Normally, comparisons are made of the item-difficulty estimates and presented in graphical form (scattergrams). Random splits of the population into subgroups the same size provide a basis for obtaining plots which can serve as a baseline for interpreting the plots of principal interest (Angoff, 1982b; Lord, 1980a; Hambleton and Murray, 1983). Graphical displays of distributions of standardized differences in item parameter estimates can be studied. Distributions ought to have a mean of zero and a standard deviation of one (for example, Wright, 1968).

2. Invariance of Ability Parameter Estimates (Applies to All Models)

   • Comparison of Ability Estimates Obtained in Two or More Item Samples from the Item Pool of Interest. Choose item samples which have special significance such as relatively hard versus relatively easy samples, and subsets reflecting different content categories within the total item pool. Again, graphical displays and investigation of the distribution of ability differences are revealing.

Checking Model Predictions of Actual (and Simulated) Test Results

   • Investigation of Residuals and Standardized Residuals of Model-Test Data Fits at the Item and Person Levels. Various statistics are available to summarize the fit information. Graphical displays of data can be revealing.
   • Comparison of Item Characteristic Curves Estimated in Substantially Different Ways (for Example, Lord, 1970a).
   • Plot of Test Scores and Ability Estimates (Lord, 1974a).
   • Plots of True and Estimated Item and Ability Parameters (for Example, Hambleton & Cook, 1983). These studies are carried out with computer simulation methods.
   • Comparison of Observed and Predicted Score Distributions. Various statistics (chi-square, for example) and graphical methods can be used to report results. Cross-validation procedures should be used, especially if sample sizes are small (Hambleton & Traub, 1973).
   • Investigation of Hypotheses Concerning Practice Effects, Test Speeded-ness, Cheating, Boredom, Item Format Effects, Item Order, etc.

Lissitz, and Mulaik (1977) have noted that the value of KR-20 depends on test length and group heterogeneity and that the statistic therefore provides misleading information about unidimensionality.

A more promising method involves considering the plots of eigenvalues for test item intercorrelation matrices and looking for the "breaks" in the plots to determine the number of "significant" underlying factors. To assist in locating a "break," Horn (1965) suggested that the plot of interest be compared to a plot of eigenvalues obtaining from an item intercorrelation matrix of the same size and where inter-item correlations are obtained by generating random variables from normal distributions. The same number of examinees as used in the correlation matrix of interest is simulated.

Another promising approach, in part because it is not based on the analysis of correlation coefficients, was suggested by Bejar (1980):

1. Split test items on an a priori basis (e.g., content considerations). For example, isolate a subset of test items that appear to be tapping a different ability from the remaining test items.
2. For items in the subset, obtain item parameter estimates twice: once by including the test items in item calibration for the total test and a second time by calibrating only the items in the subset.
3. Compare the two sets of item parameter estimates by preparing a plot (see Figure 8-2).

Unless the item parameter estimates (apart from sampling error) are equal, the probabilities for passing items at fixed ability levels will differ. This is not acceptable because it implies that performance on items depends on which items are included in the test, thus contradicting the unidimensionality assumption.

Finally, McDonald (1980a, 1980b) and Hattie (1981) have suggested the use of nonlinear factor analysis and the analysis of residuals as a promising approach. The approach seems especially promising because test items are related to one another in a nonlinear way anyway, and the analysis of residuals, after fitting a one-factor solution, seems substantially more revealing and insightful than conducting significance tests on the amount of variance accounted for.

8.3.2 Equal Discrimination Indices

This assumption is made with the one-parameter model. There appear to be only descriptive methods available for investigating departures from this

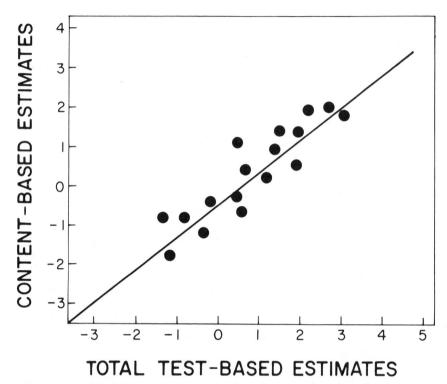

TOTAL TEST-BASED ESTIMATES

Figure 8-2.   Plot of Content-Based and Total Test Based Item Difficulty Parameter Estimates

model assumption. A rough check of its viability is accomplished by comparing the similarity of item point-biserial or biserial correlations. The range (or the standard deviation) of the discrimination indices should be small if the assumption is to be viable.

8.3.3 Guessing

There appears to be no direct way to determine if examinees guess the answers to items in a test. Two methods have been considered: (1) nonlinear item-test score regression lines, and (2) the performance of low test score examinees on the hardest test items. With respect to the first method, for each test item, the proportion of correct answers for each test score group (small test score groups can be combined to improve the accuracy of results) is plotted. Guessing is assumed to be operating when test performance for the low performing score groups exceeds zero. For method two, the performance of the low-scoring examinees on the hardest test questions is of central concern. Neither method, however, is without faults. The results will be misleading if the test items are relatively easy for the low-ability group and/ or if the low-ability group is only relatively low in ability in relation to other examinees in the population for whom the test is intended but not low ability in any absolute sense (i.e., very low scorers on the test).

8.3.4 Speededness of the Test

Little attention is given to this seldom stated assumption of many item response models. When it operates it introduces an additional factor to influence test performance and can be identified by a factor analytic study. Interestingly, with some of the new ability estimation methods (Lord, 1980a), the failure of examinees to complete a test can be handled so that the speededness factor does not "contaminate" ability score estimates. The appropriateness of the assumption in relation to a set of test results can be checked by determining the number of examinees who fail to finish a test and the number of items they fail to complete. The ideal situation occurs when examinees have sufficient time to attempt each question in a test.

Donlon (1978) provided an extensive review of methods for determining the speededness of tests. Three of the most promising are cited in figure 8–1. One of the methods Donlon describes involves obtaining an estimate of the correlation between scores obtained under power and speed conditions and correcting the correlation for attenuation due to the unreliability associated with the power and speed scores:

$$\rho(T_p, T_s) = \frac{\rho(X_p, X_s)}{\sqrt{\rho(X_p, X_p')}\sqrt{\rho(X_s, X_s')}}.$$

The speededness index proposed by Cronbach and Warrington (1951) is

$$\text{Speededness Index} = 1 - \rho^2(T_s, T_p).$$

The index is obtained in practice by administered parallel forms of the test of interest under speed and power conditions to the same group of examinees.

8.4 Checking Model Features

When item response models fit test data sets, three advantages are obtained:

1. Examinee ability estimates are obtained on the same ability scale and can be compared even though examinees may have taken different sets of test items from the pool of test items measuring the ability of interest.
2. Item statistics are obtained that do not depend on the sample of examinees used in the calibration of test items.
3. An indication of the precision of ability estimates at each point on the ability scale is obtained.

Item response models are often chosen as the mode of analysis in order to obtain the advantages. However, whether these features are obtained in any application depends on many factors—model-data fit, test length, precision of the item parameter estimates, and so on. Through some fairly straight-forward methods, these features can be studied and their presence in a given situation determined.

The first feature can be addressed, for example, by administering examinees two or more samples of test items that vary widely in difficulty (Wright, 1968). In some instances, items can be administered in a single test and two scores for each examinee obtained: The scores are based on the easier and harder halves of the test. To determine if there is substantial difference in test difficulty, the distributions of scores on the two halves of the test can be compared. Pairs of ability estimates obtained from the two halves of the test for each examinee can be plotted on a graph. The bivariate plot of ability estimates should be linear because expected ability scores for examinees do not depend on the choice of test items when the item response model under investigation fits the test data. Some scatter of points about a best fitting line, however, is to be expected because of measurement error. When a linear relationship is not obtained, one or more of the underlying assumptions of the item response model under investigation are being violated by the test data set. Factors such as test characteristics, test lengths, precision of item statistics, and so on can also be studied to determine their influence.

The second feature is studied in essentially the same way as the first. The difference is that extreme ability groups are formed and item parameter estimates in the two samples are compared. Wright (1968) and Lord (1980a) have carried out extensive studies in this area. Again, if the test data are fit by the item response model under investigation, there should be a linear relationship between item parameter estimates from the two examinee samples, even if the samples differ in ability, race, or sex (Lord & Novick, 1968). The comparison is carried out for each of the item parameters in the model of interest. This check would be a stiff one, but a linear relationship must still be obtained or it must be said that the item response model does not fit the test data for one or two of the groups.

Perhaps the most serious weakness of the approaches described above (and these are the only ones found in the literature) is that there are no baseline data available for interpreting the plots. How is one to know whether the amount of scatter is appropriate, assuming model-data fit? In the next chapter one approach utilizing the notion of "random plots" will be introduced for interpreting plots of statistics obtained from two or more groups. Alternatively, statistical tests are performed to study the differences between, say, b values obtained in two groups. But, as long as there is at least a small difference in the true-parameter values in the groups, statistically significant differences will be obtained when sample sizes are large. Thus, statistically significant differences may be observed even when the practical differences are very small.

The third feature of item response models is a harder one to address. Perhaps it is best answered via simulation methods. According to the theory, if a test is "long enough," the conditional distribution of ability estimates at each ability level is normal (mean = ability; sd = $1/\sqrt{\text{information}}$). It appears that a test must include about 20 items (Samejima, 1977a).

8.5 Checking Additional Model Predictions

Several approaches for checking model predictions were introduced in figure 8–1. One of the most promising approaches for addressing model-data fit involves the use of residual analyses. An item response model is chosen; item and ability parameter estimates are obtained; and predictions of the performance of various ability groups on the items on the test are made, assuming the validity of the chosen model. Finally, comparisons of the predicted results with the actual results are made.

By comparing the average item performance levels of various ability groups to the performance levels predicted by an estimated item characteristic curve, a measure of the fit between the estimated item characteristic curve and the observed data can be obtained. This process, of course, can and is repeated for each item in a test. In figure 8–3 a plot of the residuals (difference between the observed data and an estimated item characteristic curve) across ability groups for four items is reported along with likely explanations for the results. The average item performance of each ability group is represented by the symbols in the figure. If, for example, 25 of 75 examinees in the lowest ability group answered an item correctly, a symbol would be placed at a height of .33 above the average ability score in the

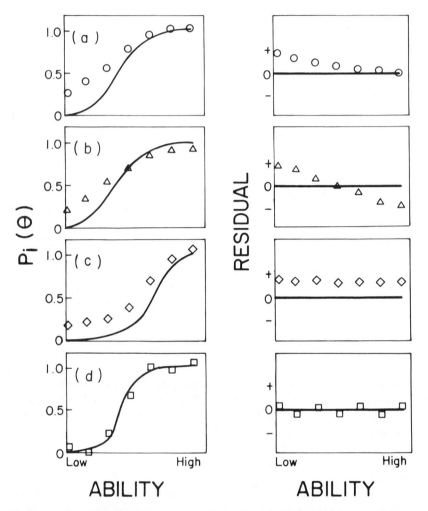

Figure 8-3.   Four Item Residual Plots. Possible Explanations: (a) failure to account for examinee guessing, (b) failure to adequately account for a highly discriminating item, (c) biased item, and (d) adequate fit between the model and the item performance data

ability group where the performance was obtained. (The width of each ability group should be wide enough to contain a reasonable number of examinees.) With items (a), (b), and (c) in figure 8–3, there is substantial evidence of a misfit between th available test data and the estimated item characteristic curves (Hambleton, 1980). Surprisingly, given their apparent usefulness, residuals have not received more attention from item response model researchers. Many examples of residual plots will be described in the next chapter.

Lord (1970a, 1974a) has advanced several approaches for addressing model-data fit. In 1970, Lord compared the shape of item characteristic curves estimated by different methods. In one method he specified the curves to be three-parameter logistic. In the other method, no mathematical form of the item characteristic curves was specified. Since the two methods gave very similar results (see figure 8–4), he argued that it was reasonable to impose the mathematical form of three-parameter logistic curves on his data. Presumably, Lord's study can be replicated on other data sets as well although his second method requires very large examinee samples. In a second study, Lord (1974a) was able to assess, to some extent, the suitability of ability estimates by comparing them to raw scores. The relationship should be high but not perfect.

Simulation studies have been found to be of considerable value in learning about item response models and how they compare in different applications (e.g., Hambleton, 1969, 1983b; Hambleton & Cook, 1983; Ree, 1979). It is possible to simulate data with known properties and see how well the models recover the true parameters. Hambleton and Cook (1983) found, for example, when concerned with estimating ability scores for ranking, description, or decisions, that the one-, two-, and three-parameter models provided highly comparable results except for low-ability examinees.

Several researchers (for example, Hambleton & Traub, 1973; Ross, 1966) have studied the appropriateness of different mathematical forms of item characteristic curves by using them, in a comparative way, to predict observed score distributions (see figures 8.5 and 8.6). Hambleton and Traub (1973) obtained item parameter estimates for the one- and two-parameter models from three aptitude tests. Assuming a normal ability distribution and using test characteristic curves obtained from both the one- and two-parameter logistic models, they obtained predicted score distributions for each of the three aptitude tests. A χ^2 goodness-of-fit index was used to compare actual test score distributions with predicted test score distributions from each test model. Judgment can then be used to determine the suitability of any given test model and the desirability of one model over another. While Hambleton and Traub (1973) based their predictions on a normal ability distribution assumption, it is neither desirable nor necessary to make such an assumption to obtain predicted score distributions.

Finally, it is reasonable and desirable to generate testable hypotheses concerning model-data fit. Hypotheses might be generated because they seem interesting (e.g., Are item calibrations the same for examinees

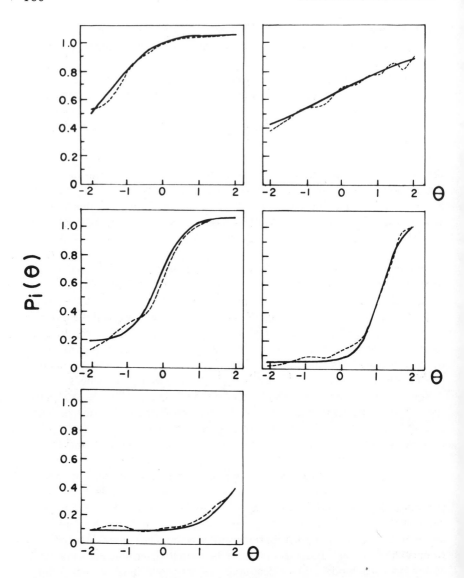

Figure 8-4.   Five Item Characteristic Curves Estimated by Two Different Methods (From Lord, F. M. Estimating item characteristic curves without knowledge of their mathematical form. *Psychometrika*, 1970, *35*, 43-50. Reprinted with permission.)

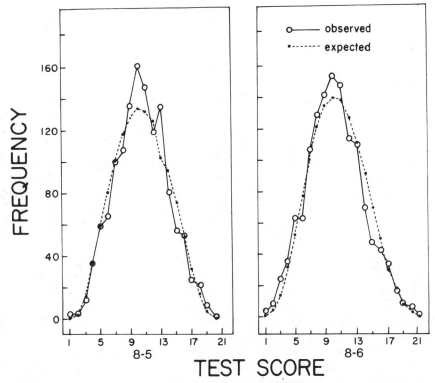

Figure 8-5. Observed and Expected Distributions for OSAT-Verbal Using the Two-Parameter Logistic Model

Figure 8-6. Observed and Expected Distributions for OSAT-Verbal Using the One-Parameter Model

receiving substantially different types of instruction?) or because questions may have arisen concerning the validity of the chosen item response model and testing procedure (e.g., What effect does the context in which an item is pilot tested have on the associated item parameter estimates?) On this latter point, see, for example, Yen (1980).

8.6 Summary

The potential of item response theory has been widely documented but that potential is certainly not guaranteed when applied to particular tests, with particular samples of examinees, or when used in particular applications. Item response theory is not a magic wand to wave over a data set to fix all of the inaccuracies and inadequacies in a test and/or the testing procedures. But, when a bank of content valid and technically sound test items is available, and goodness of fit studies reveal high agreement between the chosen item response model and the test data, item response models may be useful in test development, detection of biased items, score reporting, equating test forms and levels, item banking, and other applications as well.

With respect to addressing the fit between an item response model and a set of test data for some desired application, our view is that the best approach involves (1) designing and implementing a wide variety of analyses, (2) interpreting the results, and (3) judgmentally determining the appropriateness of the intended application. Analyses should include investigations of model assumptions, the extent to which desired model features are obtained, and comparisons between model predictions and actual data. Statistical tests can be carried out but care must be shown in interpreting the statistical information. Extensive use should be made, whenever possible, of replication, of cross-validation, of graphical displays of model predictions and actual data, etc. Also, fitting more than one model and comparing (for example) the residuals provides information that is invaluable in determining the usefulness of item response models. Whenever possible it is also helpful to assess the consequences of model misfit. There is no limit to the number of investigations that can be carried out. The amount of effort extended in collecting, analyzing, and interpreting results must be related to the importance and nature of the intended application. For example, a small school district using the one-parameter model to aid in test development will not need to expend as many resources on goodness of fit studies as (say) the Educational Testing Service when they use an item response model to equate forms of the Scholastic Aptitude Test.

With respect to testing model assumptions, unidimensionality is clearly the most important assumption to satisfy. Many tests of unidimensionality are available, but those that are independent of correlations (Bejar) and/or incorporate the analysis of residuals (McDonald) seem most useful. In category two, there is a definite shortage of ideas and techniques. Presently, plots of, say, item parameter estimates obtained in two groups are compared but without the aid of any "baseline plots." Or statistical tests are used to compare the two sets of item parameter estimates, but such tests are less than ideal for reasons offered in section 8.2. Several new techniques seem possible, and these will be introduced in the next chapter. In the third category, a number of very promising approaches have been described in the literature, but they have received little or no attention from researchers. Perhaps the problem is due to a shortage of computer programs to carry out necessary analyses or to an overreliance on statistical tests. In any case, the problem is likely to be overcome in the near future. We will focus our attention in the next chapter on several of the more promising approaches in this category.

In summary, our strategy for assessing model-data fit is to accumulate a considerable amount of evidence that can be used to aid in the determination of the appropriateness of a particular use of an item response model. Judgment will ultimately be required and therefore the more evidence available, the more informed the final decision about the use of an item response model will be. Information provided in Figure 8-1 will be useful as a starting point for researchers interested in designing goodness-of-fit investigations.

9 EXAMPLES OF
MODEL-DATA FIT STUDIES

9.1 Introduction

In the previous chapter, a set of steps and techniques were introduced for
conducting goodness-of-fit investigations. The purpose of this chapter is to
highlight the applications of several of those techniques to the analysis of real
data. Specifically, the results of fitting the one- and three-parameter logistic
models to four mathematics tests in the 1977–78 National Assessment of
Educational Progress will be described. This chapter is intended to serve as a
case-study for how a researcher might approach the problem of assessing
model-data fit.

9.2 Description of NAEP Mathematics Exercises

In the 1977–78 NAEP assessment of mathematics skills of 9-, 13- and 17-
year-olds, approximately 650 test items (called "exercises" by NAEP) at

---

Some of the material in this chapter is from a report by Hambleton, Murray, & Simon (1982)
and a paper by Hambleton and Murray (1983).

each age level were used. Available test items at a given age level were randomly assigned to one of ten forms. Each test form was administered to a carefully chosen sample of (approximately) 2,500 examinees. Elaborate sampling plans were designed and carried out to ensure that each form was administered to a nationally representative sample of examinees.

Item statistics play only a minor part in NAEP mathematics test development. Test items are included in test forms if they measure what national panels of mathematics specialists believe should be included in the NAEP testing program. Content considerations are dominant in the item selection process. In this respect, test development parallels the construction of criterion-referenced tests (Popham, 1978; Hambleton, 1982b). Math calculations, story problems, and geometry appear to be the most frequently occurring types of test items in the NAEP tests.

Test items in the NAEP mathematics assessment were of two types: multiple-choice and open-ended. Among the multiple-choice test items, it was also interesting to note that the number of answer choices varied from two to nine.

9.3 Description of Data

Four NAEP mathematics test booklets from the 1977–78 assessment were selected for analysis:

9-Year-Olds:

   Booklet No. 1, 65 test items
   Booklet No. 2, 75 test items

13-Year-Olds:

   Booklet No. 1, 58 test items
   Booklet No. 2, 62 test items

Between 2,400 and 2,500 examinees were used in item parameter estimation, which was carried out with the aid of LOGIST (Wingersky, 1983; Wingersky, Barton, & Lord, 1982).[1]

9.4 Checking Model Assumptions

Checking on two model assumptions, unidimensionality and equal item discrimination indices, with respect to the NAEP math booklets was carried

Table 9-1.   Largest Eigenvalues for NAEP Math Booklet No. 1 (9-year-olds, 1977-78)[1]

Eigenvalue Number	Value
1	10.21
2	2.85
3	1.73
4	1.50
5	1.38
6	1.26
7	1.21
8	1.12
9	1.09
10	1.05
11	1.03
12	1.02
13	1.00
14	.99
15	.97
16	.96
17	.96
18	.93
19	.92
20	.91
% Variance Accounted For By the First Factor	17.60

[1] The sample included 2422 examinees.

out. The results will be presented next. It was not necessary to check the level of test speededness because test items were administered one at a time to examinees, who were given sufficient time on each one to provide answers.

9.4.1 Unidimensionality

A check on the unidimensionality of one of the math booklets, NAEP Math Booklet No. 1 for 13-year-olds, is reported in table 9-1. A study of the eigenvalues was carried out with a sample of 2,422 examinees. About 17.6 percent of the total variance was accounted for by the first factor or component, and the ratio of the first to the second eigenvalue was (approximately) 3.6. Similar results were obtained for the other tests as well. These statistics do not meet Reckase's (1979) minimal criteria for unidimensionality. However, since his criteria are arbitrary and other goodness-of-fit evidence would be available, the decision made was to move on to other types of analyses.

9.4.2 Equal Item Discrimination Indices

Tables 9–2 and 9–3 provide item difficulty and discrimination (biserial correlations) information for two of the four NAEP math booklets. The item statistics for the remaining two math booklets were similar. The following results were obtained:

Booklet	Sample Size	Test Length	Item Discrimination Indices[2]	
			Mean	SD
Booklet No. 1, 9-year-olds	2,495	65	.565	.260
Booklet No. 2, 9-year-olds	2,463	75	.565	.260
Booklet No. 1, 13-year-olds	2,500	58	.585	.250
Booklet No. 2, 13-year-olds	2,433	62	.615	.252

The results above show clearly that the assumption of equal item discrimination indices is violated to a considerable degree. This finding is not surprising because item statistics play only a small part in NAEP mathematics test development. It would be reasonable, therefore, to expect a wider range of values than might be found on a standardized achievement or aptitude test, where items with low discrimination indices are usually deleted. Also, it would be reasonable to suspect based on the results above that the two- or three-parameter logistic models would provide a more adequate fit to the test results. This point is addressed in more detail in section 9.6.

9.5 Checking Model Features[3]

When an item response model fits a test data set, at least to an adequate degree, two advantages or features are obtained: (1) Item parameter estimates do not depend on the samples of examinees drawn from the

Table 9-2. NAEP Math Booklet No. 1 Basic Item Statistical and Classificatory Information (9-year-olds, 1977–78)

Test Item	Absolute-Valued Standardized Residuals[1]		Item Difficulty[2]	Item Discrimination[3]	Content Category[4]	Format[5]
	1-p	3-p				
1	1.27	0.62	.55	.62	3	1
2	1.73	0.60	.47	.69	3	1
3	1.27	0.85	.55	.65	1	1
4	3.50	2.24	.91	.34	2	1
5	2.28	1.57	.89	.39	2	1
6	3.26	1.08	.70	.33	2	1
7	2.00	0.88	.12	.37	2	2
8	0.59	0.82	.33	.56	2	2
9	1.73	0.63	.46	.47	2	1
10	1.53	0.63	.39	.65	5	1
11	2.18	0.79	.89	.77	4	2
12	2.03	1.01	.84	.75	4	2
13	2.45	0.84	.88	.80	4	2
14	2.35	1.73	.73	.76	4	2
15	2.61	1.06	.81	.80	4	2
16	3.05	2.16	.75	.79	4	2
17	3.20	1.00	.46	.35	1	1
18	0.49	0.59	.81	.59	1	2
19	0.86	1.30	.85	.51	2	1
20	0.85	0.73	.63	.63	4	2
21	2.35	0.48	.40	.75	4	2
22	2.26	0.74	.20	.60	5	1
23	1.84	0.65	.53	.62	1	1
24	2.50	0.58	.82	.79	4	2
25	1.55	0.86	.40	.68	4	2
26	2.64	0.88	.49	.77	4	2
27	1.85	0.86	.68	.72	4	2
28	1.08	0.94	.36	.63	4	2
29	1.41	0.40	.77	.69	4	2
30	2.67	0.88	.68	.78	4	2

(continued on next page)

Table 9-2 *(continued)*

Test Item	Absolute-Valued Standardized Residuals[1]		Item Difficulty[2]	Item Discrimination[3]	Content Category[4]	Format[5]
	1-p	3-p				
31	1.92	0.99	.69	.72	6	1
32	4.48	1.33	.03	.14	3	1
33	4.92	0.69	.19	.14	3	1
34	1.12	0.92	.64	.54	5	1
35	0.92	1.13	.80	.62	6	1
36	1.41	1.10	.65	.67	4	2
37	1.25	0.56	.09	.60	4	2
38	1.33	0.84	.94	.43	3	1
39	3.53	0.72	.20	.26	1	1
40	4.00	0.58	.17	.22	4	1
41	2.26	1.12	.20	.73	1	2
42	0.69	0.38	.17	.57	4	2
43	1.22	0.58	.02	.61	4	2
44	1.10	1.10	.01	.59	4	2
45	3.55	0.87	.29	.28	5	2
46	1.72	0.60	.36	.51	4	1
47	2.63	1.11	.54	.40	5	1
48	1.18	0.61	.83	.67	6	1
49	2.36	0.93	.29	.50	6	1
50	4.38	0.47	.66	.27	1	1
51	4.18	0.69	.25	.21	1	1
52	5.51	0.88	.35	.19	2	1
53	3.19	0.66	.09	.22	2	1
54	2.67	0.97	.09	.31	2	1
55	0.58	0.65	.01	.49	6	2
56	1.43	0.68	.12	.64	1	2
57	1.51	1.16	.48	.53	2	1
58	1.11	0.91	.24	.53	2	1
59	2.32	0.44	.28	.48	2	1
60	0.99	0.76	.21	.51	1	2
61	1.54	0.92	.10	.53	5	2
62	1.46	1.47	.85	.60	3	2

(continued on next page)

Table 9-2 *(continued)*

Test Item	Absolute-Valued Standardized Residuals[1]		Item Difficulty[2]	Item Discrimination[3]	Content Category[4]	Format[5]
	1-p	3-p				
63	1.53	1.17	.48	.67	4	2
64	1.16	0.53	.35	.49	2	1
65	3.71	0.94	.27	.24	3	1

1. 1-p ≡ one-parameter logistic model; 3-p ≡ three-parameter logistic model.
2. Item difficulty ≡ proportion of examinees in the NAEP sample answering the test item correctly ($N = 2495$).
3. Item discrimination ≡ biserial correlation between item and the total test score.
4. Content Categories: 1 — Story Problems, 2 — Geometry, 3 — Definitions, 4 — Calculations, 5 — Measurement, 6 — Graphs and Figures.
5. Format: 1 — multiple choice, 2 — open response.

Table 9-3. NAEP Math Booklet No. 1 Basic Item Statistical and Classificatory Information (13-year-olds, 1977–78)

Test Item	Absolute-Valued Standardized-Residuals[1]		Item Difficulty[2]	Item Discrimination[3]	Content Category[4]	Format[5]
	1-p	3-p				
1	1.47	.84	.85	.70	1	2
2	.68	.44	.93	.61	3	1
3	.71	.85	.95	.62	3	1
4	3.11	1.94	.52	.81	5	2
5	1.74	.89	.65	.72	4	1
6	1.80	.96	.36	.48	2	1
7	1.70	.64	.40	.49	2	1
8	3.80	1.47	.70	.29	2	1
9	2.13	.72	.30	.43	1	1
10	1.59	.64	.81	.72	5	1
11	1.47	.86	.95	.75	4	2
12	1.47	1.31	.94	.74	4	2

(continued on next page)

Table 9-3 *(continued)*

Test Item	Absolute-Valued Standardized-Residuals[1]		Item Difficulty[2]	Item Discrimination[3]	Content Category[4]	Format[5]
	1-p	3-p				
13	1.61	1.11	.93	.75	4	2
14	1.21	.77	.92	.70	4	2
15	.97	.88	.89	.66	4	2
16	1.11	1.39	.88	.58	4	2
17	1.86	.98	.73	.47	5	1
18	.96	.83	.14	.54	1	2
19	2.42	1.42	.62	.75	4	2
20	3.30	.42	.59	.84	4	2
21	3.08	.53	.56	.82	4	2
22	.68	.48	.93	.46	3	1
23	2.85	.71	.36	.38	3	1
24	1.88	.89	.33	.48	3	1
25	1.15	.98	.52	.64	1	2
26	2.32	.46	.73	.41	2	1
27	1.06	.81	.10	.51	2	1
28	4.62	.77	.22	.18	2	2
29	.92	.77	.18	.57	5	2
30	1.92	.83	.46	.60	1	1
31	.80	.73	.74	.64	2	1
32	2.06	1.56	.58	.64	1	1
33	1.13	.64	.42	.49	1	1
34	.75	.56	.96	.46	2	1
35	2.36	1.87	.66	.44	2	1
36	7.08	1.19	.21	−.01	1	1
37	1.36	.66	.37	.47	2	1
38	2.63	.67	.78	.80	3	1
39	3.37	.73	.70	.36	3	1
40	1.72	.85	.66	.70	1	1
41	1.16	.96	.27	.62	3	1
42	.60	.93	.69	.60	2	1
43	.87	.81	.78	.60	2	1
44	1.58	1.93	.68	.59	4	2
45	1.16	1.62	.45	.61	4	2

(continued on next page)

Table 9-3 (continued)

Test Item	Absolute-Valued Standardized Residuals[1]		Item Difficulty[2]	Item Discrimination[3]	Content Category[4]	Format[5]
	1-p	3-p				
46	2.01	.90	.34	.63	1	1
47	4.63	.98	.11	.10	2	1
48	1.69	1.11	.15	.48	3	1
49	1.20	.83	.49	.64	4	2
50	.77	.80	.84	.62	1	1
51	3.30	.57	.18	.27	1	1
52	5.03	.96	.60	.26	1	1
53	1.37	.31	.82	.45	2	1
54	1.19	1.19	.73	.63	4	2
55	1.83	.83	.25	.68	6	2
56	.49	.74	.72	.59	1	1
57	2.48	.95	.31	.73	5	2
58	.83	.71	.74	.62	4	2

1. 1-p ≡ one-parameter logistic model; 3-p ≡ three-parameter logistic model.
2. Item difficulty ≡ proportion of examinees in the NAEP sample answering the test item correctly ($N \approx 2500$).
3. Item discrimination ≡ biserial correlation between item and the total test score.
4. Content Categories: 1 ≡ Story Problems, 2 ≡ Geometry, 3 ≡ Definitions, 4 ≡ Calculations, 5 ≡ Measurement, 6 ≡ Graphs and Figures.
5. Format: 1 ≡ multiple-choice, 2 ≡ open response.

population of examinees for whom the test is designed (i.e., item parameter invariance) and (2) expected values of ability estimates do not depend on the choice of test items. The extent to which the first feature was obtained with NAEP math data will be presented next.

9.5.1 Item Parameter Invariance

Item parameter estimates, aside from sampling errors, will be the same regardless of the samples of examinees chosen from the population of examinees for whom the items are intended when the item response model of interest fits the test data. Therefore, it is desirable to identify sub-groups of

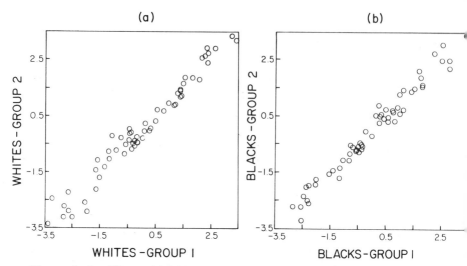

Figure 9-1. Plots of b-Values for the One-Parameter Model Obtained from Two Equivalent White Student Samples (N = 165) in (a), and Black Student Samples (N = 165) in (b)

special interest in the examinee population and study item invariance. For example, it would be meaningful to compare item parameter estimates obtained with examinees from different geographic regions, ethnic groups, age groups or instructional groups in the examinee population of interest. The invariance of item difficulty estimates for Whites and Blacks with the one-parameter model was investigated by Hambleton and Murray (1983) initially with Math Booklet No. 1 for 13 Year Olds. Three hundred and thirty Black examinees were located on the NAEP data tape. All these examinees were used in the analysis. An equal number of White students were selected at random from the same data tape. Next, the Black and the White student samples were divided at random into two halves so that four equal-sized groups of students (N = 165) were available for the analyses. These groups were labelled "White 1," "White 2," "Black 1," and "Black 2." A one-parameter analysis was carried out with each group. The plots of "b" values in the two White and Black samples are shown in figure 9-1. The idea for obtaining base-line plots was suggested by Angoff (1982). The plots show high relationships between the sets of b values (r ≅ .98). What variation there is in the plots is due to model-data misfit and examinee sampling errors. These plots provide a basis for investigating hypotheses concerning the invariance of item parameter estimates. If the feature of item invariance is present, similar plots should be obtained when the Black and White item

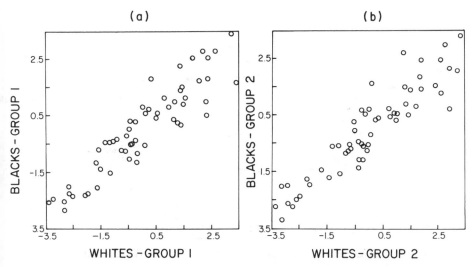

Figure 9-2.   Plots of b-Values for the One-Parameter Model Obtained from the First White and Black Samples in (a) and the Second White and Black Samples in (b)

parameter estimates are compared. Figure 9-2(a) reveals clearly when that item difficulty estimates differ substantially in the first Black and White samples ($r \cong .74$) compared to the plots in figure 9-1. Figure 9-2(b) provides a replication of the Black-White comparison of item difficulty estimates in two different samples. The plot of b values in figure 9-2(b) is very similar to the plot in figure 9-2(a) and both plots differ substantially from the baseline plots shown in figure 9-1.

Figure 9-3(a) provides a plot of the differences in item difficulty estimates between the two White and the two Black samples ($r \cong .06$). The item parameter estimates obtained in each ethnic group should estimate the same item parameter values if the feature of item invariance is obtained (although the value may be different in the two ethnic groups because of scaling). Therefore, after any scaling factors are taken into account, the expected difference for any pair of item difficulty indices should be zero and the correlation of these differences across the set of test items in these two groups should also be zero. In fact, the correlation is very close to zero. If the feature of item invariance is present it should exist for any pairings of the data. Figure 9-3(b) shows that the correlation between b value differences in the first and second Black and White samples is not zero (in fact, $r \cong .72$!). Clearly, item difficulty estimates obtained with the one-parameter model are not invariant in the Black and White examinee samples. The test items

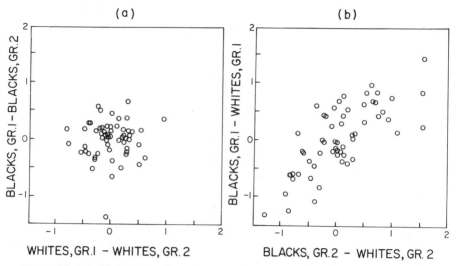

Figure 9-3.   Plots of b-Value Differences B1-B2 vs. W1-W2 in (a) and B1-W1 vs. B2-W2 in (b)

located in the bottom left hand corner and the top right hand corner of the plot in Figure 9-3(b) are the ones requiring special review. These test items show a *consistent* and *substantial difference* in difficulty level in the two groups.

We stop short here of attributing the problem to ethnic bias in the test items. The analyses shown in figures 9-1, 9-2, and 9-3 do suggest that the test items are functioning differently in the two ethnic groups. The finding was observed also in a replication of the study. But, there are at least two plausible explanations besides ethnic bias in the test items: (1) The problem is due to a variable which is confounded with ethnicity (e.g., regarding achievement scores—Blacks did perform substantially lower on the math booklets than Whites) or (2) failure to consider other important item statistics such as discrimination (a) and pseudo-chance level (c) in fitting the item response model to the test data. With respect to the second point, in other words, the problem maybe due to model-data misfit. But whatever the correct explanation, the feature of item parameter invariance was not obtained with the one-parameter model. Unfortunately the same analyses could not be carried out with the three-parameter model because of the very small sample sizes. An alternate methodology to handle small samples was recently proposed by Linn and Harnisch (1981).

No attempt was made in the Hambleton and Murray study to bring closure to the question of whether or not the item invariance was due to (1) model-data misfit, (2) methodological shortcomings (*not* matching the two groups on ability, or failure to account for variation in the standard errors associated with the item difficulty estimates), or (3) ethnic background. However, based on some recent analyses it appears now that the first two explanations are more plausible than the third.

It should be recognized that a similar methodology to that described above can be used to address ability invariance. Baseline plots can be obtained by estimating examinee abilities from randomly equivalent parts of the test. Then, abilities can be estimated and plotted using more interesting splits of the test items. Possible splits might include "hard" versus "easy" items, "first half" versus "second half" items, "items which appear to be measuring a second trait" versus "the remaining items", etc.

One criticism of the earlier analyses is that no attempt was made to account for variation in the items due to their discriminating power and pseudo-chance level. The analysis described next with Math Booklet No. 1 with 13-year-olds was carried out to address this deficiency. A group of 2,400 examinees was found with the 1,200 lowest ability students and 1,200 highest ability students. The (approximately) 22 middle-ability students were deleted from the analysis. Next, the 2,400 examinees were divided on a random basis into two equal subgroups of 1,200 examinees, with each subgroup used to obtain the three-parameter model item estimates. Figure 9-4(a) provides the plot of b-values in the two randomly-equivalent samples obtained with the three-parameter logistic model. The item parameter estimates in the two samples are nearly identical, thus establishing item parameter invariance across random groups and providing a graphical representation of the size of errors to be expected with a sample size of 1200. Next, the 2,400 examinees were divided into two equal-sized low- and high-ability groups (again, $N = 1,200$), and the analyses and the same plot carried out with the random groups was repeated. The results for the three-parameter model are reported in figure 9-4(b).

If the feature of item invariance was present, the two plots in figure 9-4 should have looked the same. In fact, the plots in figure 9-4 are substantially different. However, it is not plausible this time to explain the differences in terms of a failure to account for essential item statistics (i.e., discrimination and pseudo-level) since these statistics were calculated and used in the analysis. One possible explanation that remains is that item parameter estimation is not done very well when extreme groups are used.[4] Of course another possibility is that the test items are functioning differently in the two ability groups; i.e., item parameters are not invariant across ability groups.

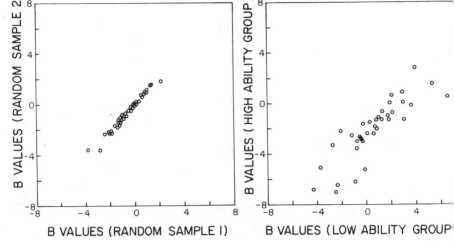

Figure 9-4. Plots of Three-Parameter Model Item Difficulty Estimates Obtained in Two Equivalent Samples in (a) and Low and High Ability Samples in (b) with NAEP Math Booklet No. 1 (13 Year Olds, 1977-78, N = 1200)

9.6 Checking Additional Model Predictions

In this section, the results from two analyses will be described: Residual analyses and research hypothesis investigations.

9.6.1 Residual Analyses

To carry out residual analyses with the math booklets, a computer program was prepared (Hambleton, Murray, & Simon, 1982). The program was prepared by Linda Murray to be compatible with the item and ability parameter estimation output from LOGIST and provides both residuals and standardized residuals for each test item at various ability levels (the number is selected by the user). Twelve ability levels were chosen for the investigation. In addition, fit statistics are available for each test item (found by summing over ability levels), for each ability level (found by summing over test items), and for the total test (found by summing over ability levels and test items).

Standardized residuals for items 2, 4, and 6 in Math Booklet No. 1 for 13 year olds obtained with the one-parameter model and three-parameter models are shown in figures 9-5, 9-6, and 9-7, respectively. Two features of the plots in figures 9-6 and 9-7 are the cyclic patterns and the large size of the standardized residuals. Residual plots like those in figure 9-6 for the one-parameter model were obtained for items with relatively high biserial correlations. Residual plots like those in figure 9-7 for the one-parameter model were obtained for items with relatively low biserial correlations. Also, the standardized residuals tended to be high. From table 9-4 it can be seen that (approximately) 25% of the standardized residuals exceeded a value of 3 when the one-parameter model was fit to the test data. This result was obtained with four test booklets. If the model data fit had been close, the distribution of standardized residuals would have been approximately normal.

The standardized residual plots obtained from fitting the three-parameter model and shown in figures 9-5 and 9-6 reveal dramatically different patterns. The cyclic patterns which were so evident with the residuals for the one-parameter model are gone, and the sizes of the standardized residuals are substantially smaller. For item 2, the standardized residual plots were very similar for the two models. For this item, guessing played a minor role in test performance and the level of item discrimination was average.

An analysis of the standardized residual results shows clearly that the three-parameter model fits the test data and the one-parameter model did not. Table 9-4 provides a complete summary of the distributions of standardized residuals obtained with the one- and three-parameter models for four Math Booklets. In all cases, the standardized residuals were considerably smaller with the three-parameter model and the distributions of the three-parameter model standardized residuals were approximately normal.

9.6.2 Research Hypothesis Investigations

The residual analysis results in the last section are valuable for evaluating model-data fit but additional insights can be gained from supplemental analyses of the residuals. A preliminary study showed a relationship between the one-parameter model absolute-valued standardized residuals and classical item difficulties (see figure 9-8). The outstanding features were the large size of the residuals and the tendency for the most difficult items to have the highest residuals. Possibly this latter problem was due to the guessing behavior of examinees on the more difficult test items. In a plot of three-

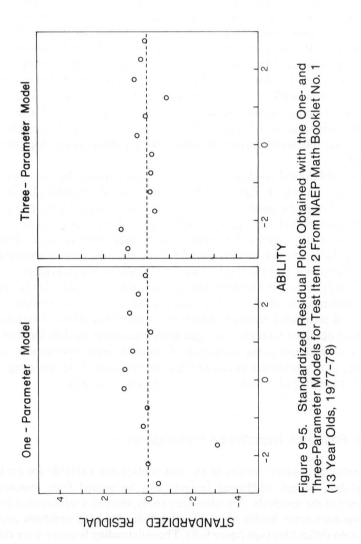

Figure 9-5. Standardized Residual Plots Obtained with the One- and Three-Parameter Models for Test Item 2 From NAEP Math Booklet No. 1 (13 Year Olds, 1977–78)

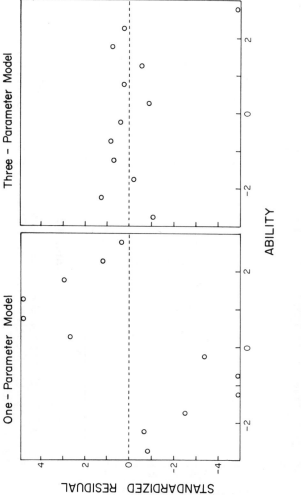

Figure 9-6. Standardized Residual Plots Obtained with the One- and Three-Parameter Models for Test Item 4 From NAEP Math Booklet No. 1 (13 Year Olds, 1977–78)

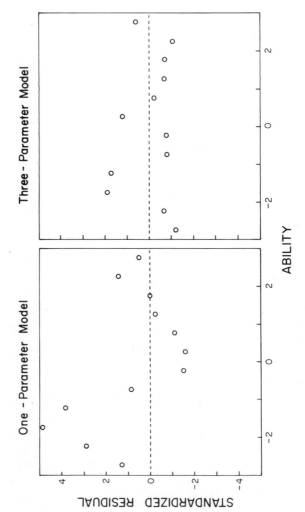

Figure 9-7. Standardized Residual Plots Obtained with the One- and Three-Parameter Models for Test Item 6 From NAEP Math Booklet No. 1 (13 Year Olds, 1977–78)

Table 9-4. Analysis of Standardized Residuals with the One- and Three-Parameter Logistic Models for Four 1977-78 NAEP Mathematics Booklets

NAEP Booklet	Logistic Model	Percent of Standardized Residuals*			
		$\mid 0\ to\ 1\mid$	$\mid 1\ to\ 2\mid$	$\mid 2\ to\ 3\mid$	$\mid over\ 3\mid$
Booklet 1	1	35.9	21.5	17.3	25.3
(9-year-olds)	3	66.7	24.4	6.7	2.3
Booklet 2	1	37.1	25.3	13.8	23.8
(9-year-olds)	3	67.4	24.7	5.7	2.2
Booklet 1	1	40.7	22.1	16.5	20.7
(13-year-olds)	3	65.4	25.1	.78	1.7
Booklet 2	1	42.6	24.2	16.3	16.9
(13-year-olds)	3	67.2	26.1	5.7	1.1

*At the 9-year-old level, there were 780 standardized residuals (65 test items $\times$ 12 ability levels). At the 13-year-old level, there were 690 standardized residuals (58 test items $\times$ 12 ability levels) (From Hambleton, Murray, & Simon, 1982).

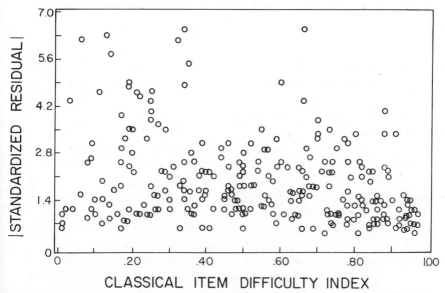

CLASSICAL ITEM DIFFICULTY INDEX

Figure 9-8. Scatterplot of One-Parameter Model Standardized Residuals and Classical Item Difficulties for 9 and 13 Year Old Math Booklets Nos. 1 and 2

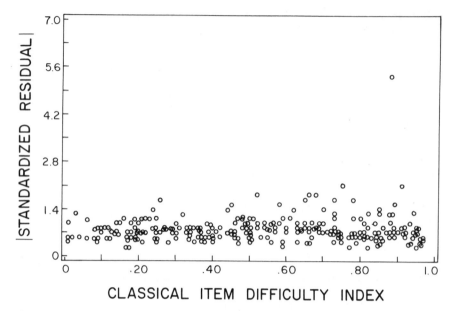

CLASSICAL ITEM DIFFICULTY INDEX

Figure 9-9. Scatterplots of One-Parameter Model Standardized Residuals and Classical Item Difficulties for 9 and 13 Year Olds, Math Booklets Nos. 1 and 2

parameter model absolute-valued standardized residuals and classical item difficulty estimates shown in figure 9-9, residuals were substantially smaller *and* it appeared that by estimating item pseudo-chance level parameters, the tendency for the highest residuals to be obtained with the most difficult items was removed.

Figure 9-10 provides the results of a second preliminary analysis: a plot of one-parameter model absolute-valued standardized residuals and classical item biserial correlations for four of the Math Booklets combined. A strong curvilinear relationship was evident. Items with relatively high or low biserial correlations had the highest standardized residuals. Figure 9-11 provides the same information as the plot in figure 9-10 except that the three-parameter model standardized residuals were used. The curvilinear relationship appeared. Substantially better fits were obtained when variations in discriminating powers of test items were accounted for by the three-parameter logistic model.

These initial analyses were encouraging because they provided several insights into possible reasons for item misfit. It appeared that the one-

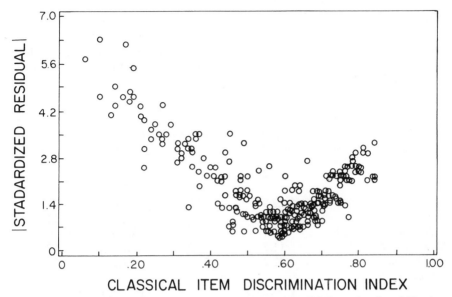

Figure 9-10. Scatterplot of One-Parameter Model Standardized Residuals and Classical Item Discrimination Indices for 9 and 13 Year Olds, Math Booklets Nos. 1 and 2

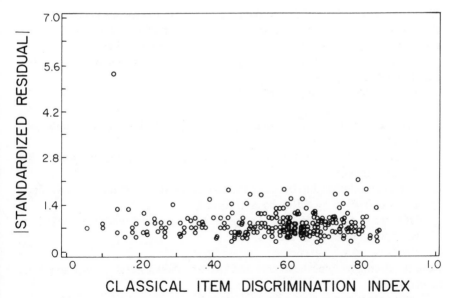

Figure 9-11. Scatterplot of Three-Parameter Model Standardized Residuals and Classical Item Discrimination Indices for 9 and 13 Year Olds, Math Booklets Nos. 1 and 2

Table 9-5.   Association Between Standardized Residuals and NAEP Item
Content Classifications (Booklets No. 1 and 2, 260 Items, 9- and 13-year
olds, 1977-78)[1]

Content Category	Number of Items	Standardized Residuals			
		$SR(\leq 1.0)^{1-p}$ (n = 48)	$SR(>1.0)$ (n = 212)	$SR(\leq 1.0)^{3-p}$ (n = 197)	$SR(>1.0)$ (n = 63)
Story Problems	52	21.2	78.8	82.7	17.3
Geometry	48	22.9	77.1	75.0	25.0
Definitions	42	16.7	83.3	78.6	21.4
Calculations	83	15.7	84.3	69.9	30.1
Measurement	17	11.8	88.2	82.4	17.6
Graphs and Figures	18	22.2	77.8	72.2	27.8
		$\chi^2 = 2.08$ d.f. = 5	$p = .838$	$\chi^2 = 3.65$ d.f. = 5	$p = .602$

[1]From Hambleton, Murray, & Simon (1982).

parameter model did not fit the data well because the model was unable to account for variation in the discriminating power of test items and/or the guessing behavior of examinees on the more difficult test items.

Next, a more comprehensive analysis of the test items was initiated on the four NAEP test booklets.

Two hypotheses were investigated:

1. Is there a relationship between the size of the standardized residuals and the content of the items in the test?
    (If there is, the assumption of unidimensionality is possibly violated in the test items.)
2. Is there a relationship between the size of the standardized residuals and items classified by difficulty and format?
    (If there is, the results would suggest that the model could be revised to provide a better fit to the test data.)

Results relating to hypothesis one and two are shown in tables 9-5 and 9-6, respectively.

For hypothesis one, the pattern of standardized residuals was the same across content categories. Misfit statistics for both the one- and three-parameter models were clearly unrelated to the content of the test items. Of

Table 9-6. Descriptive Statistical Analysis of Standardized Residuals
(Booklets No. 1 and 2, 260 Items, 9- and 13-year-olds, 1977-78)

Difficulty Level	Format	Number of Items	1-p Results		3-p Results	
			$\bar{X}$	SD	$\bar{X}$	SD
Hard ($p < .5$)	Multiple-Choice	70	2.73	1.55	.82	.23
	Open-Ended	54	1.64	.81	.86	.28
Easy ($p \geq .5$)	Multiple-Choice	70	1.79	1.10	.90	.64
	Open-Ended	66	1.67	.72	.97	.38

From Hambleton, Murray, & Simon (1982).

course, the standardized residuals are substantially smaller for the three-parameter model because the fit was considerably better. For hypothesis two, the hard multiple-choice items had substantially larger absolute-valued standardized residuals when fit by the one-parameter model than easy items in either format, or hard items in an open-ended format. This result suggests that the problem with the one-parameter model was due to a failure to account for guessing behavior (note, the fit was better for hard open-ended items where guessing behavior was not operative). The differences between standardized residual, except for the hard multiple-choice test items, were probably due to the difference in the way item discriminating power was handled. With the hard multiple-choice test items, the difference was due to a failure to account for both item discriminating power *and* examinee guessing behavior in the one-parameter model. There were no relationships among item difficulty level, item format, and absolute-valued standardized residuals obtained from fitting the three-parameter model.

In summary, the results of the hypothesis testing showed clearly that the test items in the content categories were not in any way being fit better or worse by the item response models, and failure to consider examinee guessing behavior and variation in item discriminating power resulted in the one-parameter model providing substantially poorer fits to the various data sets than the three-parameter model.

9.7 Summary

A number of conclusions can be drawn from the analyses described in the chapter:

1. The findings of this investigation clearly support the desirability of conducting a wide range of analyses on a data set, and on several data sets. Were a narrow set of analyses to be conducted on (possibly) a single model and data set, the interpretation of results would have been more confusing and difficult. The approaches described in figure 8–1 should provide some direction to researchers with an interest in IRT applications.

2. It seems clear that the three-parameter model performed substantially better than the one-parameter model. The results were not especially surprising, given information about the ways in which the NAEP exercises are constructed (i.e., relatively little use is made of item statistical information in test development). While the utility of the three- over the one-parameter model was not too surprising, the actual fits of the three-parameter model to the data sets were. The study of standardized residuals at the item level revealed a very good fit of the three-parameter model.

3. Not all analyses revealed high three-parameter model-test data fit. The studies of item invariance were the most confusing. Regardless of whether the three-parameter model or the one-parameter model was fitted to the data, a number of potentially "biased" items were identified. Several possible explanations exist: Several test items are biased against one group or another (e.g., race, or high and low performers) or there are problems in item parameter estimation (e.g., the c parameters cannot be properly estimated in high performing groups, or in any groups—black or white or hispanic—if group size is of the size used in this investigation).

4. Perhaps the most important finding is that it is highly unlikely that the one-parameter model will be useful with NAEP mathematics exercises. This is in spite of the fact that many other organizations are very pleased with their work with the one-parameter model. With NAEP mathematics booklets, it appears there is too much variation among mathematics items in their discrimination power and too much guessing on the hard multiple-choice test items for the one-parameter model to provide an adequate fit to the test data.

The results in this chapter provide information that can influence the future use of item response models in NAEP. There is considerable evidence in this chapter to suggest that the three-parameter logistic model provides a very good accounting of the actual mathematics test results. The one-parameter logistic model did *not*. It may be that NAEP will now want to consider utilizing the three-parameter model in some small-scale item bias, item banking, and test-development efforts to determine the utility and appropriateness of the three-parameter model. Such investigations seem highly worthwhile at this time. Of course, it may be that with other content areas, the one-parameter model may suffice, and for problems of score reporting, new models being developed by Bock, Mislevy, and Woodson (1982) may be substantially better than the three-parameter logistic model.

Notes

1. The most recent references to LOGIST are given, but the 1976 version of the computer program was used in our analysis.

2. Correlations were transformed via Fisher's Z-transformation prior to calculating the descriptive statistics. The mean is reported on the correlation scale. The standard deviation is reported on the Z_r scale.

3. Some of the material in this section is from a paper by Hambleton and Murray (1983).

4. The close fit between the three-parameter model and several data sets reported in section 9.6 suggest that this explanation is highly plausible.

10 TEST EQUATING

10.1 Introduction

In some testing situations it is necessary to convert or relate test scores obtained on one test to those obtained on another. The need for such "equating" typically arises in the following two situations:

1. The tests are at comparable levels of difficulty and the ability distributions of the examinees taking the tests are similar;
2. The tests are at different levels of difficulty and the ability distributions of the examinees are different.

Equating in the above situations are termed *horizontal* and *vertical* equating, respectively.

Horizontal equating is appropriate when multiple forms of a test are required for security and other reasons. The various forms of the test will not be identical but can be expected to be parallel. Moreover, the distributions of abilities of the examinees to whom these forms are administered will be approximately equal.

In contrast, in a vertical equating situation, it is of interest to construct a single scale that permits comparison of the abilities of examinees at different levels, e.g., at different grades. The tests that have to be administered at the various levels will not usually be multiple forms of one particular test and will typically be at different levels of difficulty. Moreover, unlike the horizontal equating situation, the ability distributions of the examinees at the various levels will be different. Clearly, the problem of vertical equating is considerably more complex than that of horizontal equating.

In the above two situations, the issue of primary importance is that of equating the scores of individuals on two or more tests. A related problem occurs in the construction of item banks. In this case, it is of interest to place the item on a common scale without any reference to the group of examinees to which the items were administered.

10.2 Designs for Equating

Equating of scores of examinees on various tests or scaling of items can be carried out only under certain circumstances. For example, two different tests administered to two different groups of examinees cannot be equated. The following designs permit equating of scores of examinees (Lord, 1975d; Cook & Eignor, 1983):

1. *Single-group Design.* The two tests to be equated are given to the same group of examinees. Since the same examinees take both tests, the difficulty levels of the tests are not confounded with the ability levels of the examinees. However, practice and fatigue effects may affect the equating process.

2. *Equivalent-group Design.* The two tests to be equated are given to equivalent but not identical groups of examinees. The groups may be chosen randomly. The advantage of this method is that it avoids practice and fatigue effects. However, since the groups are not the same, differences in ability distributions, small as they may be, introduce an unknown degree of bias in the equating procedure.

3. *Anchor-test Design.* The tests to be equated are given to two different group of examinees. Each test contains a set of common items, or a common external anchor test is administered to the two groups simultaneously with the tests. The two groups do not have to be equivalent, hence the difficulties encountered with the previous two designs are overcome.

Clearly, variations of the above basic designs may be used to equate two tests. For example, instead of using the anchor-test method, the two tests to be equated may be administered with a common group of examinees taking both tests.

10.3 Conditions for Equating

Lord (1977a) has argued that in equating test scores, it should be a matter of indifference to the examinees whether they take test X or Y. More recently, Lord (1980a, p. 195) has elaborated on this by introducing the notion of "equity" in equating tests:

> If an equating of tests X and Y is to be equitable to each applicant, it must be a matter of indifference to applicants at every given ability level whether they are to take test X or test Y.

This equity requirement has several implications as documented in Lord (1977b, 1980a, pp. 195–198):

1. Tests measuring different traits or abilities cannot be equated.
2. Raw scores on unequally reliable tests cannot be equated (since otherwise scores from an unrealiable test can be equated to scores on a reliable test, thereby obviating the need for constructing reliable tests!).
3. Raw scores on tests with varying difficulty levels, i.e., in vertical equating situations, cannot be equated (since in this case the true scores will have a nonlinear relation and the tests therefore will not be equally reliable at different ability levels).
4. The conditional frequency distribution at ability level θ, $f[x|\theta]$ of score θ on test X is the same as the conditional frequency distribution for the transformed score $x(y)$, $f[x(y)|\theta]$, where $x(y)$ is a one-to-one function of y.
5. Fallible scores on tests X and Y cannot be equated unless tests X and Y are strictly parallel (since the condition of identical conditional frequency distributions, under regularity conditions, implies that the moments of the two distributions are equal).
6. Perfectly reliable tests can be equated.

The concept of equity introduced above plays a central role in the problem of equating test scores. While this requirement may appear stringent in itself, it is only one of the requirements that must be met before test scores can be equated.

The requirements other than equity that have to be met have been noted by Angoff (1971) and Lord (1980a, p. 199). These involve the nondependence of the equating on (1) the specific sample used (invariance), and (2) the test that is used as the base (symmetry). In addition, when item response theory provides the basis for equating, it must be assumed that the latent space is complete. Since, currently, only unidimensional item response models are feasible, it must be assumed that the tests to be equated are unidimensional. To summarize, the following are the requirements for the equating of two tests:

1. Equity;
2. Invariance across groups;
3. Symmetry;
4. Unidimensionality of the tests.

10.4 Classical Methods of Equating

Classical methods of equating have been described in detail by Angoff (1971, 1982a). It suffices to note here that these can be categorized as (1) equipercentile equating, (2) linear equating, and (3) regression method.

Equipercentile equating is based on the definition that scores on test X and test Y are considered equivalent if their respective frequency distributions for a specific population of examinees are identical. According to Angoff (1982a), scores on test X and test Y may be considered equivalent "if their respective percentile ranks in any given group are equal."

While equipercentile equating ensures that the transformed score distributions are identical, it does not meet the requirements for equating, set forth in the previous section, when raw scores are used. This can be seen by noting that a nonlinear transformation is needed to equalize all moments of two distributions. This will result in a nonlinear relation between the raw scores and hence in a nonlinear relation between the true scores. As pointed out previously, this implies that the tests will not be equally reliable; consequently, it is not a matter of indifference to the examinees which test is taken. Thus, the requirement of equity is not met. A further problem with equipercentile equating of raw scores is that the equating process is group dependent.

When two tests to be equated are similar in difficulty, as in the horizontal equating situation, the raw score distributions will be different only with respect to the first two moments when administered to the same group of examinees. When this is the case, a linear transformation of the raw scores will ensure that the moments of the two distributions are identical. Scores x and y on test X and test Y can then be equated through the linear transformation:

$$y = ax + b. \tag{10.1}$$

The coefficients a and b can be determined from the following relations:

$$\mu_y = a\mu_x + b \tag{10.2}$$

$$\sigma_y = a\sigma_x, \tag{10.3}$$

where μ_y and μ_x are the means of scores on tests Y and X, respectively, while σ_y and σ_x are the respective standard deviations. Thus,

$$y = \frac{\sigma_y}{\sigma_x} x + \left(\mu_y - \frac{\sigma_y}{\sigma_x} \mu_x \right). \tag{10.4}$$

The linear equating procedure described above can be thought of as a special case of the equipercentile equating procedure when the assumptions regarding the moments are met. Otherwise, it may be considered as an approximation to the equipercentile equating procedure. Given this, it follows that linear equating of raw scores is subject to the objections raised earlier with equipercentile equating.

In view of the above mentioned difficulties with equipercentile and linear equating procedures, it may be tempting to use regression approaches to equate test scores. The following are two possible approaches:

1. Predict one test score from the other.
2. Determine the relation between the two scores through the use of an external criterion.

The first approach, straightforward as it may seem, it not acceptable since in a regression situation the "dependent" and "independent" variables are not symmetrically related. To understand the limitations of the second approach, let $R_x(\omega|x)$ denote the value of the external criterion ω predicted from x through the usual regression equation. Similarly, let $R_y(\omega|y)$ denote the value of ω predicted from y. Then the relation between x and y is determined such that

$$R_x(\omega|x) = R_y(\omega|y). \tag{10.5}$$

The curve relating x and y can be plotted and the conversion from one score to the other obtained.

Lord (1980a, p. 198) has pointed out the problems with this procedure. Recall that when raw scores are being equated, the equity requirement will not be met unless the tests are parallel or perfectly reliable. In predicting from x (or y), it is customarily assumed that x (or y) is measured without error. Even if this were true, it will not be a matter of indifference to the examinees which test they take unless the two tests correlate equally with the criterion variable since otherwise one test score will predict the criterion more accurately than the other. A second problem is that the relation between x and y found with this method will vary from group to group unless the two tests correlate equally with the criterion (Lord, 1980a, pp. 208–209). Since in this discussion we had to assume that tests X and Y are perfectly reliable, the situation is far worse in practice where this assumption is usually not tenable. Thus, the regression approach to equating is not viable.

10.5 Equating Through Item Response Theory

The above discussion indicates that the equating of tests based on raw scores is not desirable for reasons of equity, symmetry, and invariance. Equating based on item response theory overcomes these problems if the item response model fits the data (Kolen, 1981).

It was pointed out in chapter 1 (figure 1–4) that according to item response theory, the ability θ of an examinee is independent of the subset of items to which he or she responds. Since the estimator of θ is consistent (with respect to items) when item parameters are known, the estimate $\hat{\theta}$ of θ will not be affected by the subset of items to which the examinee responds. Hence, it is of no consequence whether an examinee takes a difficult test or an easy test. The ability estimates will be comparable subject to sampling fluctuations. Thus, within the framework of item response theory, the need for equating test scores does not arise. This is true in both horizontal and vertical equating situations.

It has been noted by several psychometricians that reporting of scores on the ability metric may prove to be uninterpretable for the consumer. Scaled scores, as indicated in chapter 4, may be of use in this situation. Alternatively, the ability score may be transformed to be on the test score metric (see section 4.6). Either the true score ξ or the proportion correct score π can be obtained once θ is known from the relations:

$$\xi = \sum_{i=1}^{n} P_i(\theta)$$

$$\pi = \xi/n, \tag{10.6}$$

where n is the number of items on the test. Since θ is not known, the estimate $\hat{\theta}$ can be substituted for θ to yield $\hat{\xi}$ and $\hat{\pi}$. Clearly, $0 < \hat{\pi} < 1$, while $0 < \hat{\xi} < n$ when the one- or the two-parameter model is employed. The lower limit changes for the three-parameter model. Since $P_i(\theta) \geq c_i$, the pseudo-chance level parameter,

$$\sum_{i=1}^{n} c_i < \hat{\xi} < n, \tag{10.7}$$

while

$$\left(\sum_{i=1}^{n} c_i \right) \bigg/ n < \hat{\pi} < 1.$$

To summarize, in the context of item response theory, the need for equating does not arise when item parameters are known. Either the ability scores or transformed scores on the test score metric can be reported.

The above discussion applies even when the item parameters are unknown, with one difference: When the item parameters are known, the metric for θ is fixed although it can be transformed (see section 4.3). However, when item and ability parameters are unknown, the item response function is invariant up to a linear transformation in the ability and item parameters. It is, therefore, necessary to choose an arbitrary metric for either the ability parameter θ or the item difficulty parameter b. For the one-parameter model, it is sufficient to fix the scale so that the mean of θ (or difficulty) is zero. Customary practice with the two- and three-parameter models is to set the mean of θ (or difficulty) to zero and the standard deviation of θ (or difficulty) to one.

In earlier chapters, much was made of the invariance features of item response models, such as the ability of an examinee not being affected by the items administered, and the item parameters remaining invariant across groups of examinees. However, the item parameters for items that are administered to two separate groups may appear to be different. This apparent discrepancy arises because of the arbitrary fixing of the metric for θ (or b). A linear relationship, however, exists between the item parameters and ability parameters in the two groups.

To illustrate this, suppose that the same examinees took two tests, X and Y, measuring the same trait. Then the following relation holds in the one parameter model when the metric of b is fixed such that its mean is zero:

$$\theta_x - \mu_{\theta x} = \theta_y - \mu_{\theta y} \tag{10.8}$$

or,

$$\theta_y = \theta_x + (\mu_{\theta y} - \mu_{\theta x}). \tag{10.9}$$

For the two- and the three-parameter models, since the mean is zero and the standard deviation of b is one,

$$(\theta_x - \mu_{\theta x})/\sigma_{\theta x} = (\theta_y - \mu_{\theta y})/\sigma_{\theta y} \tag{10.10}$$

or

$$\theta_y = \frac{\sigma_{\theta y}}{\sigma_{\theta x}} \theta_x + \left(\mu_{\theta y} - \frac{\sigma_{\theta y}}{\sigma_{\theta x}} \mu_{\theta x} \right). \tag{10.11}$$

Here $\mu_{\theta x}$ and $\sigma_{\theta x}$ denote the mean and standard deviation of θ for test X. Similar notation holds for test Y.

The above establish the relation between θ on the two tests. This relationship should be compared with the linear relation between raw scores in the linear equating procedure. While the similarity is clear, the linear relationship that exists between θ_x and θ_y is a consequence of the theory, whereas in the linear equating procedure, this relationship is assumed.

Equation (10.11) can be expressed as

$$\theta_y = \alpha \theta_x + \beta. \tag{10.12}$$

(Note that for the one-parameter model, $\alpha = 1$.) Once the constants α and β are determined, the equating of abilities for the two tests is accomplished.

It is a matter of indifference whether the metric is fixed according to θ or b for the estimation of parameters. However, this has implications when equating or linking is attempted. The two common situations that should be distinguished are design 1 and design 3 described in section 10.2.

In design 1, where two tests are administered to the same group of examinees, the simplest procedure is to treat the two tests as if they were administered at the same time, combine the responses, and estimate the item and ability parameters concurrently. This places the estimates of the ability and item parameter on a common scale and obviates the need for equating.

In the event that the concurrent calibration of the two tests is not possible, equating may be necessary to relate the abilities. Since each examinee has a pair of ability values (θ_x, θ_y), the relation between these ordered pair provides the equating constant α and β in equation (10.12).

If the metric for θ is fixed in the two calibration situations, then $\mu_{\theta x} = \mu_{\theta y} = 0$, and $\sigma_{\theta x} = \sigma_{\theta y} = 1$. Thus, substituting in equation (10.11), we obtain $\theta_y = \theta_x$! No equating is necessary. If on the other hand, the metric of b

is fixed, then the use of equation (10.11) will yield the equating constants.

In design 3, the difficulty (and discrimination) parameters for the common items will be linearly related. Since there are pairs of values for the difficulty and discrimination parameters, (b_x, b_y) and (a_x, a_y), the relationship between the parameters can be obtained by fixing the metric of θ in each group.

In this case

$$b_y = \alpha b_x + \beta \qquad (10.13)$$

and

$$a_y = a_x/\alpha, \qquad (10.14)$$

where

$$\alpha = \sigma_{by}/\sigma_{bx} \qquad (10.15)$$

and

$$\beta = \mu_{by} - \alpha\mu_{bx}. \qquad (10.16)$$

The situation is similar to that described for design 1 except for the fact that additional information is available: the slope of the line for the item difficulties is the reciprocal of the slope of the line for item discrimination.

A design similar to the above is one in which a subset of examinees take two distinct tests. This "common person" equating design is a variation on design 1. Through this subset of common examinees, it is possible to place the items on a common scale and also to equate the ability estimates. In this case the metric of either the abilities or the item parameters can be fixed.

To summarize, the metric for the parameters may be fixed in the following manner to carry out the necessary equating:

1. *Single group design*: Fix the metric for ability parameters in each test. Equating is not necessary in this case.
2. *Anchor test design*: Fix the metric for ability in each group.
3. *Common-person design*: Fix either the metric of ability or item parameters.

10.6 Determination of Equating Constants

When pairs of values such as (θ_x, θ_y), (b_x, b_y), (a_x, a_y) are available, plotting one value against another will yield a linear relationship from which the slope and intercept values can be determined. Unfortunately, since only estimates of the parameters are available, the pairs of values will not fall on a straight line but will be scattered about the line of relationship. The constants in the linear equation can be determined in this case through the following:

a. Regression methods;
b. "Mean and sigma" procedure;
c. Robust "mean and sigma" procedure;
d. Characteristic curve methods.

10.6.1 Regression Methods

The linear relationship between two variables can be found most directly by using regression techniques. In this case,

$$y = \alpha x + \beta + e, \qquad (10.17)$$

where $y = \theta_y$ and $x = \theta_x$ when equating is carried out with respect to ability. When item difficulties are used, $y = b_y$ and $x = b_x$. The error, e, is an independently and identically distributed random variable. The estimates of the regression coefficients, α and β, can be determined from the following:

$$\hat{\alpha} = r_{xy} s_y / s_x \qquad (10.18)$$

and

$$\hat{\beta} = \bar{y} - \hat{\alpha}\bar{x}, \qquad (10.19)$$

where r_{xy} is the correlation between x and y, $\bar{y}$ and $\bar{x}$ are the means of y and x, and s_y and s_x are the respective standard deviations.

This approach is not viable since the relationship is not symmetric. The regression coefficient will be affected by which test is chosen as the base test. A further point is that x is assumed to be measured without error. Since there is no valid reason for choosing one test as a base test, this approach will result in a nonsymmetric equating procedure. Furthermore, the errors are not necessarily identically distributed since each item and ability parameter estimate has a different standard error of estimate (section 7.4).

The only exception to the lack of symmetry is when the Rasch model is considered appropriate. In this case $\alpha = 1$, and hence $\hat{\beta} = \bar{y} - \bar{x}$. In this case

$$y = x + (\bar{y} - \bar{x}),$$

and

$$x = y + (\bar{x} - \bar{y}),$$

a relationship that is symmetric.

10.6.2 Mean and Sigma Method

This method exploits the relationship given by equation (10.11). If

$$y = \alpha x + \beta,$$

then

$$\bar{y} = \alpha \bar{x} + \beta \qquad (10.20)$$

and

$$s_y = \alpha s_x. \qquad (10.21)$$

From these two relationships,

$$\alpha = s_y / s_x \qquad (10.22)$$

and

$$\beta = \bar{y} - \alpha \bar{x}. \qquad (10.23)$$

This relationship is symmetric (note that for the Rasch model, this approach and the regression approach yield identical results).

10.6.3 Robust Mean and Sigma Method

While the mean and sigma method is symmetric in that

$$x = (y - \beta)/\alpha,$$

there is no provision to take into account the fact that each item and ability parameter is estimated with varying accuracy. Furthermore, outliers will unduly affect the calculation of the coefficients.

The robust mean and sigma method was proposed by Linn, Levine, Hastings and Wardrop (1981). Since the (x, y) pair is a pair of estimates of either the ability on two tests or item difficulty in two groups, each x and y has its own standard error of estimate. The weight for each pair is the inverse of the larger of the two estimated variances.

If the abilities are used for obtaining the equating constants, the estimated variances are the reciprocals of the information functions evaluated at the ability levels. Since the larger the estimated variance, the smaller the information function values, the abilities with larger variances will receive small weights. When difficulty estimates in the two groups are used to obtain the equating constants, the information matrix (table 7–2) for each item has to be inverted, and the appropriate diagonal element is taken as the variance of the estimate. The dimension of the information matrix depends on the model, e.g., it is (3×3) for the three-parameter model.

The procedure can be summarized as follows:

1.   Determine w_j for each (x_j, y_j) pair. Here

$$w_j = \max\{v(x_j), v(y_j)\}, \qquad j = 1, \ldots, k,$$

where $v(\theta)$ denotes the variance of the jth estimate.

2.   Scale the weights:

$$w_j' = w_j / \left(\sum_{j=1}^{n} w_j \right).$$

3.   Compute

$$x_j' = w_j' x_j, \qquad (j = 1, \ldots, k)$$

and

$$y_j' = w_j' y_j. \qquad (j = 1, \ldots, k).$$

4.   Determine

$$\bar{x}', \bar{y}', s_x', s_y',$$

where $\bar{x}'$, $\bar{y}'$, $\bar{s}_x'$, and s_y' are the mean and standard deviations of the weighted scores.

5.   Determine α and β using equation (10.23) but with the weighted means and standard deviations.

Stocking and Lord (1983) have pointed out that although this procedure is an improvement over the mean and sigma method, it does not take into account outliers. They have suggested using robust weights based on perpendicular distances to the equating line. For this procedure, computations outlined in steps (1) through (5) are carried out. In addition, the following computations are carried out:

6.   Once α and β, and hence the line is determined, obtain the perpendicular distance of each point (x_j, y_j) to the line, where

$$d_j = (y_j - \alpha x_j - \beta_j)/[\alpha^2 + \beta^2]^{\frac{1}{2}}$$

and their median, M.

7. Compute Tukey weights defined as

$$T_j = \begin{cases} [1 - (d_j/6M)^2]^2 & \text{when } d_j < 6M \\ 0 & \text{otherwise.} \end{cases}$$

8. Reweight each point (x'_j, y'_j) using the weight

$$u_j = w'_j T \left\{ \sum_{j=1}^{n} w'_j T_j \right\}.$$

9. Repeat step 3 using u_j instead of w'_j and compute α and β as in step 5.
10. Repeat steps 6, 7, 8, and 9 until the changes in α and β are less than a prescribed value.

This "robust iterative weighted mean and sigma method" (Stocking and Lord, 1983) gives low weights to poorly estimated parameters and to outliers.

10.6.4 Characteristic Curve Method

While the robust mean and sigma methods are attractive, they suffer from one flaw; namely, when estimates of item parameters are used to obtain the equating line, only the relationship that exists for the item difficulties is used, i.e.,

$$b_y = \alpha b_x + \beta.$$

The relationship that exists between discriminations, i.e.,

$$a_y = a_x/\alpha,$$

is not used in determining α. This important piece of information could be used through a weighted procedure similar to the one described above, and an "average" value for α can be determined. Alternatively, the "characteristic curve method" suggested by Haebara (1980) and Stocking and Lord (1983) can be used.

The true score ξ_a of an examinee with ability θ_a on test X is

$$\xi_{xa} = \sum_{i=1}^{n} P(\theta_a, a_{xi}, b_{xi}, c_{xi}). \qquad (10.24)$$

The true score of examinee a with ability $_a$ on test Y is

$$\xi_{ya} = \sum_{i=1}^{n} P(\theta_a, a_{yi}, b_{yi}, c_{yi}), \qquad (10.25)$$

where

$$b_{yi} = \alpha b_{xi} + \beta, \qquad (10.26)$$

$$a_{yi} = a_{xi}/\alpha \qquad (10.27)$$

and

$$c_{yi} = c_{xi}. \qquad (10.28)$$

The constants α and β should be chosen to minimize the difference between ξ_{xa} and ξ_{ya}. Following Stocking and Lord (1983), the appropriate criterion may be chosen as

$$F = \frac{1}{N} \sum_{a=1}^{N} (\xi_{xa} - \xi_{ya})^2, \qquad (10.29)$$

where N is the number of examinees.

The function F is a function of α and β and is minimized when

$$\frac{\partial F}{\partial \alpha} = \frac{\partial F}{\partial \beta} = 0. \qquad (10.30)$$

These equations are nonlinear and have to be solved iteratively using either the Newton-Raphson procedure described in chapter 7 or other numerical procedures. For details of the solution of these equations, the reader is referred to Stocking and Lord (1983).

Comparison results provided by Stocking and Lord indicate that this procedure compares well with the mean and sigma methods. However, the characteristic curve procedure produced better results for transforming the item discriminations. Intuitively, the characteristic curve method is more appealing since it takes into account all available information.

10.7 Procedures to Be Used with the Equating Designs

The procedures for equating within the context of the various equating designs have been discussed partially in the previous section. In practice, existing computer programs such as LOGIST can be used to simplify the equating procedure. Given this, equating procedures are reviewed in the context of equating designs and the computer program, LOGIST.

10.7.1 Single Group Design

This design has been considered in sufficient detail in the previous section. Either of the two following procedures is appropriate when tests X and Y are administered to the same group of examinees:

Procedure I: Combine the data and estimate item and ability parameters. The abilities and the item parameters will be on the scale for tests X and Y.

Procedure II: Fix the metric of θ identically if separate calibrations of the data are necessary. The abilities will be on a common scale with this procedure.

10.7.2 Equivalent Group Design

Since neither the items nor examinees are common, it is necessary to estimate the parameters of the model separately. In this case:

1. Obtain random samples (with equal number of examinees) of examinees who have taken tests X and Y.
2. Calibrate the two samples separately, fixing the metric of θ identically in the two calibrations.
3. Rank order the estimated θ values and pair the lowest $\hat{\theta}_x$ with the lowest $\hat{\theta}_y$, etc.
4. Plot $\hat{\theta}_x$ against $\hat{\theta}_y$ values.

If the item response theory assumptions are met, the plot of θ_x against θ_y will result in a straight line. In practice, however, this will not be true when estimates are used. This is particularly true at extreme values of $\hat{\theta}_x$ and $\hat{\theta}_y$ because of larger errors of estimation.

10.7.3 Anchor Test Design

In this design N_x examinees take test X, which has n_x items and an anchor test with n_a items. Similarly, N_y examinees take test Y with n_y items and the n

anchor test items. The following two procedures are appropriate for equating:

Procedure I: The two tests, one with N_x examinees and $(n_x + n_a)$ items and the other with N_y examinees and $(n_y + n_a)$ items, are calibrated separately. The metric of θ is fixed identically for the two calibrations. The line of relationship is obtained through the n_a common items administered to two groups of N_x and N_y examinees as indicated in the previous section. The abilities of the examinees are equated using this line of relationship.

Procedure II: Using the LOGIST program estimate, the item and ability parameters in a single computer run in the following manner:[1]

1. Treat data as if $(N_x + N_y)$ examinees have taken a test with $(n_x + n_y + n_a)$ items.
2. Treat the n_y items to which the N_x examinees did not response as items that are "not reached" and code the responses as such. Treat the n_x items to which the N_y examinees did not respond similarly.
3. With this coding estimate the ability parameters for the $(N_x + N_y)$ examinees and the item parameters for the $(n_x + n_y + n_a)$ items simultaneously.

When this is done, the ability estimates will be equivalent and the item parameter estimates will be on a common scale.

10.8 True-Score Equating

If for some reason reporting of abilities on the θ-scale is not acceptable (such situations may be dictated by past practices), the θ-value may be transformed to the corresponding true values through equation (10.6). Equating of true scores on different tests is then possible.

Let θ_x denote the ability level of an examinee on test X and ξ_x the true score of the examinee, i.e.,

$$\xi_x = \sum_{i=1}^{n} P_i(\theta_x). \qquad (10.31)$$

Similarly if θ_y is the ability of the examinee on test Y, and the true score is ξ_y, then

$$\xi_y = \sum_{j=1}^{m} P_j(\theta_y) \equiv \sum_{j=1}^{m} P_j(\alpha\theta_x + \beta), \qquad (10.32)$$

where $\theta_y = \alpha\theta_x + \beta$ is the line of relationship between θ_y and θ_x. For a given value θ_x, the pair (ξ_x, ξ_y) can be determined. Thus, it is possible to equate the true scores on two tests, as is illustrated in figure 10–1.

The line of relationship between θ_x and θ_y can be determined by using one of the methods described in section 10.6. However, given the logic of the characteristic curve method and its parallel to true-score equating, this appears to be the most consistent procedure to be used with true score equating.

The graph of ξ_x against ξ_y will be nonlinear. This is not a problem when θ_x and θ_y are known since in this case the relationship between ξ_x and ξ_y can be exactly determined. However, as is usually the case, when θ_x and θ_y have to

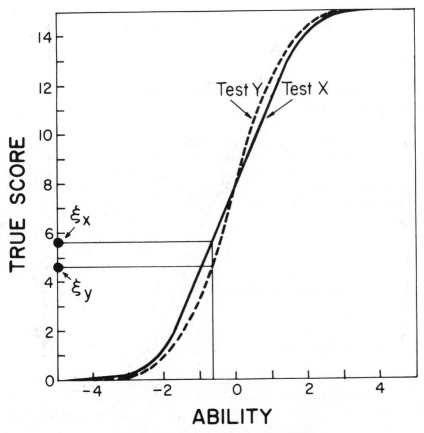

Figure 10-1. True Score Equating

be estimated, the relationship between $\hat{\theta}_x$ and $\hat{\theta}_y$ will be subjected to sampling fluctuations. The sampling fluctuations are large for extreme values of items and ability parameter estimates; hence, the nonlinear relationship between $\hat{\xi}_x$ and $\hat{\xi}_y$ will be determined with substantial error. Hence, extrapolation will be necessary in this region. The procedures described by Angoff (1982a) for extrapolating in the context of equipercentile equating can be applied in this situation. At this point, the major disadvantage of true-score equating becomes clear: The advantage gained by equating θ_x and θ_y, that of a linear relationship, is lost.

This problem can be avoided if the nonlinear relationship between ξ_x and ξ_y is not determined. Instead, for each value of $\hat{\theta}_x$, the value $\hat{\theta}_y$ can be obtained using the relationship $\theta_y = \alpha\theta_x + \beta$. From this, $\hat{\xi}_x$ and $\hat{\xi}_y$ can be computed using equations (10.31) and (10.32) and tabulated. Conversion from one test to another can be obtained through such tables without resorting to nonlinear interpolation.

10.9 Observed-Score Equating Using Item Response Theory

Equating through the use of item response theory is accomplished in a straightforward manner if the reporting of either the ability estimate $\hat{\theta}$ or true score estimate $\hat{\xi}$ is appropriate. The basic question is, should observed-score equating be carried out using item response methods?

The true score ξ is on the same scale as the observed raw score r, where

$$r = \sum_{i=1}^{n} U_i.$$

Moreover, if item response theory is valid, then

$$E(r) = \xi.$$

Thus, the temptation may be to

1. Obtain the relationship between true scores ξ_x and ξ_y on the two tests as described in the previous section;
2. Treat this relationship as a relationship between raw scores r_x and r_y and equate raw scores.

Lord (1980a) has noted that the relationship that exists between ξ_x and ξ_y is not necessarily the same as that which exists between the raw scores r_x and r_y. This can be demonstrated by observing that in the three-parameter model, $\xi_x \geq \Sigma_{i=1}^n c_i$ and $\xi_y \geq \Sigma_{i=1}^m c_i$, whereas the observed scores r_x and r_y may be zero. Thus the true scores do not provide any equating for examinees who have observed scores below the chance level. Formula scoring may be used to avoid this problem. However, in the very strict sense, the relationship between the true scores ξ_x and ξ_y (or estimated true scores ξ_x, ξ_y) should not be used to equate raw scores r_x and r_y.

Item response theory does provide the means for predicting the theoretical observed score distribution for a given test (Chapter 4). Once these theoretical observed score distributions are obtained for tests X and Y, equipercentile equating may be carried out. The most important advantage to be gained by using item response theory for this purpose is that the tests do not have to be at comparable levels of difficulty, a condition necessary in classical methods of equating.

The theoretical observed score distribution $f(r|\theta)$ on a test can be obtained from the identity (Lord, 1980a, p. 45):

$$\sum_{r=0}^n f(r|\theta)t^r = \prod_{i=1}^n [Q_i(\theta) + tP_i(\theta)]. \tag{10.33}$$

The above expression is appropriate for a given ability level θ. As an illustration, consider the case when $n = 3$. Then, the right side of equation (10.33) is

$$\prod_{i=1}^3 (Q_i + tP_i) = (Q_1 + tP_1)(Q_2 + tP_2)(Q_3 + tP_3)$$

$$= Q_1 Q_2 Q_3 + t(Q_1 Q_2 P_3 + P_1 Q_2 Q_3 + P_1 Q_2 Q_3)$$

$$+ t^2(Q_1 P_2 P_3 + P_1 Q_2 P_3 + P_1 P_2 Q_3) + t^3 P_1 P_2 P_3.$$

The left side is

$$\sum_{r=0}^3 f(r|\theta)t^r = f(r = 0|\theta) + tf(r = 1|\theta) + t^2 f(r = 2|\theta)$$

$$+ t^3 f(r = 3|\theta).$$

On equating like terms, we obtain the frequency distribution summarized in table 10–1.

Table 10-1. Distribution of Observed Scores Conditional on θ for a Three-Item Test

Raw Score	Conditional Relative Frequency $f(r\|\theta)$
0	$Q_1 Q_2 Q_3$
1	$Q_1 Q_2 P_3 + Q_1 P_2 Q_3 + P_1 Q_2 Q_3$
2	$Q_1 P_2 P_3 + P_1 Q_2 P_3 + P_1 P_2 Q_3$
3	$P_1 P_2 P_3$

The coefficient of t^r, $f(r\,|\,\theta)$, is the sum of $\binom{n}{r}$ terms. Computations of this nature were encountered in relation to conditional maximum likelihood estimation in the Rasch model (section 7.5). These computations are indeed tedious when large numbers of items are involved.

Once the value of θ is substituted, the exact relative frequency $f(r\,|\,\theta)$ can be determined. If there are N examinees with abilities $\theta_1, \theta_2, \ldots, \theta_a, \ldots, \theta_N$, the marginal distribution $f(r)$ can be found as

$$f(r) = \sum_{a=1}^{N} f(r\,|\,\theta_a). \qquad (10.34)$$

Since θ_a and the item parameters will not be known, their estimates are substituted to obtain the estimate of the item response function P_i. The marginal frequency distribution $f(r)$ given by equation (10.34) can then be estimated.

The generation of the theoretical observed score distribution is illustrated through the following example. For the purpose of illustration, it is assumed that a two-parameter logistic model is appropriate with the following difficulty and discrimination parameters for three items:

$$b = [b_1\ b_2\ b_3] = [1.0\ \ 0.0\ -1.0],$$

$$a = [a_1\ a_2\ a_3] = [1.5\ \ 1.0\ \ 0.5].$$

The probabilities of correct and incorrect responses, P_i and Q_i, for item $i(i = 1, 2, 3)$, at the given ability levels

$$\theta = [\theta_1\ \theta_2\ \theta_3\ \theta_4\ \theta_5] = [-2\ -1\ 0\ 1\ 2]$$

are provided in table 10–2. With these probabilities, the conditional relative frequency distribution for the raw score $r(0, 1, 2, 3)$ on the three-item test at the specified ability levels can be computed with the aid of table 10–1. These relative frequencies are summarized in table 10–3.

Table 10-2. Probabilities of Correct and Incorrect Responses at Five Ability Levels for Three Items

Item Number	$\theta = -2$		$\theta = -1$		$\theta = 0$		$\theta = 1$		$\theta = 2$	
	P_i	Q_i	P_i	Q_i	P_i	Q_i	P_i	Q_i	P_i	Q_i
1	.000	1.000	.006	.994	.072	.928	.500	.500	.928	.072
2	.032	.968	.154	.846	.500	.500	.846	.154	.968	.032
3	.299	.701	.500	.500	.701	.299	.846	.154	.928	.072

Table 10-3. Theoretical Conditional Relative Frequency Distribution of Raw Scores at Various Ability Levels

	Conditional Relative Frequency $f(r\|\theta)$				
Raw Score	$\theta = -2$	$\theta = -1$	$\theta = 0$	$\theta = 1$	$\theta = 2$
0	.678	.420	.139	.012	.000
1	.313	.500	.475	.143	.009
2	.010	.080	.361	.488	.158
3	.000	.000	.025	.357	.833

If we assume that the total number of examinees is $N = 100$, and the number with abilities $\theta = -2, -1, 0, 1, 2$ are 5, 15, 30, 40, and 10, respectively, then the theoretical marginal frequency distribution of raw scores can be computed. These calculations are summarized in table 10–4.

With the observed score distribution generated as described above, equating can be carried out as follows:

1. Obtain the conditional frequency distribution given by equation (10.31) $f_x(r|\theta_a)$ for each examinee in any convenient group using estimates of ability and item parameters on test X.
2. Obtain the marginal frequency distribution $f_x(r)$ from equation (10.32).
3. Repeat steps (1) and (2) for examinees taking test Y.
4. Equate raw test scores using the equipercentile method.

As Lord (1980a) points out, this procedure, attractive as it may seem, has two flaws:

Table 10-4. Theoretical Conditional and Marginal Frequency Distributions of Raw Scores

	Conditional Frequency Distribution $f(r \mid \theta)^*$					Marginal Frequency Distribution
Raw Score	$\theta = -2$	$\theta = -1$	$\theta = 0$	$\theta = 1$	$\theta = 2$	$f(r)$
0	3	6	4	0	0	13
1	2	8	14	6	0	30
2	0	1	11	20	2	34
3	0	0	1	14	8	23
Number of Examinees	5	15	30	40	10	100

*Rounded off to the nearest integer.

1. Since abilities are estimated, θ_x may have larger errors than θ_y. If this is the case, $f_x(r \mid \theta_x)$ will not be comparable to $f_y(r \mid \theta_y)$.
2. The marginal distributions $f_x(r)$ and $f_y(r)$ depend on the group that is used; hence, the procedure is group dependent.

Fortunately, it now appears that in practice observed score equating and true score equating may give very similar results. According to Lord and Wingersky (1983):

> On the data studied, [the two methods] yield almost indistinguishable results. (p. 1)

They go on to note that their finding should be reassuring to users of IRT equating methods. Their comment is important because most IRT users presently equate their tests using estimated true scores and then proceed to use their equated scores table with observed test scores.

10.10 Steps in Equating Using Item Response Theory

The first step in equating using item response theory is to determine if the tests have precalibrated items. In this case no equating is necessary. Ability estimates for individuals may be obtained using the procedures described in chapter 5.

On the other hand, if the tests are not calibrated, then the estimation procedures described in chapter 7 must be used. Equating is necessary and involves the following steps:

1. *Choose the appropriate equating design:* Depending on the nature of the test, and the group of examinees, one of the three designs described earlier may be appropriate.
2. *Determine the appropriate item response model:* This decision is usually the most difficult to make. In vertical equating situations, the one-parameter model is typically not suitable (Slinde & Linn, 1978; 1979a) when the tests are not constructed to fit the model. The two- or three-parameter models may be appropriate in such situations. Goodness-of-fit measures (chapters 8 and 9) must be used to assess model fit. While the one-parameter model may be satisfactory in horizontal equating situations, fit assessment must be conducted nevertheless.
3. *Establish a common metric for ability and item parameters:* Since the item and ability parameters are linearly related, a common metric must be established. This is carried out by determining the equating constants for relating either ability parameters or item parameters. When relating item parameters, adjustments have to be made to item parameter estimates.
4. *Decide on the scale for reporting test scores:*
   (a) If test scores are reported in terms of ability θ, the procedure is terminated.
   (b) If test scores are to be reported in terms of estimated true scores, then true scores are estimated on the tests for various ability levels and either tabulated or graphed. From this, true scores on two tests can be equated.
   (c) If observed scores are to be equated, then:
       (1) Theoretically conditioned observed-score distributions are generated for ability corresponding to a select sample of examinees.
       (2) Theoretical marginal observed-score distribution are generated.
       (3) Equipercentile equating is carried out to equate test score generated.
       (4) From a compiled table or graph, actual observed scores are equated.

The following example illustrates some of the steps listed above:

Table 10-5. Estimates of Item Difficulty for Two Tests Based on Simulated Data

	Test Y Difficulty		Test X Difficulty		Scaled Test X Difficulty	
	Unique Items	Common Items	Common Items	Unique Items	Common Items	Unique Items
Item	b_y	b_{yc}	b_{xc}	b_x	$\alpha b_{xc} + \beta$	$\alpha b_x + \beta$
1	−1.55					
2	−1.00					
3	−.78					
4	.65					
5	−.75					
6	1.72					
7	−1.27					
8		1.32	1.52		1.43	
9		.10	.32		.27	
10		−1.25	−1.24		−1.23	
11		.68	.40		.36	
12		−1.42	−1.43		−1.42	
13		−.23	−.17		−.20	
14		.57	.62		.56	
15		1.34	1.43		1.35	
16				−.31		−.34
17				−1.72		−1.70
18				.13		.09
19				.23		.18
20				.23		.18
21				−.87		−.88
22				.86		.79
Mean		.14	.18			
S.D.		1.06	1.09			

Note: $\alpha = .97$. $\beta = -.04$.

1. Data were generated to fit a two-parameter logistic model such that tests X and Y have 15 items each with 8 common items. Responses for two groups of examinees with $N_x = N_y = 100$.
2. Item and ability parameters were estimated by fixing the metric of θ in two separate calibrations. Estimates of difficulty and discrimination parameters are displayed in tables 10–5 and 10–6.

Table 10-6. Estimates of Item Discrimination for Two Tests Based on Simulated Data

	Test Y Discrimination		Test X Discrimination		Scaled Test X Discrimination	
Item	Unique Items a_y	Common Items a_{yc}	Common Items a_{xc}	Unique Items a_x	Common Items a_{xc}/α	Unique Items a_x/α
1	1.67					
2	.87					
3	1.36					
4	2.00					
5	.83					
6	1.63					
7	1.78					
8		1.75	1.76		1.82	
9		2.30	1.07		1.11	
10		.94	1.17		1.21	
11		.67	.68		.70	
12		1.76	2.00		2.07	
13		1.60	1.04		1.08	
14		1.61	.73		.75	
15		1.36	1.22		1.26	
16				1.23		1.27
17				1.35		1.40
18				2.27		2.34
19				2.39		2.47
20				1.58		1.63
21				1.69		1.75
22				.92		.95

Note: $\alpha = .97$. $\beta = -.04$.

3. Means and standard deviations for the eight common items for the two calibrations were obtained.
4. Item parameter estimates for test Y were adjusted to be on the same scale as the item parameters on test X.
    (a) Using item difficulty estimates, the means $\bar{b}_x$, $\bar{b}_y$, and standard deviations s_x and s_y were obtained.
    (b) In the line of relationship

$$y = \alpha x + \beta,$$

Table 10-7. Scaled Item Parameter Estimates on Combined Tests X and Y for Simulated Data

| | | Difficulty | | | Discrimination | |
| | | Common | | | Common | |
Item	Test Y	Items	Test X	Test Y	Items	Test X
1	−1.55			1.67		
2	−1.00			.87		
3	−.78			1.36		
4	.65			2.00		
5	−.75			.83		
6	1.72			1.63		
7	−1.27			1.78		
8		1.37			1.79	
9		.19			1.70	
10		−1.24			1.07	
11		.52			.69	
12		−1.42			1.91	
13		−.21			1.34	
14		.57			1.18	
15		1.35			1.31	
16			−.34			1.27
17			−1.70			1.40
18			.09			2.34
19			.18			2.47
20			.18			1.63
21			−.88			1.75
22			.79			.95

α and β were computed using equations (10.22) and (10.23).[2]

(c) Item parameter estimates for test X were adjusted according to the above linear equation:

$$b_y = \alpha b_x + \beta,$$

$$a_y = a_x/\alpha.$$

(Item parameter estimates for test Y are not to be adjusted.)

(d) Difficulty and discrimination parameter estimates of the eight common items were averaged since these should be the same by definition.

(e) The scaled item parameter estimates were obtained for the two tests (table 10-7).

5.   The estimated true scores ξ_x and ξ_y for tests X and Y were obtained for various ability levels. These were plotted as indicated in figure 10–1. From this, given the estimated true score of an examinee on test X, that on test Y can be computed.

10.11 Summary

In comparison with the classical methods of equating, item response theoretic methods for equating are:

1.   Linear;
2.   Group independent;
3.   Not affected by difficulty levels of the test (appropriate in the vertical equating situation).

When items have been precalibrated, the need for equating is obviated. However, when item and ability parameters are unknown, linear adjustments are necessary to relate the ability and item parameters across subgroups. One of the three equating designs—the single group design, the equivalent group design, or the anchor test design—or variations of these must be employed to place the parameters on a common scale.

   Establishing a common scale for the parameters can be carried out using one of the following: (1) the mean and sigma method, (2) robust mean and sigma method, (3) characteristic curve method. The characteristic curve method appears to be the most appropriate method for use with the two- and three-parameter models.

   While equating in terms of ability parameters is the most direct procedure, the ability parameters may be transformed to yield true scores. Since ability parameters will not be known, equating may be carried out using estimated values.

   Observed score equating carried out by replacing true score estimates by observed scores is not entirely correct. A more direct approach is to estimate observed-score distributions and then equate the observed scores using the equipercentile method. The advantages offered by item response theory, e.g., linearity, are generally lost with this approach.

Notes

1.   This is possible only with the LOGIST computer program (Wingersky, 1983).
2.   The mean and sigma procedure is used here only for illustrative purposes.

11 CONSTRUCTION OF TESTS

11.1 Introduction

The purposes of this chapter are to consider some uses of item response models in the construction of tests and to present some new research results on item selection. With the availability of invariant item statistics, the desirability of item response models for test development work seems clear. But more effective implementation of the models could be achieved if several questions were satisfactorily answered. The choice of a test model is one question that was considered in chapter 8 and will be considered again in the last chapter. It would greatly facilitate the test development process if practical guidelines existed to provide a basis for making this choice. A second question concerns the reasons for item misfit. Several techniques for identifying misfitting items were considered in chapters 8 and 9. At the present level of our technical sophistication, the test developer, faced with a misfitting item, can do little more than subjectively examine the item and hope that the reason for misfit will be apparent.

An important practical question that has been addressed in the literature is the applicability of item response theory to the types of tests typically encountered in the areas of educational and psychological measurement. Rentz and Rentz (1978), in their useful review of the literature related to the Rasch model, discussed a large number of content areas that the model had been applied to. Applications included such academic areas as reading achievement (Rentz & Bashaw, 1975, 1977; Woodcock, 1974); psychological variables (Woodcock, 1978); and mathematics, geology, and biology (Soriyan, 1971; Connolly, Nachtman & Pritchett, 1974). The Rasch model has also been used in the preparation of intelligence tests (Andersen, Kearney, & Everett, 1968), state competency tests (Hambleton, Murray, & Williams, 1983) career development measures (Rentz & Ridenour, 1978), and civil service exams (Durovic, 1970) and the new edition of the Stanford Achievement Test. Lord (1968, 1977b) and Marco (1977) described the application of the three-parameter logistic model to the analysis of such tests as the Verbal Scholastic Aptitude Test, the mathematics sections of the Advanced Placement Program (APP), and the College Level Examination Program (CLEP). Yen (1981, 1983) described the application of the three-parameter logistic model to the development of the California Tests of Basic Skills. The development of many other tests with item response models has also been described in the psychometric literature.

11.2 Development of Tests Utilizing Item Response Models[1]

The test development process consists of the following steps:

1. Preparation of test specifications;
2. Preparation of the item pool;
3. Field testing the items;
4. Selection of test items;
5. Compilation of norms (for norm-referenced tests);
6. Specification of cutoff scores (for criterion-referenced tests);
7. Reliability studies;
8. Validity studies;
9. Final test production.

The important differences between developing tests using standard methods and item response models occur at steps 3, 4, and 7. The discussion that follows in this section will center on these three steps.

11.2.1 Field Testing the Items

Standard item analysis techniques involve an assessment of item difficulty and discrimination indices and the item distractors. The major problem with the standard approach is that the item statistics are *not* sample invariant. The item statistics depend to a great extent on the characteristics of the examinee sample used in the analysis. Heterogeneous examinee samples will, generally, result in higher estimates of item discrimination indices as measured by point-biserial or biserial correlation coefficients. Item difficulty estimates rise and fall with high- and low-ability groups, respectively. But one advantage of the standard approach to item analysis is that estimation of item parameters (difficulty and discrimination) is straightforward and requires only a moderate sample size for obtaining stable parameter estimates.

Detection of bad items (for norm-referenced tests at least) using standard procedures is basically a matter of studying item statistics. A bad item is one that is too easy or too difficult or nondiscriminating (i.e., has a low item-total score correlation) in the population of examinees for whom the test is designed. Of course, because these statistics are sample dependent, an item may have relatively bad statistics for one sample of students and relatively good statistics in a second group.

The process is quite different when item response models are employed to execute the item analysis. As mentioned in chapter 1 and several subsequent chapters, the major advantage of item response model methods and procedures is that they lead, in theory, to item parameters that are sample invariant. Difficulties that have been cited are the necessity for large sample sizes in order to obtain stable item parameter estimates and the mathematical complexity of the techniques used to obtain these estimates.

The detection of bad items is not as straightforward as when standard techniques are employed. Items are generally evaluated in terms of their goodness of fit to a model using a statistical test or an analysis of residuals. Rentz and Rentz (1978) and Rentz and Ridenour (1978) have offered reviews of research related to goodness-of-fit measures used with the one-parameter logistic model. Many of their observations and interpretations of the research are applicable to the use of these measures with other logistic models as well. In addition, bad items can be identified by a consideration of their discrimination indices (the value of a_i will be negative or low positive) and difficulty indices (items should not be too easy or too difficult for the group of examinees to be assessed).

In view of the problems with the chi-square statistic, Rentz and Rentz (1978) suggest caution should be used, and that relative sizes be considered rather than absolute values. They also suggest that the practitioner disregard any probability values associated with the test statistic due to the previously mentioned fact that if sample size is sufficiently large, probabilities will almost always be less than the critical value set by the investigator. These recommendations seem eminently sensible.

Another reason for an item being judged as "bad" occurs when the chosen model does not fit the data. It is certainly true that the item statistics are of limited value when the fit is poor, but the situation can often be improved substantially by fitting a more general model to the data.

A number of studies have been conducted for the purpose of comparing the characteristics of items selected using standard test construction techniques with those of items selected according to the goodness-of-fit measures employed by item response models (Tinsley & Dawis, 1974, 1977a, 1977b). Rentz and Rentz (1978) again suggest caution on the part of test developers when interpreting the goodness-of-fit results, for reasons mentioned earlier. Basically, these studies, which have involved the Rasch model, revealed very little difference between the items selected by the two techniques. The situation is apt to be substantially different when the three-parameter model is used.

In summary, the item analysis process, when employing standard test development techniques, consists of the following steps: (1) determining sample-specific item parameters employing simple mathematical techniques and moderate sample sizes; and (2) deleting items based on statistical criteria. In contrast, item analysis using item response models involves (1) determining sample-invariant item parameters using relatively complex mathematical techniques and large sample sizes, and (2) utilizing goodness-of-fit criteria to detect items that do not fit the specified item response model. Our own view, is, however, that while item response model parameter estimates are needed for subsequent test development work, classical item analysis procedures with an assessment of distractors can provide invaluable information about test item quality.

11.2.2 Item Selection

When applying standard test development techniques to the construction of norm-referenced tests, in addition to concerns for content validity, items are selected on the basis of two characteristics: item difficulty and item discrimination. An attempt is always made to choose items with the highest discrimination parameters. The choice of level of item difficulty is usually governed by the purpose of the test and the anticipated ability distribution of the group the test is intended for. It may be that the purpose of a test is to select a small group of high-ability examinees. A scholarship examination is a good example. In this situation, items are generally selected such that an examinee whose ability places him or her at exactly a desired cut-off score on the ability scale would have a probability of .50 of answering that item correctly.

Most norm-referenced achievement tests are commonly designed to differentiate examinees with regard to their competence in the measured areas; i.e., the test is designed to yield a broad range of scores maximizing discriminations among all examinees taking the test. When a test is designed for this purpose, items are generally chosen to have a medium level and narrow range of difficulty.

The important point to note is that because standard item parameters are not sample invariant, the success of the technique described above depends directly on how closely the sample used to determine the item parameters employed in the item selection process matches the population for which the test is intended.

Item response theory offers the test developer a far more powerful method of item selection. Of course, item selection is, as when standard methods are often employed, based on the intended purpose of the test. However, the selection of items often depends on the amount of information they contribute to the total amount of information supplied by the test. For example, it is quite possible for items to be well-fit by a three-parameter model but with discrimination parameters so low that these test items would be worthless in any test.

Lord (1977b) outlined a procedure, originally conceptualized by Birnbaum (1968) for the use of item information functions in the test building process. Basically, this procedure entails that a test developer take the following steps:

1. Describe the shape of the desired test information function. Lord (1977) calls this the *target information function.*
2. Select items with item information functions that will fill up the hard-to-fill areas under the target information function.
3. After each item is added to the test, calculate the test information function for the selected test items.
4. Continue selecting test items until the test information function approximates the target information function to a satisfactory degree.

It is obvious that the use of item information functions in the manner described above will allow the test developer to produce a test that will very precisely fulfill any set of desired test specifications. Examples of the application of the above steps to the development of achievement tests (based on simulated results) are given in sections 11.4 and 11.5.

One of the useful features of item information functions is that the contribution of each item to the test information function can be determined independently of the other items in the test. With standard testing procedures, the contribution of any item to test reliability or test variance cannot be determined independently of the relationship the item has with all the other items in the test.

Using Lord's procedure with a pool of items known to fit a particular item response model, it is possible to construct a test that "discriminates" well at one particular region or another on the ability continuum. That is to say, if we have a good idea of the ability of a group of examinees, test items can be selected so as to maximize test information in the region of ability spanned by the examinees being tested. This optimum selection of test items will contribute substantially to the precision with which ability scores are estimated. To be more concrete, with criterion-referenced tests, it is common to observe lower test performance on a pretest than on a posttest. Given this knowledge, the test instructor should select easier items for the pretest and more difficult items for the posttest. Then on each testing occasion, precision of measurement will have been maximized in the region of ability where the examinees would most likely be located. Moreover, because the items on both tests measure the same ability and ability estimates do *not* depend on the particular choice of items, growth can be measured by subtracting the pretest ability estimate from the posttest ability estimate.

The following three examples are intended to demonstrate how a test developer would apply Birnbaum's technique to develop, first, a typical norm-referenced achievement test, one designed to maximize the range of examinee scores; second, a scholarship exam designed to yield maximum discrimination among high ability examinees; and, third, a test to provide maximum information for the group of examinees tested.

The items used to illustrate Birnbaum's procedure in examples one and two are those found in tables 11-1 and 11-2. Although somewhat typical, this set of items is far from being representative of an ideal item pool. Since the discrimination parameters of all items are fairly low, most of the items afford only a limited amount of information. Those items with discrimination parameters of .19 supply very limited usable information at all ability levels and so they can be eliminated from serious consideration in any test development work. Elimination of the six items with discrimination parameters of .19 leaves an item pool of 12. Of course, no test developer would

Table 11-1. Item Characteristic Functions for a Set of Typical Test Items

Number (i)	Item Parameters			Probabilities* of Ability Level						
	Diffi-culty (b_i)	Discri-mination (a_i)	Pseudo-Chance (c_i)	-3	-2	-1	0	1	2	3
1	-1.5	.19	.00	38	46	54	62	69	76	81
2	0.0	.19	.00	28	34	42	50	58	66	72
3	1.5	.19	.00	19	24	31	38	46	54	62
4	-1.5	.59	.00	18	38	62	82	92	97	99
5	0.0	.59	.00	05	12	27	50	73	88	95
6	1.5	.59	.00	01	03	08	18	38	62	82
7	-1.5	.99	.00	07	30	70	93	99	100	100
8	0.0	.99	.00	01	03	16	50	84	97	99
9	1.5	.99	.00	00	00	01	07	30	70	93
10	-1.5	.19	.25	54	59	66	71	77	82	86
11	0.0	.19	.25	46	51	56	63	69	74	79
12	1.5	.19	.25	39	43	48	54	59	66	71
13	-1.5	.59	.25	39	53	72	86	94	98	99
14	0.0	.59	.25	29	34	45	63	80	91	96
15	1.5	.59	.25	26	27	31	39	53	72	86
16	-1.5	.99	.25	31	48	77	94	99	100	100
17	0.0	.99	.25	25	28	37	63	88	97	100
18	1.5	.99	.25	25	25	26	31	48	77	94

*Decimal points have been omitted.

attempt to develop a test with a pool of only 12 items, but the number of items is sufficient for illustrative purposes.

The first example to be considered is the development of a typical norm-referenced achievement test. The initial consideration is Birnbaum's first step, the establishment of the target information curve. The test developer would most probably desire a test of this type to provide maximum discrimination or information in the ability range of -2 to $+2$; i.e., as abilities are scaled to have a mean of zero and a standard deviation of one, this ability range would contain approximately 95 percent of examinee

Table 11-2. Item Information Functions for a Set of Typical Test Items

	Item Parameters			Item Information* Ability Level						
Number (i)	Diffi- culty (b_i)	Discri- mination (a_i)	Pseudo- Chance (c_i)	−3	−2	−1	0	1	2	3
1	−1.5	.19	.00	02	03	03	02	02	02	02
2	0.0	.19	.00	02	02	03	03	03	02	02
3	1.5	.19	.00	02	02	02	02	03	03	02
4	−1.5	.59	.00	15	24	24	15	07	03	01
5	0.0	.59	.00	15	11	20	25	20	11	05
6	1.5	.59	.00	01	03	07	15	24	24	15
7	−1.5	.99	.00	19	60	60	19	04	01	00
8	0.0	.99	.00	02	09	37	71	37	09	02
9	1.5	.99	.00	00	01	04	19	60	60	19
10	−1.5	.19	.25	01	02	02	02	02	01	01
11	0.0	.19	.25	01	01	01	02	02	02	01
12	1.5	.19	.25	01	01	01	01	02	02	02
13	−1.5	.59	.25	05	13	15	11	05	02	01
14	0.0	.59	.25	01	03	09	15	14	08	03
15	1.5	.59	.25	00	00	01	05	13	15	11
16	−1.5	.99	.25	04	28	40	14	03	01	00
17	0.0	.99	.25	00	01	12	42	27	07	01
18	1.5	.99	.25	00	00	00	04	28	40	14

*Decimal points have been omitted.

abilities (if ability is normally distributed). Once the area of maximum test information is determined, the next decision to be made is the accuracy with which it is desired to estimate abilities within this range. Suppose the test developer could tolerate an error of .40 (standard error of estimation = .40).

Since the standard error of estimation (SEE) equals $1/\sqrt{\text{Information}}$, if SEE = .40, then Information = 6.25. Thus, to obtain estimates of ability to the desired degree of precision across the ability scale (from −2.0 to +2.0), items must be selected from the item pool to produce a test information function with a height of over 6.25 from −2.0 to +2.0 on the ability scale. The tails of the target information function, those sections below −2 and above +2, are of no interest to the test developer and can take on any form.

After the target information function is specified, the next step is to select items with ordinates that, when summed, approximate the target information function as closely as possible. Trial and error is involved in this step of the process. It is important that the test developer select the fewest possible items to fulfill the test requirements. For this particular example, the most useful items would be those supplying a reasonable amount of information over a wide ability range, e.g., items 5, 8, and 17. Items such as 7 or 9, which supply relatively more information but for a narrower range of abilities, will be reserved for hard-to-fill areas under the target information function.

Suppose the test developer began by selecting 10 items similar to item 8 in the item pool; the amount of information supplied at each ability level would be the following:

Ability Level	Test Information Curve (10 items)
−3	.20
−2	.90
−1	3.70
0	7.10
1	3.70
2	.90
3	.20

But, after the selection of the first 10 items, additional information is required at ability levels −2, −1, 1, and 2. Appropriate choices of items to fill the problem areas under the target information curve would be items similar statistically to 7 and 9. Suppose six items similar to item 7, and 6 items similar to item 9, where chosen from the item pool. The test information function would now supply the following amount of information at the various ability levels:

Ability Level	Test Information Curve (22 items)
−3	1.34
−2	4.56
−1	7.54
0	9.38
1	7.54
2	4.56
3	.32

At this point, areas under the target information function that are still deficient are those corresponding to ability levels -2 and 2. What is required to fill these areas are several easy and difficult test items with fairly high discrimination parameters (items that presently are not contained in the item pool). To continue to attempt to fill these areas with the existing items would probably result in a final test which is overly long for many examinees taking it.

The target information function for a test designed as a scholarship examination would be one that produced substantial information at the high end of the ability scale. Suppose this time the test designer was satisfied with estimating ability to an accuracy of $\pm .33$; the information level desired in this area would be approximately equal to 9. The target information function for this type of test would be one with an ordinate of 9 at high levels of ability. The height of the target information function at other points on the ability scale is of considerably less interest. Items would be selected to fulfill the requirements of this test in the manner described in the first example.

For the third example, table 11–3 provides some results revealing the advantages of selecting test items matched to the ability level of a group of examinees. From a typical pool of items ($-2 \leq b_i \leq 2$; $.60 \leq a_i \leq 1.40$; $c_i = .20$), three 20-item tests were constructed: a wide-range test (random selection of items), an easy test (random selection of items with $b_i < 0$), and a difficult test (random selection of items with $b_i > 0$). At seven equally spaced points on the ability scale, test information functions for the three tests and efficiency functions for the easy and difficult tests in relation to the wide-range test are reported in table 11-3. As expected, the easy test provides more precise ability estimates at the low end of the ability continuum than does the wide-range test or the difficult test. Therefore, it would be a more useful test than the other two for low-performing examinees. In fact, from the last section of table 11–3, it is seen that at $\theta = -3$, the easy test is equivalent to a wide-range test that is increased in length by about 58 percent (or 12 items). Compared to the wide-range test, the difficult test is doing a very poor job of assessing low ability scores. The difficult test is functioning about as well as a test consisting of 35% of the items in the wide range test.

For the hard test, it can be seen from table 11–3 that it is considerably better than the wide-range test for estimating ability scores at the high end of the ability scale. For example, at $\theta = 2$ the wide range test would need to be increased in length by 36 percent to equal the difficult test in terms of measurement precision.

Perhaps one final point is worth making. With the availability of a set of items and corresponding parameter estimates, a variety of hypothetical tests

Table 11-3. Comparison of Test Information and Efficiency Functions for Three Types of Tests (Easy, Wide Range, Difficult) Built from a Common Pool of Items

Ability Level	Test Information Function*			Test Efficiency Function (Relative to the Wide Range Test)		Improvement (Decrease) (Relative to the Wide Range Test)	
	Wide Range	Easy	Difficult	Easy	Difficult	Easy	Difficult
-3.0	.24	.37	.08	1.58	.35	58%	(65%)
-2.0	.86	1.27	.37	1.48	.44	48%	(56%)
-1.0	2.02	2.71	1.27	1.35	.63	35%	(37%)
0.0	2.94	3.18	2.71	1.08	.92	8%	(8%)
1.0	2.65	2.16	3.18	.81	1.20	(19%)	20%
2.0	1.59	1.06	2.16	.67	1.36	(33%)	36%
3.0	.75	.46	1.06	.61	1.41	(39%)	41%

*Based on 20-item tests.

can be constructed and their information functions compared. These comparisons greatly facilitate the task of determining the best test to accomplish some specified purpose.

A useful discussion of item selection, as it pertains to tests developed according to Rasch model procedures, is presented by Wright and Douglas (1975) and Wright (1977a). The item selection procedure basically consists of specifying the ability distribution of the group for whom the test is intended and then choosing items such that the distribution of item difficulties matches the distribution of abilities. This procedure is equivalent to that originally introduced by Birnbaum (1968) since, in this case, the item information functions depend only on the difficulty parameters.

11.2.3 Test Reliability

When standard test development methods are employed, one or more of the following approaches to reliability are used: (1) parallel-form reliability; (2) test-retest reliability; and (3) corrected split-half reliability. All three measures of reliability are sample specific. This unfortunate property of standard estimates of reliability reduces their usefulness. Another problem is that the well-known classical model estimates of reliability lead to a group estimate of error in individual test scores. It is called the *standard error of measurement*. Intuitively, it does not seem to be reasonable to assume that the size of errors in examinee test scores is unrelated to the "true scores" of examinees taking the test.

The item response theory analog of test score reliability and the standard error of measurement is the test information function. The concept of information was described in chapter 6, and its use in the selection of test items was illustrated for the three examples given in the previous section. The use of the test information function as a measure of accuracy of estimation is appealing for at least two reasons: (1) Its shape depends *only* on the items included in the test, and (2) it provides an estimate of the error of measurement at each ability level.

An excellent discussion of the use of test information functions as a replacement for the traditional concepts of reliability and the standard error of measurement is given by Samejima (1977a). Information functions for two scoring methods with the Raven Colored and Standard Progressive Matrices, Sets A, B, and C, are shown in figure 11–1. The figure is from a paper by Thissen (1976).

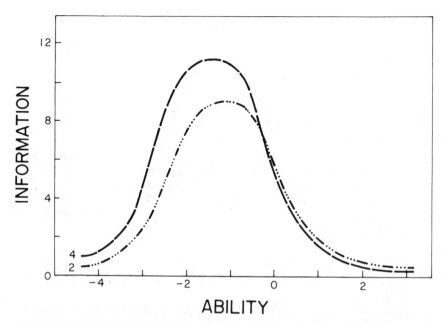

Figure 11-1.   Test Information Functions for Two Scoring Methods with the Raven Colored and Standard Progressive Matrices, Sets A, B, and C (From Thissen, D. M. Information in wrong responses to Raven's Progressive Matrices. *Journal of Educational Measurement*, 1976, *13*, 201-214. Copyright 1976, National Council on Measurement in Education, Washington, D.C. Reprinted with permission.)

11.3 Redesigning Tests

In the last section, several of the problems associated with test construction were considered. Occasionally, however, there is some interest in revising an existing test. With the aid of IRT, the consequences of various types of changes can be evaluated. Unlike problems of test development, when redesigning a test, item statistics are almost always available so that the consequences of various changes in the test design can be studied quickly and in an informative way.

Utilizing item response data for a version of the SAT, Lord (1974c, 1977b) considered the impact of eight typical test revision questions: How would the relative efficiency of the original test be changed by

1. shortening the test by removing randomly equivalent parts?
2. adding five items similar to the five easiest items in the original test?
3. removing five items of medium difficulty?
4. replacing five medium-difficult items by five very easy items?
5. replacing all reading items by a typical set of nonreading items?
6. removing the easiest half of the items?
7. removing the hardest half of the items?
8. replacing all items by items of medium difficulty?

Lord answers the eight questions by computing the *relative efficiency* of the two tests of interest: the original test and the revised test. Lord's (1977b) figure is reproduced in figure 11–2. For convenience of interpretation, he replaced the usual ability scale (−4 to +4) with the college board scaled scores. The answers are as follows:

1. If the test is shortened to n_2 from n_1 items by removing a random selection of items, the relative efficiency will be n_2/n_1 relative to the original test.
2. Adding five very easy items increases the relative efficiency across the scale slightly, but the influence at the lower end of the ability scale is substantial.
3. Deleting five items of medium difficulty lowers the relative efficiency of the revised test across most of the scale but especially near the middle of the scale.
4. Deleting five items of medium difficulty and adding five very easy items results in a new test that provides more information at the lower end of the ability scale and less information in the middle of the ability scale.
5. As Lord noted, the results of this revision were not generalizable to other tests, but the question does describe a type of question that can be addressed through relative efficiency. For example, there may be interest in determining the relative efficiency of a test consisting of true-false items with respect to a test consisting of multiple-choice items in a common domain of content.
6. Deleting the easiest items dramatically affects the measurement precision of the revised test at the lower end of the ability scale. There is even some loss (about 10 percent) in measurement precision at the upper end of the ability scale.
7. Removing the hardest items has the predicted effect: Measurement precision is lost at the high end of the ability scale. But there is also a surprise. Because the most difficult items are removed, low-ability examinees do less guessing, and the revised test, therefore, actually

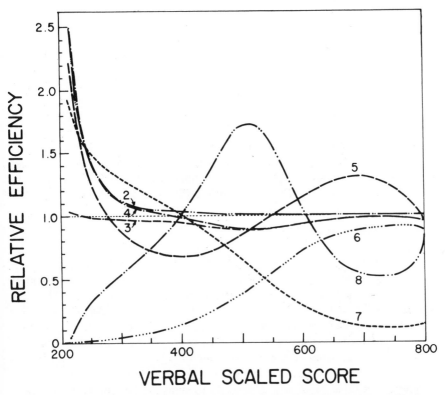

Figure 11-2. Relative Efficiency of Various Modified SAT Verbal Tests (From Lord, F. M. Practical applications of item response theory. *Journal of Educational Measurement*, 1977, *14*, 117-138. Copyright 1977, National Council on Measurement in Education, Washington, D.C. Reprinted with permission.)

functions substantially better at the lower end of the ability scale even though the revised test is only half as long as the original test.

8. Loading the test with items of medium difficulty results in a revised test with substantially more measurement precision in the middle of the scale and less measurement precision at the ends of the ability scale.

Lord (1974d) has demonstrated how the consequences of test revisions can be studied with the aid of relative efficiency. A variety of new test designs can be proposed, relative efficiency curves can be computed, and then the best of the designs can be selected and implemented.

11.4 Comparison of Five Item Selection Methods[2]

The purpose of this section is to compare the types of tests that are produced by five substantially different item selection methods using the test information function. In order to make the results of the five methods comparable, a fixed test length was used. Each method was used to select 30 items, and the amount of information provided by the 30 selected test items, at five ability levels, -2, -1, 0, $+1$, $+2$, was calculated. The information functions obtained from the item selection methods were then used to compare the methods. The five methods investigated were designated: (1) random, (2) standard, (3) middle difficulty, (4) up and down, and (5) maximum information. These procedures will be described later.

11.4.1 Generation of the Item Pool

A computer program, DATAGEN (Hambleton & Rovinelli, 1973) was used to generate a "pool" of 200 test items. Each test item was described by the item parameters in the three-parameter logistic test model. The item statistics for the first 75 items are reported in table 11–4. The average value and range of the item statistics were chosen to correspond to values that have been observed in practice (see, for example, Lord, 1968; Ross, 1966). Ability scores from a normal distribution (mean $= 0$, sd $= 1$) for 200 examinees were generated, and using the item response model item statistics reported in table 11–4, it was possible to simulate the item performance of the 200 examinees, assuming the validity of the three-parameter logistic test model. With the availability of examinee item scores and total test scores, conventional item statistics (proportion-correct, and item-test score correlations) were calculated. These item statistics are also reported in table 11–4.

11.4.2 Item Selection Methods

Random. No norm-referenced test developer would ever select items at random, but the results from such a procedure do provide a base line for comparing the results obtained with other methods. To apply this method, a table of random numbers was used to select 30 test items from the pool.

Standard. This method employed classical item statistics (item difficulty and item discrimination). Items were chosen such that their difficulties varied between .30 and .70. Of the total number of items with difficulty values

Table 11-4. Item Pool Parameters and Item Information at Five Ability Levels (b, −2.00 to +2.00; a, .19 to 2.00; c, .00 to .25)

Item	Item Parameters			Ability Level					Classical Statistics	
	b	a	c	−2	−1	0	1	2	p	r
1	.49	.49	.07	.04	.09	.14	.15	.11	.44	.36
2	−1.68	1.04	.25	.38	.39	.11	.02	.00	.93	.30
3	.09	1.11	.22	.00	.10	.55	.35	.07	.61	.48
4	1.73	1.70	.22	.00	.00	.00	.22	1.28	.30	.20
5	.81	1.44	.16	.00	.00	.25	1.10	.25	.37	.49
6	−1.41	1.32	.17	.42	.80	.15	.02	.00	.90	.41
7	1.38	.55	.13	.01	.03	.08	.15	.17	.39	.28
8	−.88	1.94	.19	.02	1.67	.43	.02	.00	.83	.62
9	1.45	.87	.12	.00	.01	.09	.35	.39	.27	.32
10	.47	1.21	.24	.00	.02	.39	.56	.13	.47	.48
11	.18	.32	.12	.03	.05	.06	.06	.05	.62	.22
12	.58	1.04	.25	.00	.03	.27	.46	.16	.50	.43
13	−.55	1.78	.22	.00	.62	.91	.06	.00	.78	.49
14	1.09	1.70	.23	.00	.00	.04	1.20	.40	.46	.37
15	1.01	1.39	.08	.00	.00	.22	1.19	.41	.28	.50
16	.88	.52	.12	.02	.06	.12	.15	.13	.45	.31
17	1.47	1.59	.04	.00	.00	.04	1.03	1.08	.14	.31
18	−.49	1.88	.04	.01	1.13	1.40	.08	.00	.71	.65
19	−1.00	1.45	.04	.28	1.39	.42	.04	.00	.82	.59
20	−1.80	.57	.18	.16	.14	.09	.04	.02	.89	.31
21	.73	1.21	.11	.00	.02	.37	.81	.24	.37	.50
22	.23	.72	.02	.06	.20	.35	.29	.13	.49	.44
23	.85	.96	.05	.00	.06	.34	.60	.29	.33	.45

(continued on next page)

Table 11-4 (continued)

Item	Item Parameters			Ability Level					Classical Statistics	
	b	a	c	-2	-1	0	1	2	p	r
24	-.37	1.10	.14	.03	.38	.63	.20	.03	.67	.58
25	1.21	.58	.17	.01	.03	.09	.17	.16	.38	.31
26	-.21	1.67	.19	.00	.20	1.36	.20	.01	.65	.57
27	-1.40	1.00	.04	.49	.60	.21	.05	.01	.86	.56
28	.82	.45	.09	.03	.06	.10	.12	.10	.53	.32
29	1.89	1.40	.13	.00	.00	.00	.23	1.11	.18	.30
30	-.11	1.70	.16	.00	.15	1.53	.26	.02	.63	.59
31	.27	1.94	.20	.00	.01	1.23	.64	.03	.49	.59
32	-.62	1.56	.22	.01	.67	.71	.07	.01	.77	.49
33	-.82	1.52	.09	.09	1.25	.58	.05	.00	.81	.55
34	1.93	.20	.09	.01	.02	.02	.02	.02	.48	.06
35	-1.54	1.34	.09	.72	.80	.13	.01	.00	.92	.36
36	-1.63	.68	.14	.23	.24	.13	.05	.02	.85	.37
37	.08	1.36	.23	.00	.08	.79	.38	.05	.60	.59
38	-.46	1.39	.16	.02	.52	.84	.14	.01	.77	.49
39	1.17	.91	.03	.00	.04	.24	.55	.39	.25	.41
40	-1.29	1.92	.04	.58	2.04	.14	.01	.00	.87	.62
41	.18	.20	.12	.02	.02	.02	.02	.02	.53	.29
42	.34	1.58	.22	.00	.02	.75	.68	.06	.54	.54
43	-1.44	.36	.02	.09	.09	.08	.06	.04	.68	.33
44	-.49	1.40	.20	.01	.49	.78	.12	.01	.74	.56
45	-.28	.98	.01	.13	.48	.65	.26	.06	.64	.60
46	-1.90	.88	.11	.45	.32	.10	.03	.01	.91	.31
47	-.84	1.20	.15	.11	.72	.45	.08	.01	.78	.58

48	1.92	.71	.19	.00	.00	.03	.14	.25	.31	.31
49	1.62	.72	.20	.00	.01	.05	.18	.25	.32	.19
50	1.47	.64	.24	.00	.01	.06	.15	.18	.38	.31
51	1.77	1.40	.02	.00	.00	.03	.59	1.27	.13	.43
52	-1.26	1.56	.03	.59	1.49	.23	.02	.00	.87	.51
53	-1.13	1.62	.12	.22	1.50	.27	.02	.00	.89	.57
54	1.65	1.18	.23	.00	.00	.01	.28	.61	.33	.24
55	-1.15	1.59	.11	.25	1.44	.27	.02	.00	.87	.55
56	-.26	1.54	.01	.04	.71	1.52	.23	.02	.63	.69
57	1.52	.24	.15	.01	.02	.03	.03	.03	.48	.22
58	-1.88	1.22	.07	.91	.48	.08	.01	.00	.95	.30
59	-.33	1.26	.14	.02	.38	.81	.20	.03	.72	.57
60	.42	1.52	.22	.00	.01	.61	.74	.09	.55	.55
61	-.76	1.66	.12	.04	1.28	.65	.05	.00	.78	.59
62	-.44	.72	.21	.05	.19	.25	.14	.05	.68	.48
63	.11	.86	.15	.02	.14	.38	.29	.10	.55	.44
64	.90	1.82	.22	.00	.00	.09	1.57	.23	.44	.41
65	-1.21	1.14	.15	.27	.69	.25	.04	.01	.90	.43
66	.69	1.41	.13	.00	.01	.40	1.03	.20	.38	.50
67	.46	.42	.20	.02	.05	.08	.09	.07	.53	.29
68	.39	.40	.06	.05	.08	.10	.10	.08	.46	.33
69	-.07	1.83	.08	.00	.18	2.06	.29	.01	.63	.70
70	-1.66	.20	.02	.03	.03	.03	.02	.02	.68	.10
71	1.77	.20	.18	.01	.01	.02	.02	.02	.52	.21
72	.62	1.67	.16	.00	.00	.44	1.23	.13	.41	.46
73	-.08	.79	.23	.02	.14	.29	.21	.08	.65	.33
74	.79	1.47	.13	.00	.00	.30	1.19	.24	.32	.42
75	-.33	.69	.12	.07	.20	.26	.17	.07	.65	.34

[1] Obtained from a normally distributed set of ability scores.

falling in this range, the thirty items with the highest item discrimination parameters were chosen. The selected items had discrimination parameters (as estimated by point-biserial correlations) that ranged between .53 and .70.

Middle Difficulty.   The 30 test items that provided the maximum amount of information at an ability level of 0.0 were selected from the pool.

Up and Down.   This method consisted of a three-step process that was repeated until 30 items were selected. The first step involved selecting the item from the pool that provided the maximum amount of information at an ability level of -1.0, and the second step involved proceeding to an ability level of 0.0 and selecting the item that provided the maximum amount of information at this ability level. The third step was to select the item at an ability level of $+1.0$ that provided the maximum amount of information. This three-step process, repeated until 30 items were selected, was intended to build a test that would provide maximum information across the center portion of the ability scale, where a high percentage of examinees were expected to be located.

Maximum Information.   The fifth item selection method employed involved the averaging of information provided by each of the 200 items across three ability levels, -1.0, 0.00, and 1.0. The 30 test items providing the highest average levels of information across the three ability levels were selected for the test.

11.4.3 Results

The test information at five ability levels of interest for each of the five item selection methods are presented in table 11–5. Table 11–5 also reports the numbers of the test items selected by each of the methods. These results are not surprising, but the size of the differences in information curves obtained with the five methods was not known, and the results therefore are interesting. Figure 11–3 provides a graphical representation of the test information functions resulting from the five item selection methods. As was expected, the method employing a random selection of items provided less information than any of the other methods, at the ability levels of primary interest $(-1, 0, +1)$. It is interesting to note, however, that the test information function resulting from this process is unimodal with maximum

Table 11-5. Test Composition and Information Using Five Item Selection Methods

Item Selection Method	Selected Test Items (n = 30)										Test Information Ability Level				
											−2.0	−1.0	0.0	1.0	2.0
Random	1	2	9	11	13	15	45	54	56	58	2.61	5.99	12.43	10.14	4.57
	65	71	76	81	82	93	97	108	118	121					
	131	139	143	148	161	163	170	172	176	186					
Standard	24	26	30	31	37	42	45	56	60	69	.48	6.50	35.12	16.59	2.01
	81	86	87	88	91	100	104	111	114	131					
	147	163	168	169	170	172	177	184	186	197					
Middle Difficulty	13	18	26	30	31	37	38	42	44	56	.27	11.38	40.68	10.24	.82
	59	69	81	87	88	91	104	113	114	122					
	125	139	145	168	169	170	172	177	196	197					
Up and Down	8	19	30	40	52	53	55	56	64	69	2.84	19.00	27.48	18.06	2.35
	80	81	86	87	104	105	106	111	113	114					
	129	145	155	156	163	168	177	186	194	197					
Maximum Information	8	18	33	40	56	61	69	81	86	87	1.00	17.74	35.02	15.78	1.61
	88	91	104	105	111	113	114	122	125	145					
	155	163	168	169	170	177	180	186	194	197					

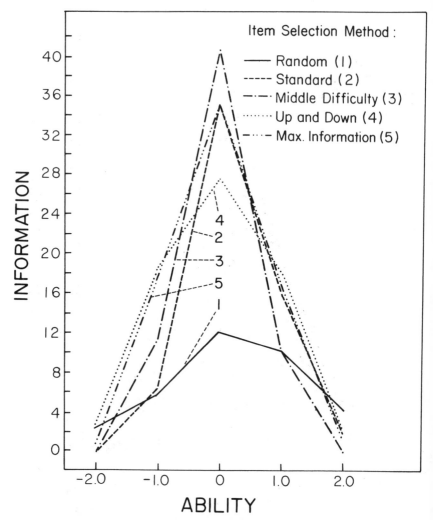

Figure 11-3.   Test Information Curves Produced with Five Item Selection Methods (30 Test Items) (From Cook & Hambleton, 1978b)

information provided at the center of the ability distribution. This result is due to the characteristics of the item pool.

The "standard method" also resulted in a test information function that provided maximum information for abilities at the center of the ability distribution. The amount of information provided at this point is considerably

Table 11-6. Overlap of Test Items Selected Using the Five Item Selection Methods (Number of Common Test Items/Percent of Common Test Items)

Item Selection Method	Item Selection Method			
	2	3	4	5
Random (1)	8 (26.7%)	6 (20.0%)	4 (13.3%)	5 (16.7%)
Standard (2)	—	19 (63.3%)	14 (46.7%)	17 (56.7%)
Middle Difficulty (3)	—	—	12 (40.0%)	17 (56.7%)
Up and Down (4)	—	—	—	19 (63.3%)
Maximum Information (5)	—	—	—	—

higher than that provided by the random approach. The information provided at an ability level of +1 is also considerably greater than that provided by the random selection method. This is not the case, however, for the amount of information provided at an ability level of −1. There is really very little difference between the two methods, in the values obtained at this ability level.

The third method, which involves selecting only those items that provided maximum information at an ability level of 0.0 resulted, as to be expected, in a test information function that provides more information at $\theta = 0.0$ than any of the other methods. This method also resulted in an appreciable amount of information at the two adjacent ability levels.

The up-and-down method provided the least amount of information at $\theta = 0.0$ with the exception of the random method, but it provides considerably more information at ability levels of −1.0 and +1.0 than did any of the other methods.

The maximum information method provided an appreciable amount of information at three ability levels −1.0, 0.0, and 1.0. It did not provide as much information at the ability level of 0.0 as did the middle-difficulty method, although it did provide more information at the adjacent ability levels of +1 and −1 than did any of the other methods with the exception of the up-and-down method.

An interesting point to consider is the amount of overlap (in terms of percentage of items) that might be expected to result from each of these methods. Table 11–6 lists the number of overlapping items along with the percentage of overlap that this number represents. The smallest amount of overlap observed is four items. This occurred between the random method and the up-and-down method. A surprisingly large amount of overlap was found between the standard and the middle-difficulty methods and between the up-and-down and maximum information methods. Both pairs of methods had an overlap of 19 items (or 63.3 percent).

11.5 Selection of Test Items to Fit Target Curves[3]

In this section of the chapter, the merits of several item selection methods for producing (1) a scholarship exam and (2) a test to optimally separate examinees into three ability categories are considered.

The first situation, designated case I, refers to the development of a test that is to be used for awarding scholarships. The maximum amount of information is desired at the upper end of the ability continuum. The second situation, designated case II, refers to the development of a test to be used to make decisions at two different points on an ability continuum. This situation arises when, for example, a test is used to award "passing" as well as "honors" grades to students. For each situation (case I and case II), several item selection methods were developed and compared.

11.5.1 Method

Case I. The development of a scholarship selection test was initiated by setting a target information function. This task was accomplished by specifying the size of the SEE that we considered desirable at each of the five ability levels ranging from -2 to $+2$. Using the relationship between the SEE and test information that was discussed in chapter 6, the amount of information required at each ability level was determined. The resulting target information function is summarized in table 11-7 and presented graphically in figure 11-4.

Four item selection methods were compared: (1) random, (2) standard, (3) high difficulty, and (4) up and down. Methods 3 and 4 are based on the use of item information functions. The high-difficulty method was one that involved choosing items that provided maximum information at an ability level of $+1.0$ (the ability level of primary interest). The up-and-down method involved the following steps: (1) choose the item that provides maximum information at an ability level of $+2$, (2) proceed to the adjacent ability level of $+1$ and select the item that provides maximum information at this ability level, (3) continue to work down the ability continuum in this manner until an item is chosen that provides maximum information at an ability level of -2, (4) go back to an ability level of $+2$ and repeat the cycle. As the desired

Table 11-7. Target and Score Information Functions for the Two Test Development Projects

Case	Target/Method	Ability Level					Number of Test Items Selected
		−2.0	−1.0	0.0	1.0	2.0	
I	Target	2.70	2.70	4.00	35.00	6.25	—
	Random	2.73	6.15	12.79	10.73	4.88	32
	Standard	.13	.60	4.25	18.14	17.18	32
	High Difficulty	.01	.44	13.18	35.01	9.29	32
	Up and Down	2.65	3.83	16.22	34.94	15.28	38
II	Target	4.00	25.00	4.00	25.00	4.00	—
	Random	3.47	8.65	13.65	11.36	5.29	36
	Standard	3.27	18.84	16.23	21.19	4.83	36
	Low-High Difficulty	4.77	25.26	15.39	24.86	5.27	36

amount of information is obtained at a particular ability level, delete this ability level from consideration in the cycle.

The two remaining methods, which were not based on item information functions, were similar to the random and standard methods described in an earlier part of this chapter, with the following exceptions: (1) The number of test items for each of these methods was set to be the same as the number of items required by the "best" of methods 3 and 4, and (2) the specifications for the item difficulty values for the standard method were changed so that no item with an item difficulty value greater than .35 was chosen.

Case II. The target information function for this testing situation was established by the same procedure described for case I. The values for the resulting bimodal target information curve are summarized in table 11-7 and presented graphically in figure 11-5. It should be noted that maximum information is desired at two points on the ability continuum, −1.0 and 1.0.

Three item selection methods were compared for this testing situation. The only method based on the use of item information functions is the one designated low-high difficulty. This method is similar to the up-and-down technique that was described previously and consists of selecting items alternately that provide maximum information at ability levels of +1.0 and −1.0. This back-and-forth procedure is continued until the area under the target information function is filled to a satisfactory degree. The random and

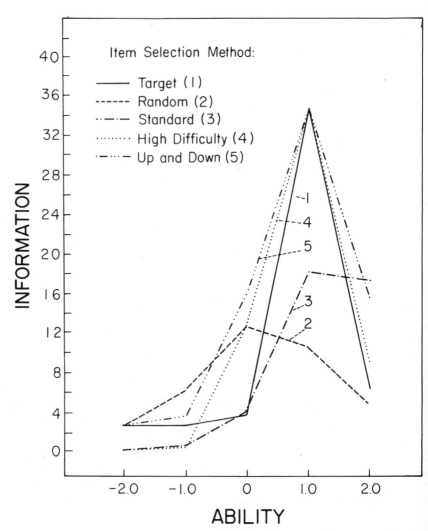

Figure 11-4.   Scholarship Test Information Curves Produced with Five Item Selection Methods (From Cook & Hambleton, 1978b)

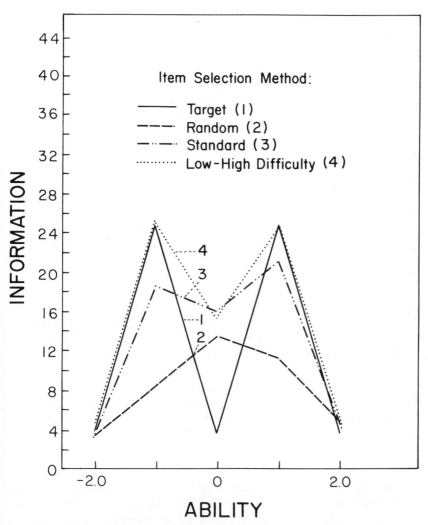

Figure 11-5.   Bimodal Test Information Curves Produced with Four Item Selection Methods (From Cook & Hambleton, 1978b)

standard methods are similar to those previously described. The number of items used for both methods was set to be the number of items required by the low-high-difficulty method. The specifications for selecting items using classical item difficulty and item discrimination values were, first, to choose items with discrimination values greater than .40 and second, from this subset of items, to choose 18 items with difficulty values in the range of .70 to .90 and 18 items with difficulty values in the range of .20 to .40.

11.5.2 Results

Case I. The results of the four item selection methods are summarized in table 11–7. A comparison of the two methods based on test information functions (high difficulty and up and down) shows that the high-difficulty method required six fewer items than the up-and-down method required to provide the desired amount of information at the ability level of interest (+1.0). The random and standard methods were clearly inferior. These results were certainly expected for the random method, but the dramatic difference between the amount of information at the ability level of interest obtained using the classical item statistics and that obtained using either of the other two methods is quite surprising. It was interesting to note that the up-and-down method provides maximum information over a broader range of abilities than does the high-difficulty method; therefore, it could possibly be a more appropriate technique for developing a selection test if moderate discrimination were also required at ability levels other than the one of major interest.

Case II. A summary of the results of the three item selection methods investigated is presented in table 11–7. As expected, the random method is totally inappropriate. The contrast between the standard method and the method based on the use of item information curves is not as dramatic as in the case I situation. Although clearly inferior, the results of the standard method might possibly be useful in some situations. It is clear from figure 11–5 that none of the methods provides test information functions that match closely the target information function at points on the ability continuum other than those of major interest. However, the low-high-difficulty method did provide a good test information–target information match at these points.

11.5.3 Summary

In all cases, the item selection methods based on either the random selection of items or the use of classical item statistics produced results inferior to those produced by methods utilizing item response model item parameters. And the appropriateness of each method was situation specific. If maximum information is required at only one point on an ability continuum, it is clear that a method that chooses items that maximize information at this particular point will be the best. If information is required over a wider range of abilities, methods involving averaging the information values across the ability levels of interest or choosing items in some systematic method that considers each point of interest on the ability continuum appear to be quite promising.

Only a limited number of methods and testing situations have been investigated, but the results indicate that it may be possible to prespecify item selection methods that are situation specific and that will enable a practitioner to develop a test quickly and efficiently without going through a lengthy trial-and-error process.

11.6 Summary

In this chapter we have highlighted the differences in test development between standard or classical methods and item response model methods. Item response models appear to be especially useful in test design (or redesign). It becomes possible with the aid of IRT models to build tests to fit particular specifications and without major concern for the similarity between the examinee sample used to calibrate the test items and the examinee samples who will be administered the constructed tests. The last two sections of the chapter were included to provide practitioners with several examples of how tests constructed using different item selection methods compared.

Notes

1. Some of the material in this section is from papers by Cook and Hambleton (1978a) and Hambleton (1979).
2. The material in this section is based on a research report by Cook and Hambleton (1978b).
3. The material in this section is based on a research report by Cook and Hambleton (1978b).

12 ITEM BANKING

12.1 Introduction

The concept of item banking has attracted considerable interest in recent years from both public and private agencies (Hiscox & Brzezinski, 1980). In fact, the military, many companies, school districts, state departments of education, and test publishing companies have prepared (or are preparing) item banks. Item banks consist of substantial numbers of items that are matched to objectives, skills, or tasks and can be used by test developers to build tests on an "as needed" basis. When a bank consists of content-valid and technically sound items, the test developer's task of building tests is considerably easier and the quality of tests is usually higher than when test developers prepare their own test items. Item banks, especially those in which items are described by item-response model parameter estimates, offer considerable potential:

- Test developers can easily build tests to measure objectives of interest.
- Test developers, within the limits of an item bank, can produce tests with the desired number of test items per objective.

- If item banks consist of content-valid and technically sound items, test quality will usually be better than test developers could produce if they were to prepare the test items themselves.

It seems clear that in the future, item banks will become increasingly important to test developers because the potential they hold for improving the quality of testing, while at the same time reducing the time spent in building tests, is substantial.

The availability of computer software for storing and retrieving test items (in a multitude of formats), and for making changes to the test items and for printing tests, has further enhanced the utility of item banks. In addition, guidelines for preparing and reviewing objectives and test items for item banks are readily available (Hambleton, Murray, & Anderson, 1982; Popham, 1978).

The purposes of this chapter are (1) to consider the selection of criterion-referenced test items, (2) to highlight a promising application of item response models to item banks for providing both norm-referenced and criterion-referenced test score information, and (3) to describe a research study in which this new application of item response models was evaluated.

12.2 Item Response Models and Item Banking

Depending on the intended purpose of a test, items with desired characteristics can be drawn from an item bank and used to construct a test with statistical properties of interest. This point was clearly demonstrated in the last chapter. Although classical item statistics (item difficulty and discrimination) have been employed for this purpose, they are of limited value for describing the items in a bank because these statistics are dependent on the particular group used in the item calibration process. Item response model item parameters, however, do not have this limitation, and, consequently, are of much greater use in describing test items in an item bank (Choppin, 1976; Wright, 1977a). The invariance property of the item parameters makes it possible to obtain item statistics that are comparable across dissimilar groups. Let us assume that we are interested in describing items using the two-parameter logistic test model. The single drawback is that because the mean and standard deviation of the ability scores are arbitrarily established (see chapters 4 and 5), the ability score metric is different for each group. Since the item parameters depend on the ability scale, it is not possible to directly compare item parameter estimates derived from different groups of examinees until the ability scales are equated in some way. Fortunately, the problem is not too hard to resolve, as can be seen in chapter 10, since the item parameters in the two groups are linearly related. Thus, if a subset of calibrated items is administered to both groups, the linear relationship between the estimates of the item parameters can be obtained from the two separate bivariate plots, one establishing the relationship between the estimates of item discrimination parameters for the two groups, and the second, the relationship between the estimates of the item difficulty parameters. Having established the linear relationship between item parameters common to the two groups, a prediction equation can then be used to obtain item parameter estimates for those items not administered to the first group. In this way, all item parameter estimates can be equated to a common group of examinees and reported on a common ability scale. Recently, Stocking and Lord (1983) reported some even better approaches for equating item parameter estimates obtained in different groups. These methods were considered in Chapter 10.

12.3 Criterion-Referenced Test Item Selection[1]

The common method for selecting test items for criterion-referenced tests (CRTs) is straightforward: First, a test length is selected and then a random (or stratified random) sample of test items is drawn from the pool of acceptable (valid) test items measuring the content domain of interest. A random (or stratified random) selection of test items is satisfactory when an item pool is statistically homogeneous since for all practical purposes the test items are interchangeable. When items are similar statistically, the particular choice of test items will have only a minimal impact on the statistical properties of the test scores. But when item pools are statistically hetero- geneous (as they often are), a random selection of test items may be far from optimal for separating examinees into mastery states.[2] For a fixed test length, the most valid test for separating examinees into mastery states would consist of test items that discriminate effectively near the cutoff score on the domain score scale. With a randomly selected set of test items from a heterogeneous pool, the validity of the resulting classifications will, generally, be lower since not all test items will be optimally functioning near the cutoff score. For example, test items that may be very easy or very difficult or have low discriminating power are as likely to be selected with the random-selection method as are other more suitable items in the pool. These less than ideal test items, however, must not be deleted from a pool because they will often be useful at other times.

When constructing tests to separate examinees into two or more mastery states in relation to a content domain of interest, it seems clear that it is desirable to select items that are most discriminating within the region of the cutoff score. But criterion-referenced measurement specialists have not usually taken advantage of optimal items for a test even though test developers commonly assume that the item pools from which their items will be drawn are heterogeneous. On occasion, classical item statistics are used in item selection but, as will be demonstrated next, these statistics have limited usefulness.

The classical item statistics are item difficulty (p) and item discrimination (r). Item difficulty is usually reported on the scale (0, 1) and defined over a population of examinees. Examinee domain scores (π) are also reported on the scale (0, 1), but they are defined over a population of test items. The nature of the inferences to these two scales is totally different. In the case of the classical item difficulty scale, inferences are made from item difficulty estimates to item difficulty parameters for a well-defined population of examinees (for example, the population consisting of ninth-grade students in Maryland). In the case of the domain score scale, inferences are made from domain score estimates based on a sample of the test items to examinee domain scores in a well-defined content domain. The first inference is to a pool of examinees; the second inference is to a domain of content.

The cutoff score (π_o) is almost always set on the π scale. Unfortunately, there is no connection between the π scale and the p scale; therefore, even when π_o is known, item statistics cannot be used to optimally select test items. Suppose $\pi_o = .80$. That test items are answered correctly by, say, 80 percent of the examinee population does *not* mean that the items are ideal for separating examinees with more from those with less than 80 percent mastery of the test content.

Consider the hypothetical performance of five groups of 20 examinees each on three test items: the first is easy; the second is of medium difficulty, and the third is hard. The performance of each group on each test item is reported in table 12–1, which shows that all groups answered the easy item correctly, the top four groups answered the medium-difficulty item correctly, and only the top three groups answered the hard item correctly.

The p-values for the easy, medium, and hard items are 1.00, .80, and .60, respectively. Suppose also that there are equal numbers of items of each type in the total item pool. Then, the domain scores for the five groups (from top to bottom) in the total item pool are 1.00, 1.00, 1.00, .67 and .33, respectively. If $\pi_o = .80$, then 60 of the 100 examinees are masters and should pass the test. But, if items with $p = .80$ are chosen, 20 additional examinees will be incorrectly passed. The best items to choose in the example are the ones with $p = .60$, since with these items, the separation of

Table 12-1. Number of Examinees in Each of Five Groups Answering Each of Three Items Correctly

Group	Sample Size	Item Difficulty			Domain Score
		Easy	Medium	Hard	
A	20	20	20	20	1.00
B	20	20	20	20	1.00
C	20	20	20	20	1.00
D	20	20	20	0	.67
E	20	20	0	0	.33
Item p-value		1.00	.80	.60	

Note: From Hambleton, R.K., & deGruijter, D.N.M. Application of item response models to criterion-referenced test item selection. *Journal of Educational Measurement*, 1983, *20*, in press. Copyright 1983, National Council on Measurement in Education, Washington, D.C.

true masters from true nonmasters will be perfect! This example demonstrates clearly that test items selected because their difficulty levels match a cutoff score are not necessarily the best ones for enhancing the validity of classificatory decisions.

Classical item discrimination values have some usefulness in item selection. In general, items with high item-test score correlations (*r*-values) will be more useful than items with low *r* values. But from only the *p* and *r* values, the region on the domain score scale where an item functions (discriminates) best will be unknown. It is even possible that an item with a moderate *r* value but functioning optimally near π_o will be more useful in a test than an item with a high *r* value but which is *not* functioning optimally near π_o.

Item response models, unlike classical item statistics, appear useful to the problem of item selection because they lead to item statistics, which are reported on the same scale as examinee abilities and the chosen cutoff score. Thus, it becomes possible to select test items that are maximally discriminating in the region of the cutoff score.

The contribution of each test item to measurement precision, referred to as the *item information function*, is approximately given as

$$I_i(\theta) = \frac{[P_i'(\theta)]^2}{P_i(\theta)Q_i(\theta)}, \qquad (12.1)$$

where $P_i'(\theta)$ is the first derivative of $P_i(\theta)$ and $Q_i(\theta) = 1 - P_i(\theta)$. As given by equation (6.16) $I_i(\theta)$ has its maximum at the point θ^*, where

$$\theta_i^* = b_i + \frac{1}{Da_i} \ln .5(1 + \sqrt{1 + 8c_i}). \tag{12.2}$$

When $c_i = 0$, it can be seen from equation (12.2) that item i makes its biggest contribution to measurement precision at the point b_i on the ability scale.

The influence of an item's statistics on equation (12.1) can be seen if several substitutions offered by Lord (1980a) are used. Then,

$$I_i(\theta) = \frac{D^2 a_i^2(1 - c_i)}{(c + e^{Da_i(\theta - b_i)})(1 + e^{-Da_i(\theta - b_i)})^2} \tag{12.3}$$

(from Lord, 1980a, p. 61, Eq. 4–43). From a study of equation (12.3), it can be seen that highly discriminating items are more useful than lower discriminating items, and the lower the value of c, the more an item contributes to measurement precision regardless of the value of θ.

Once the item parameters are estimated and it can be determined that the chosen item response model provides an accurate accounting of the item performance data, θ_i^* and $I_i(\theta)$ provide the basic elements necessary for optimal item selection.

When the item parameters of all items from an item domain, or at least a large representative sample of items from the domain, are known, the relationship between domain scores, π, and latent ability scores, θ, can be specified. This is due to the fact that the domain score is defined as the expected score over all items from the domain (equation 4.10)

$$\pi = \frac{1}{n} \sum_{i=1}^{n} E(u_i | \theta). \tag{12.4}$$

With a large representative sample of items, the estimated relationship between π and θ is

$$\pi = \frac{1}{m} \sum_{i=1}^{m} P_i(\theta), \tag{12.5}$$

where m is the total number of test items in the sample (Lord, 1980a; Lord & Novick, 1968). The cutoff score, usually set on the π-scale (π_o), can be transformed to the θ-scale and vice-versa using equation (12.5). This results in a standard on the ability scale, θ_o.

The item selection problem is to find the smallest number of test items from an item pool to satisfy a specified criterion. With the Wilcox (1976) criterion, an indifference zone on the π-scale (π_1 to π_u) is specified. Within the indifference zone, the test designer is indifferent to misclassifications, but at π_l and π_u, a maximum acceptable probability for misclassifications is specified. The probabilities associated with incorrectly passing a nonmaster at π_1 (denoted P_1), or failing a master at π_u (denoted P_u) on an n-item test with a cutoff score C_x, can easily be computed with the aid of the binomial model (Wilcox, 1976). In order to implement the Wilcox method, it is necessary to set the maximum acceptable value for P_1 and P_u, denoted P^*. Finally, the minimum test length is the shortest test length for which

$$P_m = \max(P_l, P_u) \leq P^*.$$

Hambleton and deGruijter (1983) and deGruijter and Hambleton (1983) demonstrated the advantages of optimal over random item selection. Shorter tests can be used to achieve acceptable levels of misclassification when optimal items are selected. Item response models provide the necessary item statistics for item selection, while at the same time the use of complex item scoring weights associated with the more general item response models are *not* necessary.

The item selection method described in this section can easily be applied in practice. To derive the misclassification probabilities, it is necessary to assume that selected test items are homogeneous, i.e., equivalent statistically or substantial computational complexities will be encountered (Lord, 1980a). But, the assumption of item equivalence among selected test items seems reasonable since the intent of the optimum item selection algorithm is to choose test items that are optimally discriminating near the cutoff score. These items are apt to have relatively similar difficulty and discrimination indices. Of course, it is not necessary for the selected test items to be equivalent statistically to the remaining items in the pool. In fact, optimal item selection will be most effective when the selected items are substantially different from the remaining items in the pool.

Basically, the method of optimal item selection proceeds in the following manner:

1. Prepare a large bank of valid test items.
2. Obtain item response model parameter estimates with a large examinee sample.
3. Determine the fit between the item response model and the response data. Do not proceed if the fit is poor.
4. Choose a cutoff score and an indifference zone on the domain score scale.
5. Transform π_l, π_o, and π_u to θ_l, θ_o, and θ_u, respectively, with equation (12.5).
6. Set the value of P^*.
7. Identify the test item for selection providing the most information at θ_o with the aid of equation (12.2).

8. Transform θ_l, θ_o, and θ_u, to π_l^*, π_o^*, and π_u^*, respectively, using the test characteristic curve consisting of selected test items. Calculate P_1 and P_u and P_m (which is the maximum of P_1 and P_u) with several cutoff scores. Consider integers close to $\Sigma_{g=1}^n P_g(\theta_o)$ as possible cutoff scores.

9. If $P_m > P^*$, select the next test item providing the most information at θ_o. Repeat the calculations required in step 8. If $P_m \leq P^*$, the item selection process can be stopped. The test at this point meets the required specifications.

One legitimate criticism of the approach is that resulting tests, where items are selected on the basis of their statistical characteristics, may lack content validity. A similar criticism is made of adaptive tests. Of course, the item selection algorithm can be revised so that within the region of useful items, items are selected to enhance content validity. In addition, ultimately the ability estimates are interpreted in relation to the total pool of test items, which presumably was constructed to be content valid. If it can be demonstrated that the item response model fits the test data, then any set of test items will estimate the same ability parameter for an examinee. And, of course, if the model data fit is poor, then the model should not be used to aid in item selection anyway.

12.4 An Application of Item Response Theory to Norming

Item banks are used frequently at the classroom level by teachers in the construction of criterion-referenced tests (CRTs) or mastery tests or competency tests, as these tests are sometimes called (Popham, 1978). Teachers (or other test builders) can choose (1) the competencies they desire to measure in their tests and (2) corresponding sets of test items from their item banks to match the competencies of interest. These CRTs are typically used to assess student performance in relation to the competencies measured in the tests and to make instructional decisions. For example, an examinee's level of performance in relation to three objectives—A, B, C—might be 75 percent, 90 percent, and 60 percent, respectively. If the minimum performance level is set at 70 percent, then instructional decisions of the following type might be made: Pass the examinee on objectives A and B, and assign remedial instruction to the examinee on objective C.

One consequence, however, of providing teachers with the flexibility for constructing tests to meet their specific instructional needs is that norms tables cannot be provided at the local level since, in theory, each teacher will construct a different test. The loss of local normative information (or national norms in other situations) may be important since often school personnel, parents, and students desire such information and some United States governmental programs even require it for the purpose of program evaluation.

The problem faced by school districts who require information for (1) diagnosing and monitoring student performance in relation to competencies, and (2) comparing examinees, is, in one sense, easy to solve. Teachers can use their item banks to build criterion-referenced tests on an "as-needed" basis, and when derived scores are needed, they can administer appropriately chosen, commercially available, standardized norm-referenced tests. But this solution has problems: (1) The amount of testing time for students is increased, and (2) the financial costs of school testing programs is increased. Of course, the amount of time allocated for testing by a school district can be held constant, but when norm-referenced tests are administered, there will be less time available for criterion-referenced testing. A compromise solution adopted by many school districts is to select a suitable norm-referenced test to provide (1) normative scores and (2) criterion-referenced information through the interpretation of examinee performance on an item by item basis (Popham, 1978). But this solution does not lead to very suitable criterion-referenced measurements. It is unlikely that any norm-referenced test will measure all the competencies of immediate interest to a teacher, and those that are measured will be measured with only a few test items.

Hambleton (1980) suggested that item response models may be useful in helping to provide both instructional information and normative information from a single test. His solution requires a large pool of test items referenced to an ability scale (Lord, 1980a) and a set of norms prepared from the administration of a sample of items in the bank. The norms table can then be used successfully, subject to conditions that will be specified, with any tests that are constructed by drawing items from the bank. Generally speaking, examinee ability estimates are obtained from the administration of a set of test items of interest to a teacher, and then these ability estimates are used to predict examinee test scores on the set of test items that are in the normed test. With the predicted test scores in hand, norms tables can be used to locate corresponding percentiles, etc. In addition, teachers will have the performance levels of examinees on the competencies they chose to measure in their tests.

Local norms can be prepared by districts who build their own item banks, or test publishing companies can prepare national norms for selected tests constructed from their item banks. The quality of the normative information will depend on the "representativeness" of the examinee samples used in constructing the norms tables, the fit between items in the bank and the item response model used to construct the ability scale, the precision of the item parameter estimates, and the number and quality of items in the normed tests. With respect to the problem of model-data fit, it is especially important to address the invariance property of item parameters. For the normative information to be valuable, it is essential to show that the values of the item parameters are not dependent on (1) the time of the school year when the item parameters are estimated, (2) the types of instruction examinees in the population of interest receive, or (3) characteristics of the examinee samples in which items are calibrated such as race, sex, geographic region, ability level, etc.

An ability scale to which a large pool of test items are referenced can be very useful in providing norms for tests constructed by drawing items from the pool. Interestingly, a norms table (see table 12–2 for an example) can be prepared from the administration of only a sample of the items in the pool, while the norms table can be used successfully, subject to conditions to be specified later, with any tests constructed by drawing items from the pool.

Suppose a set of calibrated items[3] appropriate for a clearly identified population of examinees is drawn from an item pool and administered to a representative sample of the examinee population under standardized testing conditions. By utilizing the expression,

$$E(\hat{X}|\theta) = \sum_{i=1}^{n} P_i(\theta), \tag{12.6}$$

where n is the number of test items, and $E(\hat{X}|\theta)$ is the expected test score for an examinee with ability estimate $\hat{\theta}$, it is possible to obtain expected test scores. The accuracy of these predicted scores under a variety of conditions can be investigated by comparing the predicted scores to actual scores on the test. The prediction of a test score from a test characteristic curve is depicted in figure 12–1. It probably is clear to the reader that the expected test scores for an examinee on the set of items in the normed test is obtained by summing the probability for an examinee, with ability level, θ, answering each item correctly. Equation (12.6) provides a method for obtaining an expected score on the normed test for an examinee when an ability estimate is available. The mathematical form of the item characteristic curves in the expression is the user's choice. In theory, an examinee's ability in relation to any set of items drawn from the pool is the same. Of course, because of measurement errors, ability estimates obtained across different samples of test items will not be equal, but the expected value of each estimate is the same, i.e., the examinee's ability. In practice, from the examinee's responses to *any* set of test items drawn from the pool, an ability estimate is obtained, and by

Table 12-2. Conversion of Number-Right Scores to Percentile Rank and Normal Curve Equivalent Scores (Math, Grade 4)

Number Right	Fall Scores		Spring Scores		Number Right	Fall Scores		Spring Scores	
	PR	NCE	PR	NCE		PR	NCE	PR	NCE
80	99+	99.0	99+	99.0	40	9	21.8	5	15.4
79	99	99.0	98	93.3	39	8	20.4	4	13.1
78	97	89.6	96	86.9	38	8	20.4	4	13.1
77	95	84.6	91	78.2	37	7	18.9	3	10.4
76	93	81.1	86	72.8	36	6	17.3	3	10.4
75	90	77.0	81	68.5	35	6	17.3	2	6.7
74	87	73.7	75	64.2	34	5	15.4	2	6.7
73	84	70.9	70	61.0	33	4	13.1	2	6.7
72	81	68.5	65	58.1	32	4	13.1	2	6.7
71	78	66.3	60	55.3	31	3	10.4	2	6.7
70	75	64.2	56	53.2	30	3	10.4	2	6.7
69	72	62.3	52	51.1	29	3	10.4	2	6.7
68	69	60.4	48	48.9	28	2	6.7	1	1.0
67	66	58.7	45	47.4	27	2	6.7	1	1.0
66	64	57.5	41	45.2	26	2	6.7	1	1.0
65	61	55.9	38	43.6	25	2	6.7	1	1.0
64	59	54.8	36	42.5	24	2	6.7	1	1.0
63	56	53.2	33	40.7	23	1	1.0	1	1.0
62	54	52.1	31	39.6	22	1	1.0	1−	1.0
61	52	51.1	29	38.3	21	1	1.0	1−	1.0

(continued on next page)

Table 12-2 (continued)

Number Right	Fall Scores PR	Fall Scores NCE	Spring Scores PR	Spring Scores NCE
60	49	49.5	27	37.1
59	46	47.9	25	35.8
58	44	46.8	24	35.1
57	41	45.2	23	34.4
56	38	43.6	21	33.0
55	36	42.5	20	32.3
54	33	40.7	19	31.5
53	31	39.6	17	29.9
52	28	37.7	15	28.2
51	26	36.5	14	27.2
50	24	35.1	13	26.3
49	22	33.7	12	25.3
48	20	32.3	11	24.2
47	17	29.9	10	23.0
46	16	29.1	9	21.8
45	14	27.2	8	20.4
44	13	26.3	7	18.9
43	12	25.3	7	18.9
42	11	24.2	6	17.3
41	10	23.0	5	15.4

Number Right	Fall Scores PR	Fall Scores NCE	Spring Scores PR	Spring Scores NCE
20	1	1.0	1–	1.0
19	1–	1.0	1–	1.0
18	1–	1.0	1–	1.0
17	1–	1.0	1–	1.0
16	1–	1.0	1–	1.0
15	1–	1.0	1–	1.0
14	1–	1.0	1–	1.0
13	1–	1.0	1–	1.0
12	1–	1.0	1–	1.0
11	1–	1.0	1–	1.0
10	1–	1.0	1–	1.0
9	1–	1.0	1–	1.0
8	1–	1.0	1–	1.0
7	1–	1.0	1–	1.0
6	1–	1.0	1–	1.0
5	1–	1.0	1–	1.0
4	1–	1.0	1–	1.0
3	1–	1.0	1–	1.0
2	1–	1.0	1–	1.0
1	1–	1.0	1–	1.0
0	1–	1.0	1–	1.0

Note: From the *Individualized Criterion-Referenced Test Manual* (1980). Used by permission.

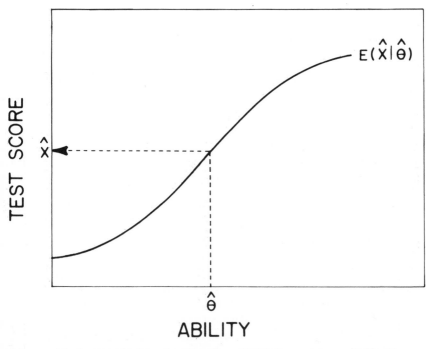

Figure 12-1. Predicting the Number Right Scores from Ability Scores and the Test Characteristic Curve

utilizing equation (12.6), an expected score on the items in the normed test is easily obtained. With the predicted raw score in hand for the examinee, the norms table can be used to obtain a percentile rank, normal curve equivalent, or whatever other derived scores are available in the table.

Why would anyone wish to administer a different set of test items from those that were normed? One reason is that instructors may wish to administer particular items to examinees because of their diagnostic value. A second reason is that with students who may be expected to do rather poorly or well on a test, better estimates of their abilities can be obtained when test items are selected to match their expected ability levels (Hambleton, 1979). Such a strategy is known as "out-of-level" testing.

A specific application of the method sketched out above will now be described. Educational Development Corporation (EDC), a test publishing company located in Tulsa, Oklahoma, publishes a set of 40 tests extending from kindergarten to grade 8 in the reading area. Each test consists of 16 test items measuring eight somewhat homogeneous objectives. So that school districts could use a selection of the tests to conduct Title I evaluations, it was necessary for EDC to compile national norms on the tests. Properly norming 40 tests, and many of the tests at several grade levels, would have been a monumental task. Instead, five tests were selected at each grade level to ensure substantial test score variability. The five 16-item tests, for the purpose of analysis, were then organized into one 80-item test. Percentile and normal curve equivalent score norms were prepared for the 80-item test at each of eight grade levels. On the average, about 1,200 students at each grade level were selected to be representative of students across the country. Details on the selection of districts, schools, and students are not needed here. It suffices to say that considerable effort was made to obtain appropriate samples of examinees.

One limitation of the general approach to norming described above is that school districts would be forced to use the 80 test items that were normed at each grade level to make use of the norm tables. This meant, for example, that out-of-level testing would not be possible since there would be no way to predict how students assigned test items to reflect their "instructional levels" would perform when they were administered the normed test items at their grade level. One solution to the problem (and to several others as well), and the one adopted by EDC, was to develop an ability scale to which all reading items in their 40 tests were referenced. When the reading test items can be fitted by an item response model, it is possible to predict how examinees would perform on any set of items of interest (in this case, the items of interest were those normed at each grade level) from ability estimates obtained from the administered items.

The continuous scale in the reading area was developed with the aid of the Rasch model. The Rasch model in recent years has been used frequently to "link" test items together to form a ability scale. The details for carrying out this statistical process are described by Wright and Stone (1979).

Item response data in reading collected in 1978 and 1979 were available on over 200,000 students. Each student was administered five tests (80 test items), but the choice of tests varied widely from one school district to the next and from grade to grade. This was fortunate because the multitude of combination of tests taken made it possible to locate some "linking" tests. For example, if district A administers tests 1 to 5, and district B administers tests 4 to 8, either test 4 or 5 can be used as a 16-item "linking" test between the two sets of tests. The following approach for obtaining item difficulty estimates on a common scale was followed:

1. Arrange the test booklets in numerical sequence (which correspond, approximately, to test booklet difficulty).

2. Fit the Rasch model to the first l test booklets (for reading, l had a value of 4) and obtain item difficulty estimates.
3. Take the next $(l - 1)$ test booklets in the sequence and the last booklet from the previous sequence (this booklet is called the "linking" test) and fit the Rasch model to obtain item difficulty estimates.
4. In order to place item difficulty estimates obtained from steps 2 and 3 on a common scale, the difference in the average item difficulty for the one test booklet common to the two sets of test booklets is obtained, and then the value of the difference is used to adjust all item difficulties in the second set.
5. Steps 3 and 4 are repeated until all test booklets are analyzed and item difficulty estimates are obtained on a common scale.

With the availability of item difficulty estimates referenced to a common scale, via the methods described in chapter 10, it is then possible to obtain ability estimates that do not depend on the particular choice of test items (Wright, 1977a). Subsequently, it is possible to predict student performance on the set of tests normed at each student's grade level.

Once the ability, θ, and the grade level to which the comparison is to be made are specified, it is possible to estimate the score the examinee would have obtained if he or she had taken the 80 test items normed at that grade level. Again, let $b_1, b_2, \ldots, b_{80}$ denote the difficulties of the 80 test items normed at the grade level. Then, the estimate of the number right score, $\hat{x}$, the individual would have obtained on the 80 test items is given by

$$\hat{x} = \sum_{i=1}^{80} \frac{e^{D(\hat{\theta}-b_i)}}{1 + e^{D(\hat{\theta}-b_i)}} \qquad (12.7)$$

Each of the terms corresponds to the probability of an examinee with ability $\hat{\theta}$ answering a particular item correctly. The expression is similar in interpretation to equation (12.6).

Once $\hat{x}$ is computed and rounded off to the nearest integer, the percentile rank or other available derived scores corresponding to the expected number correct score can be obtained from the norm tables. Another of the features of item response model analyses is that an indication of the precision (or standard error) of each ability estimate is available. If percentile bands are of interest, they can easily be constructed by determining the expected test scores corresponding to the ability estimates, $\hat{\theta} + 1$ SE and $\hat{\theta} - 1$ SE. Percentile scores corresponding to these two expected test scores provide the end points of an approximately 68 percent confidence band for the true score of an examinee with ability $\hat{\theta}$.

In this section the problem of providing normative information via the use of item response theory, ability scales, and standard norming methods has been discussed. The fit between the one-parameter model and the test data was surprisingly good in this one application. (For example, the correlation between the item difficulty estimates for fall and spring test data was .993.) Of course, much additional validation work is needed to determine the ultimate worth of this type of application with any of the test item response models. Moreover, it might be worthy of mention that the norms tables could also be set up using the ability scale metric, and the application would be somewhat easier. The disadvantage is that many tests and measurement people would not feel as comfortable working with the ability scale as the test score scale.

12.5 Evaluation of a Test Score Prediction System[4]

In the last section, an application of item response models to item banking and norming was described. However, with respect to that initial study relatively little was done to evaluate the accuracy of the predicted test scores.

The principal purpose of the investigation described in this section was to evaluate normed test score predictions through the use of item response models with reading, language arts, and mathematics tests at two grade levels. The accuracy of predictions from tests that were relatively easy, comparable in difficulty, and relatively difficult in relation to the normed tests was compared. This component was added to the Hambleton-Martois study because it seemed desirable to address the quality of normed test score predictions as a function of the difference in difficulty between tests constructed by teachers and the normed tests. A secondary purpose was to compare normed test score predictions with the one- and three-parameter logistic models. This comparison was conducted because there is substantial interest in the relative merits of these two models for various applications.

12.5.1 Method

The item banks used in the study were compiled over a four-year period by the Los Angeles County Education Center. Four 50-item achievement tests were constructed from each item bank. For the purposes of this study, these four tests were labeled "normed," "easy," "medium," and "hard." The normed test for each grade and content area was constructed by selecting test items from the appropriate test item bank to reflect, to the extent possible, school curricula. Items for the easy, medium, and hard tests were drawn from the same item banks as the normed tests and generally reflected the same content coverage. The easy, medium, and hard tests, as their names might suggest, were constructed to be relatively easy, comparable in difficulty, and relatively difficult, respectively, in relation to the normed tests. Item difficulties for the most part were judgmentally determined by curriculum specialists, but some item statistics were available to assist the test development teams. In total, 24 tests were constructed and administered as part of the study: three content areas (reading, language arts, and mathematics) $\times$ two grade levels (2, 5) $\times$ four tests (normed, easy, medium, and hard).

Each participating examinee in the spring of 1981 was administered the three normed achievement tests at his or her grade level, and *one* of the additional nine available tests for the grade level (3 content areas $\times$ 3 levels of test difficulty). The assignment of the additional test to examinees was carried out on a random basis within each classroom.

The 81 schools participating in the study were selected to be representative of the schools in the United States. Factors such as district and school size, racial composition, and geographic location were considered in school site selection.

In each content area and at each grade level, a total of 200 test items were included in the test administrations. Item parameter statistics for the 200 items in each bank were obtained from LOGIST (Wood, Wingersky, & Lord, 1976). Two LOGIST features were especially useful: (1) LOGIST can be used to obtain both one-parameter and three-parameter model item parameter estimates, and (2) LOGIST can handle the problem of missing (omitted) data, and so it is possible to organize the examinee response data in an m (total number of examinees) $\times$ k (total number of test items in an item bank) matrix and obtain parameter estimates for all test items in a single analysis. Thus, even though examinees were administered only a subset of the test items from the item bank (in this study, 100 test items), by treating examinee answers to the remaining 100 test items as "omits," all item parameter estimates could be obtained on a common scale in a single LOGIST analysis. This second feature, described by Lord (1974a), made it possible to avoid the troublesome task of calibrating test items by considering two tests at a time, and later, by linking all item parameter estimates to a common scale.

The actual numbers of examinees used in item calibration are given below:

Area	Grade	Level	Sample Size for Item Calibration
Reading	2	Normed	2,370
		Easy	1,376
		Medium	177
		Hard	1,307
	5	Normed	3,028
		Easy	1,493
		Medium	203
		Hard	1,616
Language Arts	2	Normed	2,441
		Easy	1,355
		Medium	168
		Hard	1,264
	5	Normed	2,804
		Easy	1,388
		Medium	196
		Hard	1,556
Mathematics	2	Normed	2,635
		Easy	1,352
		Medium	146
		Hard	1,356
	5	Normed	2,843
		Easy	1,399
		Medium	188
		Hard	1,892

Several criteria were used to evaluate the accuracy of normed test score predictions:

$$\bar{E} = \frac{\sum_{i=1}^{N} (X_i - X_i')}{N} \tag{12.8}$$

$$|\bar{E}| = \frac{\sum_{i=1}^{N} |X_i - X_i'|}{N} \tag{12.9}$$

In the criteria above, X is the test score for examinee i on a normed test, X' is the predicted test score for examinee i on the same normed test (the prediction is made from expression (12.6) using item parameter estimates for the normed test items, and an ability estimate obtained from administering either the easy, medium, or difficult test to the examinee), and N is the number of examinees. Statistic (12.8) provided information about the direction and size of the bias in the prediction of normed test score performance. Statistic (12.9) reflected the average value of the size of the errors in prediction without regard for the direction of the prediction errors. The average absolute deviation statistic is a practical way for summarizing the accuracy of test score predictions with the item response models.

12.5.2 Results

Descriptive Statistical Test Information. Table 12-3 provides the statistical information on the 24 tests in the study for the samples of examinees used to evaluate the accuracy of normed test score predictions. Reliability estimates for the tests ranged from .63 to .91, with 20 of the 24 estimates above .80. The lowest reliability estimates were associated with the most homogeneous test score distributions. The means for the normed and medium difficult tests were always between the means for the easy and difficult tests, but for some groups of tests the order of difficulty was reversed, and, even more importantly, the difference in difficulty between the easy and hard tests varied substantially from one group of tests to another. For example, with the grade 2 reading tests, the maximum difference in means was only 4.0 points, whereas with the grade 5 mathematics tests, the maximum difference was 11.8 points. When the means for the easy and hard tests are close, it is not possible to properly investigate the effects of test difficulty (in relation to the difficulty of the normed test) on the accuracy of predictions. For this reason, the mathematics tests were the most useful and the reading tests the least useful for investigating the influence of test difficulty on the accuracy of predictions. Also, because the grade 5 tests were somewhat more difficulty than the grade 2 tests, they provided a better basis for comparing the one- and three-parameter models.

The one- and three-parameter logistic models are based on the strong assumption of test unidimensionality. To facilitate the interpretation of prediction errors, it was desirable to have information on the extent to which prediction errors may, at least in part, be due to violations of the unidimensionality assumption in the test data. In addition, to assist in the interpretation of results comparing predictions from the one- and three-

Table 12-3. Descriptive Statistics on the 24, 50-Item Achievement Tests

Area	Grade	Level	Number of Examinees	Mean	Standard Deviation	Reliability*	SE_{meas}
Reading	2	Normed	2370	38.6	9.3	.90	3.0
		Easy	173	41.5	3.8	.63	2.3
		Medium	177	39.3	7.4	.88	2.6
		Hard	135	37.5	9.6	.91	2.9
	5	Normed	3028	30.1	10.6	.86	4.0
		Easy	215	34.7	10.6	.86	4.0
		Medium	203	32.3	10.9	.88	3.8
		Hard	214	27.9	11.4	.87	4.1
Language Arts	2	Normed	2441	38.3	8.2	.87	3.0
		Easy	123	39.6	7.9	.85	3.1
		Medium	168	37.1	8.3	.85	3.2
		Hard	110	29.8	8.2	.83	3.4
	5	Normed	2804	28.2	8.9	.83	3.7
		Easy	180	32.7	10.0	.88	3.5
		Medium	196	29.3	10.1	.87	3.6
		Hard	196	25.6	8.7	.84	3.5
Mathematics	2	Normed	2635	37.2	7.4	.80	3.3
		Easy	96	41.7	4.5	.70	2.5
		Medium	146	34.9	7.5	.82	3.2
		Hard	146	29.9	7.8	.81	3.4
	5	Normed	2843	21.4	8.6	.78	4.0
		Easy	188	29.6	9.7	.85	3.8
		Medium	188	27.0	10.4	.86	3.9
		Hard	182	17.8	7.0	.76	3.4

*Corrected split-half reliability estimates.

parameter models, it was useful to have information about the extent to which the assumption of equal item discrimination indices was violated in the test data. Tables 12–4 and 12–5 provide information pertaining to the dimensionality of the tests and the distributions of item point-biserial correlations, respectively. If the criteria developed by Reckase (1979) for describing test dimensionality are used, then, clearly, all the tests approach closely or exceed his minimum values for the adequacy of the uni-dimensionality assumption. His criteria are based on a consideration of the

Table 12-4. Summary of Eigenvalues for the 24, 50-Item Achievement Tests

Area	Grade	Level	Largest Eigenvalues λ_1	λ_2	λ_3	Var. on First Factor	$\dfrac{\lambda_1}{\lambda_2}$
Reading	2	Normed	12.12	1.93	1.43	24%	6.28
		Easy	8.75	2.76	1.96	18	2.96
		Medium	8.41	2.22	2.10	17	3.79
		Hard	11.95	1.93	1.55	24	6.19
	5	Normed	11.00	2.00	1.41	22	5.50
		Easy	11.88	1.94	1.46	24	6.12
		Medium	11.81	1.97	1.88	24	5.99
		Hard	11.68	1.87	1.40	23	6.25
Language	2	Normed	9.60	1.96	1.36	19	4.90
		Easy	10.88	1.99	1.44	22	5.47
		Medium	9.60	2.42	2.08	19	3.97
		Hard	8.56	1.63	1.39	17	5.25
	5	Normed	7.71	1.88	1.38	15	4.10
		Easy	9.23	1.78	1.56	19	5.19
		Medium	9.54	2.01	1.83	19	4.75
		Hard	8.18	1.60	1.36	16	5.11
Mathematics	2	Normed	7.70	1.92	1.73	15	4.01
		Easy	7.52	2.15	1.75	15	3.49
		Medium	8.12	2.78	2.42	17	2.92
		Hard	8.31	1.90	1.54	17	4.37
	5	Normed	7.33	2.01	1.83	15	3.65
		Easy	8.29	1.96	1.63	15	4.23
		Medium	9.59	2.08	1.85	19	4.61
		Hard	10.33	1.87	1.55	21	5.52

Table 12-5.   Summary of Item Point-Biserial Correlations

			Point-Biserial Correlations*				
Area	Grade	Level	$\overline{X}$	SD	Min.	Max.	Range
Reading	2	Normed	.47	.11	.17	.65	.48
		Easy	.38	.13	.07	.60	.53
		Medium	.39	.12	.07	.61	.54
		Hard	.46	.09	.23	.62	.39
	5	Normed	.45	.11	.15	.65	.50
		Easy	.49	.09	.22	.62	.40
		Medium	.47	.10	.26	.67	.41
		Hard	.47	.10	.15	.64	.49
Language Arts	2	Normed	.43	.08	.21	.59	.38
		Easy	.45	.12	.18	.66	.48
		Medium	.42	.11	.19	.66	.47
		Hard	.41	.08	.24	.58	.34
	5	Normed	.37	.09	.08	.54	.46
		Easy	.41	.11	.00	.58	.58
		Medium	.42	.12	.10	.60	.50
		Hard	.39	.10	.08	.55	.47
Mathematics	2	Normed	.38	.09	.12	.54	.42
		Easy	.37	.12	.13	.58	.45
		Medium	.38	.16	−.03	.59	.62
		Hard	.39	.10	.13	.53	.40
	5	Normed	.36	.11	−.02	.52	.54
		Easy	.39	.10	−.02	.53	.55
		Medium	.42	.10	.06	.59	.53
		Hard	.44	.11	.18	.65	.47

*Strictly speaking, it is incorrect to treat correlation coefficients as if they were on an equal interval scale. However, it seemed reasonable to make the assumption here since, for the most part, all correlations were on the same portion of the scale (~.00 to .67), and only a rough indication of the variability of point-biserial correlations was needed.

proportion of variance associated with the first eigenvalue and the ratio of the first to the second eigenvalue of the interitem correlation matrix.

The item point-biserial correlations reported in table 12–5 revealed substantial variation among the items in each test. Such a result would suggest that the three-parameter model should provide a better fit to the test data than the one-parameter model and produce somewhat better test score predictions.

Predictions of Normed Test Score Performance. The main results of the study as reported in table 12–6 reveal several important findings:

1. There is almost no bias in test score predictions with the one-parameter model. The average prediction error ranged from $-.04$ to $.10$. The average size of the bias in prediction errors was somewhat higher with the three-parameter model, and the direction of the bias was associated with the difficulty of the tests used to obtain ability estimates. The average bias ranged from $-.41$ to $.31$. The errors were generally negative for predictions using the easy tests (the predictions were, on the average, too high) and positive for predictions using the hard tests (the predictions were, on the average, too low).

Table 12-6. Summary of Normed Test Score Predictions

				Evaluation Criteria			
				One-Parameter Model		Three-Parameter Model	
Area	Grade	Level	Sample Size	$\bar{E}$	$|\bar{E}|$	$\bar{E}$	$|\bar{E}|$
Reading	2	Easy	142	$-.03$	1.38	$-.41$	1.66
		Middle	173	.00	1.73	.10	1.80
		Hard	124	$-.03$	1.60	.31	1.53
	5	Easy	214	$-.02$	2.47	$-.18$	2.74
		Middle	203	$-.03$	2.17	.01	2.31
		Hard	214	.02	2.29	.19	2.25
Language Arts	2	Easy	123	$-.03$	1.73	$-.15$	1.92
		Middle	167	.00	1.45	.13	1.53
		Hard	108	.08	1.63	.19	1.49
	5	Easy	179	$-.02$	2.11	$-.08$	2.33
		Middle	196	.00	2.04	.11	2.17
		Hard	195	.02	2.06	$-.05$	1.96
Math	2	Easy	96	$-.04$	1.42	.00	1.55
		Middle	145	.00	1.64	$-.06$	1.82
		Hard	145	.10	1.71	.14	1.41
	5	Easy	188	$-.02$	2.26	.27	2.51
		Middle	189	.00	2.29	$-.02$	2.39
		Hard	181	.02	2.07	$-.32$	1.72

2. The information provided by the summary statistic $|\bar{E}|$ suggested that both the one- and three-parameter models resulted in what seemed to be quite accurate predictions.

3. With the one- and three-parameter models, the standard error of prediction (standard deviation of prediction errors) across the 18 data sets ranged from 1.79 to 3.24 and 1.76 to 3.63, respectively.

4. Across all 18 predictor tests, the predictions were slightly better with the one-parameter model (the average value of $|\bar{E}|$ was 1.89 as compared to 1.94 with the three-parameter model). However, there was a clear pattern in the differences that did exist. The one-parameter model did a somewhat better job with the easy and medium difficult tests, and the three-parameter model performed better than the one-parameter model with the hard tests. Not only did the three-parameter model result in reduced prediction errors over the one-parameter model for all six difficult tests, but the improvements were largest for those difficult tests that differed most from the means of the normed tests to which predictions were made (see the mathematics tests).

12.5.3 Conclusions from the Study

The results from this study showed clearly that when item response model assumptions are met, at least to an adequate degree, item response models can be used to predict normed test score performance from samples of test items that vary to a moderate degree in difficulty from the normed test. Thus, it would appear that item response models may be useful with item banks to permit the accurate prediction of score performance on one set of test items from examinee performance on another set of test items in the same bank as long as the total set of items in the bank can be fitted by an item response model and the number of test items in each test is not too small or the two samples of test items do not differ too much in difficulty. The extent of differences in test difficulty that can be tolerated was not addressed in the study. This area needs to be investigated in subsequent research.

At the individual score level, the average prediction error was typically between 2 and 3 points (maximum test score = 50 points). This size of prediction error seems tolerable for many uses of individual test scores. When group information is of most concern to the user, the results reported in this study suggest that X and X' will be very close (as reflected in the bias statistics) and that program evaluation uses of the predicted normed test scores, therefore, will suffice, in most cases, for the actual test scores. But the generalizability of this conclusion must await additional evidence.

Overall, the one- and three-parameter model predictions were similar, although the three-parameter model did a better job with the hard tests and the one-parameter model did a better job with easy and medium difficult tests. It was surprising to observe the one-parameter model performing better than the three-parameter model with several of the test data sets since there is no theoretical reason to expect such a result. There are two plausible explanations: First, sample sizes for the medium difficult tests were definitely too small to result in suitable item parameter estimates. The problem of small examinee samples would be most acute for the three-parameter model. Second, three-parameter model item parameter estimates (especially the pseudochance level parameters) may not have been estimated properly with the easy and medium difficult tests because there were relatively few examinees with low test scores (see, for example, Hambleton, 1983b). Although item response model parameters are invariant across different samples of examinees from the population of examinees for whom the test items are intended, suitable item parameter estimation with the three-parameter model requires a reasonable sample size and a substantial number of examinees toward the lower end of the ability continuum. Otherwise, the c parameters cannot be estimated properly; when the c parameters are not estimated properly, problems arise in the estimation of the other two item parameters as well. Possibly, then, methodological shortcomings in the study were responsible for the observed advantages of the one-parameter model with the easy and medium-difficult tests.

How well the type of item response model application described in this section will work in practice remains to be assessed. If, for example, the amount and/or the type of instruction influences item calibration, the usefulness of the item statistics and associated predictions will be limited. The problem is apt to be more acute with achievement tests (CRTs, for example) than with aptitude tests because achievement tests are more likely to be influenced by the instruction to which they are more closely tied. The problem of item x instruction interaction has not been encountered to any extent because most of the IRT applications have been conducted to date with aptitude tests.

Notes

1. This section is based on material found in Hambleton and deGruijter (1983).
2. In a pool of "statistically heterogeneous" items, items vary substantially in their difficulty levels and discriminating power.
3. Calibrated items are those for which item parameter estimates are available.
4. This section is based on material found in Hambleton and Martois (1983).

13 MISCELLANEOUS APPLICATIONS

13.1 Introduction

The purpose of this chapter is to describe briefly four additional promising applications of IRT models: Item bias, adaptive testing, differential weighting of response alternatives, and estimation of power scores.

13.2 Item Bias

The fact that certain items in a test may be biased against certain groups has become a matter of considerable concern to the examinees, the users of tests, and the testing community (Berk, 1982). While the existence of item and test bias has been acknowledged for some time, until recently there has been little agreement regarding the definition of item and test bias on the part of measurement specialists and legal experts. Consequently, the procedures for detecting item bias have been flawed.

The most extreme definition of item and test bias is that a test is biased to the extent that the means of two populations of interest are different. The obvious problem with this definition is that other variables besides item bias contribute to these differences (see Hunter, 1975). By this definition a measuring stick is biased because it shows that females are, on the average, shorter than males.

A second definition of item bias that can be advanced is that an item is unbiased if the item difficulty index (or p value) for one population is the same as that for the second population of interest. This definition raises the same difficulty as the one given above. Angoff (1982b) has indicated that the disparity that may be found between the p value for the two populations may be the result of social and educational bias. If the content of the test is reflective of general educational bias, then item bias should be based on item-group interaction (Angoff, 1982b).

The definition of item bias in terms of item-group interaction has also been suggested by Cleary and Hilton (1968). In this method a comparison is made between groups of interest in their performance on the test item and the total test. When the patterns are different, as they are in illustrations (1) and (2) in figure 13-1, items are suspected as being biased. However, Hunter (1975) has clearly pointed out that a perfectly unbiased test can show item-group interaction if the items are of varying item difficulty.

By considering the item difficulties for the two groups and taking into account the variation among the item difficulties within each group, the objection raised with the Cleary-Hilton definition of item bias may be overcome. The import of these observations leads to a further refined definition of item bias. When a set of items is unbiased, it is reasonable to expect the rank ordering of the p-values to be the same for two groups. A more stringent expectation is that the correlation between the p-values is one. When this happens all the p values lie on a straight line. In this case it could be said that the items are unbiased (or, equally biased). Thus items that do not fall on the best fitting line of the scatterplot of item difficulty values may be taken as biased items.

Lord (1980a, p. 214) has demonstrated that a plot of the p-values will necessarily be non-linear. This is because the line connecting the p-values should pass through the point $(1, 1)$ for the item which is answered correctly by everyone in the two groups and through $(0, 0)$, or through (c, c) where c is the chance level, for the item that is most difficult for everyone in the two groups. If the two groups were of equal ability, then p-values would fall on the $45°$ line joining $(0, 0)$, or (c, c) to $(1, 1)$. However, if the two groups were different in ability level, with one group consistently doing better than the other group, then the points would fall on a curve.

This problem of non-linearity can be overcome partly through an inverse normal transformation of the p value. The resulting Δ values yield the Δ-plot (Angoff & Ford, 1973, Angoff, 1982b). Instead of obtaining a regression line

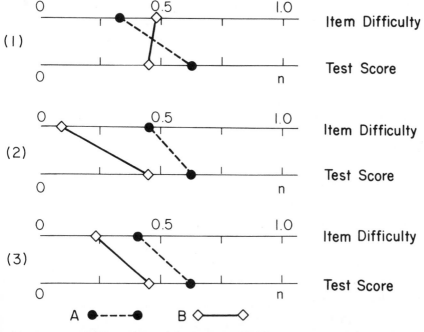

Figure 13-1. Detection of Biased Items Using the Item x Test Score Interaction Method. Compared to overall test performance of the two groups, in (1) the pattern of item performance is reversed, in (2) the difference in item performance is substantially greater, and in (3) the pattern of item performance is parallel

(for reasons indicated in section 10.6), the principal axis of the bivariate Δ-plot is determined. An item whose perpendicular distance from this line is large suggests that the item has different difficulties in the two populations relative to the other items, and hence is biased. Lord (1980a) and Angoff (1982b), however, point out that the failure of points to lie on a straight line could be attributed to such factors as guessing, and variations in item discrimination and ability differences between the groups, rather than to item bias. Lord (1980a, p. 127) notes that the item difficulties " . . . however, transformed, are not really suitable for studying item bias."

One definition of item bias that shows promise is

A test item is unbiased if all individuals having the same underlying ability have equal probability of getting the item correct, regardless of subgroup membership. (Pine, 1977)

This definition has obvious implications in terms of item response theory. However, non-item-response theoretic procedures based on the above definition have been given by Scheunemann (1979), and Shepard, Camilli, & Averill (1981). With these procedures, an item is defined as biased if individuals from different populations, but who have the same total score on the test, have different probabilities of responding correctly to that item. Clearly this approach is an approximation to the item response theoretic approach in that the total score rather than the ability is used.

The procedure proposed by Camilli (Shepard et al., 1981) involves dividing the total score range into J discrete intervals, (usually five) while ensuring that there are sufficient number of observations within each score interval. For item i, the following two-way classification is obtained for score interval j ($j = 1, \ldots, J$).

		Population 1	Population 2	Total
	Correct	N_{11j}	N_{12j}	$N_{1.j}$
Item i	Incorrect	N_{21j}	N_{22j}	$N_{2.j}$
	TOTAL	$N_{.1j}$	$N_{.2j}$	N_j

This yields the chi-square value for item i, for interval j;

$$\chi^2_{ij} = N_j(N_{11j}N_{22j} - N_{21j}N_{12j})^2/(N_{1.j}N_{2.j}N_{.1j}N_{.2j}) \qquad (13.1)$$

The chi-square value for item i is the sum across the J intervals, i.e.

$$\chi^2_i = \sum_{j=1}^{J}\chi^2_{ij}, \qquad (13.2)$$

and may be taken as a measure of bias for item i. The above quantity is approximately distributed as a chi-square with J degrees of freedom. The procedure generalizes immediately to k populations in which case the degrees of freedom is $J(k - 1)$. Using this method, bias of an item can be studied either at each level of the total score or at the aggregate level.

This procedure, known as a full chi-square method, is a modification of the procedure proposed by Scheuneman (1979) who compared the populations with respect to only the proportion of correct responses. The test statistic used by Scheuneman (for two populations) is

$$\chi_i^2 = \sum_{j=1}^{J} (N_{11j}N_{22j} - N_{21j}N_{12j})^2 / (N_{.1j}N_{.2j}N_{1.j})$$

$$(13.3)$$

and is distributed as a chi-square with J-1 degrees of freedom. Since this procedure lacks symmetry with respect to the frequency of incorrect responses, the Camilli approach is preferable.

Ironson (1982, 1983) has pointed out the problems inherent in the above mentioned procedures. The arbitrariness involved in the designation of intervals for the total score may have dramatic effect on the outcome. Furthermore, the chi-square statistics are sensitive to sample size and the cell sizes. Despite these drawbacks, this procedure can be effectively used at least at a descriptive level.

The definition of item bias in terms of the probability of correct response can be restated in terms of item response theory. Since the probability of correct response is given by the item characteristic curve, it follows that

> A test item is unbiased if the item characteristic curves across different subgroups are identical.

This means that item characteristic curves, which provide the probabilities of correct responses, must be identical, apart from sampling error, across different populations of interest. This situation is represented in figure 13-2. This further implies that when the item characteristic curves are the same, the item parameters have the same values for the groups. Figure 13-3 and 13-4 reflect two patterns of results reflecting bias. In the first, group 1 consistently performs below group 2 at all levels of θ. In the second, the pattern of bias is reversed at the two ends of the ability scale.

Shepard et al. (1981) and Ironson (1982, 1983) have provided a review of procedures based on item response theory for assessing the bias of an item. The major procedures fall into the following three categories:

1. Comparison of item characteristic curves;
2. Comparison of the vectors of item parameters;
3. Comparison of the fit of the item response models to the data.

Comparison of Item Characteristic Curves

As illustrated in figure 13-2 when an item is unbiased the item characteristic curves for the subpopulations will be identical. However, as a result of sampling fluctuations, the *estimated* item characteristic curves may not be identical even when the item is unbiased.

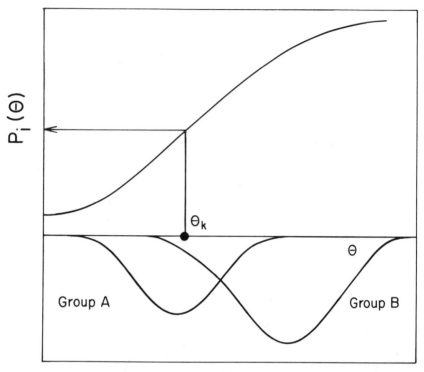

Figure 13-2.   Identical Item Characteristic Curve for Two Ability Groups

One measure of the difference between the item characteristic curves, when there are two groups, is the area between the two curves introduced by Rudner (1977) (see figure 13-5). To determine the area between the two curves, the following procedure is followed:

1. An appropriate item response model is chosen.
2. The item and ability parameters are estimated separately for the two groups (Chapter 7).
3. Since the two groups are calibrated separately, the item and ability parameters have to be placed on a common scale. However, such scaling is not required in this situation since the procedure involves determining the probabilities at various values of θ and these probabilities are invariant with respect to scale transformations. There is no harm in scaling the parameters and this may be advisable if different methods of

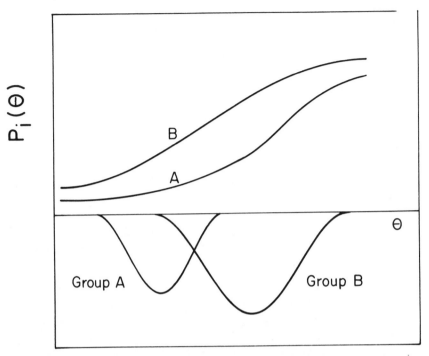

$P_i(\Theta)$

Figure 13-3.   Biased Item Against Group A At All Ability Levels

assessing item bias are studied. The direct method is to estimate the parameters separately for each group with standardizing being done on the b_i. This places all the item parameters on the same scale (compare this with the Single Group Design of section 10.5). If the standardizing is done on the θ then scaling is necessary. In this case an equating procedure (preferably the characteristic curve method) outlined in section 10.6 should be used.

4.   The ability scale say, from -3 to $+3$ is divided into intervals of width $\Delta\theta$ (e.g., $\Delta\theta = .005$).

5.   The value of θ_k in the center of interval k is determined, and the heights of the two item characteristic curves, $P_{i1}(\theta_k)$ and $P_{i2}(\theta_k)$ are calculated.

6.   The difference in the area defined as

$$A_{1i} = \sum_{\theta=-3}^{+3} |P_{i1}(\theta_k) - P_{i2}(\theta_k)| \Delta\theta \qquad (13.4)$$

is calculated (Rudner, 1977).

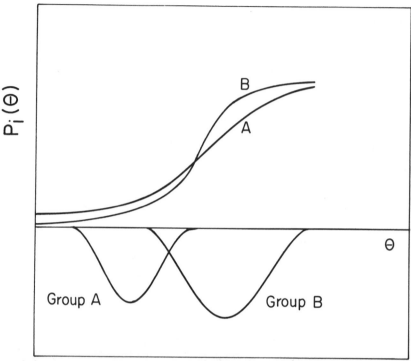

Figure 13-4. Biased Item Against Group B for Low Ability Levels; Biased Item Against Group A for High Ability Levels

Once A_{1i} is computed, a decision can be made regarding the bias present in an item. If A_{1i} is "small," bias is small, while if A_{1i} is "large," bias may be present.

Linn et al. (1981) have suggested an alternative measure of the difference between the item characteristic curves. Their measure, A_{2i}, is defined as

$$A_{2i} = \sum_{\theta=-3}^{3} \{[P_{i1}(\theta_k) - P_{i2}(\theta_k)]^2 \Delta\theta\}^{\frac{1}{2}} \qquad (13.5)$$

Linn et al. (1981) have pointed out that neither of the two measures defined above take into account the fact that the item characteristic curve is estimated with differing errors at different levels of θ. To compensate for this, these authors have suggested weighting the item characteristic curve values,

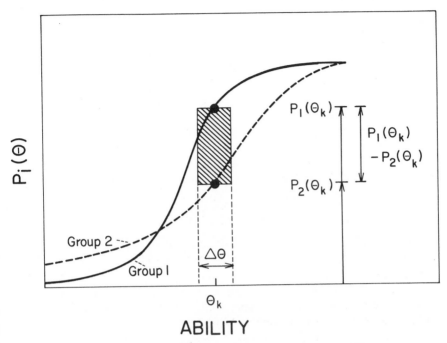

ABILITY

Figure 13-5. "Area Method" for Assessing Item Bias

$P_i(\theta_k)$, by the standard error of estimate of $P_i(\theta_k)$ at the various values of θ_k. The resulting measure of area reflects the accuracy of estimation of $P_i(\theta_k)$.

Levine, Wardrop and Linn (1982) have pointed out a further problem. Depending upon the use to which the test score is put (e.g., college admission vs. selection for scholarship), bias at different levels of θ may have different implications. These authors have suggested using weights to reflect the importance of the decision that is made. For example, if bias at a medium ability level is critical, more weight could be given at this value of θ and bias assessed.

These methods for weighting the item response function are beyond the level of the current presentation. Further details can be found in Linn et al. (1981), and Levine et al. (1982). A further point that is noteworthy is that these measures of the differences between item characteristic curves are descriptive. The importance of significance tests for these measures is clear. Work on this problem is now underway by Levine and his colleagues at the University of Illinois.

Comparison of Item Parameters

It follows that two item characteristic curves are identical across groups if and only if the item parameters that describe the curves are identical across groups. Thus bias can be established by determining if the item parameters are equal across subgroups. In the most general case, there are three item parameters for each item and these should be compared (preferably) simultaneously across the groups. The simultaneous comparison can be carried out using standard multivariate techniques.

If the vector valued random variable x of dimension $(px1)$ has a multivariate normal distribution with mean vector τ and variance-covariance matrix V, then the quadratic form

$$Q = (x - \tau)'V^{-1}(x - \tau) \tag{13.6}$$

has a chi-square distribution with degrees of freedom p (Rao, 1965, p. 443). Here x' is the $(1xp)$ vector, the transpose of x, and V^{-1} is the inverse of V. Furthermore, let x_1 and x_2 be two independent multivariate normally distributed random vectors with mean vectors τ_1 and τ_2 and variance-covariance matrices V_1 and V_2, respectively. If $x = x_1 - x_2$, then $\tau = \tau_1 - \tau_2$ and $V = V_1 + V_2$. Hence equation (13.6) becomes

$$Q = [(x_1 - x_2) - (\tau_1 - \tau_2)]'[V_1 + V_2]^{-1}[(x_1 - x_2) - \tau_1 - \tau_2)]. \tag{13.7}$$

If the hypothesis of interest is

$$H_0:\tau_1 = \tau_2, \tag{13.8}$$

then the test statistic Q reduces to

$$Q = (x_1 - x_2)'(V_1 + V_2)^{-1}(x_1 - x_2). \tag{13.9}$$

The quantity Q has a chi-square distribution with p degrees of freedom. If the calculated value of Q exceeds the tabulated chi-square value at a given level of significance, the hypothesis is rejected.

In item response models, the vectors τ_{1i} and τ_{2i} are the vectors of item parameters for item i in groups one and two respectively. The vectors x_{1i} and x_{2i} are the vectors of the estimates of item parameters for item i. The definition of item bias introduced in this section requires that the item be considered biased if the hypothesis

$$H_0: \tau_{1i} = \tau_{2i} \qquad (i = 1, \dots, n)$$

is rejected in favor of the alternate hypothesis

$$H_1: \tau_{1i} \neq \tau_{2i}.$$

As discussed in Chapter 7, the vector of maximum likelihood estimators of item parameters x_i for item i has an asymptotic multivariate normal distribution with a mean vector equal to the item parameter values. The variance-covariance matrix of the estimates is the inverse of the Information matrix whose elements are given by equation (7.21) and (7.22). Exact expressions for these elements are given in table 7-2. By substituting the values of the estimates of the item and ability parameters for each of the two groups in the expression, the Information matrix can be obtained.

The Information matrix given in table 7-2 has the item parameters in the following order: a_i, b_i, c_i. Thus

$$\tau_{1i} = \begin{bmatrix} a_{i1} \\ b_{i1} \\ c_{i1} \end{bmatrix} \quad \text{and} \quad \tau_{2i} = \begin{bmatrix} a_{i2} \\ b_{i2} \\ c_{i2} \end{bmatrix}.$$

For the three-parameter model the entire (3×3) Information matrix may be used. If the two-parameter model is chosen, the Information matrix reduces to the first two rows and columns. If the one-parameter model is used, only the diagonal element corresponding to b_i is used (this is the element in the second row and second column). In general, we denote $I_1(x_i)$ and $I_2(x_i)$ to be the Information matrices for item i in groups 1 and 2. The variance-covariance matrices for the two groups are therefore

$$V_{1i} = [I_1(x_i)]^{-1} \equiv I_{1i}^{-1}$$

and

$$V_{2i} = [I_2(x_i)]^{-1} \equiv I_{2i}^{-1}$$

for the ith item.

The test statistic for testing item bias is then given by

$$Q_i = (x_{1i} - x_{2i})'(I_{1i}^{-1} + I_{2i}^{-1})^{-1}(x_{1i} - x_{2i}). \tag{13.10}$$

This quantity has a chi-square distribution with degrees of freedom equal to the number of item parameters compared. For example, in the three-parameter model, if all the three item parameters are to be compared across the groups, the degrees of freedom is three. If, on the other hand, it is decided that in the three-parameter model only a_i and b_i are to be compared across groups (for reasons given later), then the degrees of freedom is two. Clearly, for the Rasch model, the degrees of freedom can only be one.

The simplest situation occurs with the Rasch model. In this case, the Information matrix is made up of only one element for each group. It is obtained by setting $a_i = 1$ and $c_i = 0$ in the expression located in the second row and the second column of table 7-2. Denoting these by I_1 and I_2 for the two groups respectively, the following test statistic obtains:

$$Q_i = (b_{1i} - b_{2i})'(I_{1i}^{-1} + I_{2i}^{-1})^{-1}(b_{1i} - b_{2i}).$$

Since $b_{1i} - b_{2i}$, I_{1i} and I_{2i} are scalars, Q_i becomes

$$Q_i = (b_{1i} - b_{2i})^2/(I_{1i}^{-1} + I_{2i}^{-1}) \tag{13.11}$$

$$= (b_{1i} - b_{2i})^2/(V_{1i} + V_{2i}) \tag{13.12}$$

where $V_{1i} = I_{1i}^{-1}$ and $V_{2i} = I_{2i}^{-1}$.

This quantity is distributed as a chi-square variate asymptotically with one degree of freedom (the distribution is asymptotic because the expression for the Information matrix is correct only asymptotically). Since the square root of a chi-square variate with one degree of freedom is a standardized normal variate, the above expression can be written as

$$Z_i = (b_{1i} - b_{2i})/(V_{1i} + V_{2i})^{\frac{1}{2}}. \tag{13.13}$$

The calculated value of Z_i can be compared with the tabulated standardized normal curve values, and item bias assessed. The statistic given above was proposed by Wright, Mead and Draba (1976).

The comparison of item parameters in the two- and three-parameter models can be carried out by generalizing the above procedure and by computing Q_i given by equation (13.10). The steps in carrying out this comparison for any of the three models are:

1. An appropriate model is chosen.
2. Item and ability parameters are estimated separately for each group.
3. Since the parameters are estimated separately for the two groups, they have to be placed on a common scale. Standardizing on the b_i accomplishes this. Otherwise the characteristic curve method should be used for this purpose.
4. Once the item parameter estimates are scaled, the Information matrices, using the expression given in table 7-2 are computed for the two groups.
5. The test statistic Q_i given in equation (13.10) is computed for each item.
6. Based on the test statistic a decision is made regarding the bias of the item.

The above procedure is, in principle, straightforward and easy to implement. However the following points should be borne in mind in using the procedure:

a. The test of significance is asymptotic. It is not clear how large the sample size needs to be for the chi-square test to be accurate.
b. The asymptotic distribution of the item parameter estimates is valid only if θ_a is given. When θ_a, a_i, b_i, c_i are simultaneously estimated, the asymptotic theory may not be valid (Chapter 7).

The two procedures described above for comparing item characteristic curves are logically sound, although there is some disagreement regarding their relative merits. Lord (1980a, p. 217) recommends the second procedure. Linn et al. (1981) have argued that the comparison of item parameters may lead to wrong conclusions. To illustrate this point they considered the following sets of item parameters for two groups:

$$\text{Group 1:} \quad a = 1.8 \quad b = 3.5 \quad c = .2$$
$$\text{Group 2:} \quad a = .5 \quad b = 5.0 \quad c = .2.$$

While the differences between the discrimination and difficulty parameters are substantial, the two item characteristic curves do not differ by more than .05 for θ values in the interval between -3 and $+3$. Since item bias is defined in terms of the probabilities of correct responses between groups, they concluded that the appropriate comparison is between the curves and not the item parameters.

However, this argument can be reversed to favor the parameter comparison method since the illustration demonstrates that a "truly biased" item, with unequal item parameter values across groups, may result in probabilities that are almost equal in the two groups. It can therefore be argued that item parameter comparison method is more sensitive and hence is more appropriate! The important point to note is that these two procedures are logically equivalent. Hence any discrepancy that may arise in a decision regarding the bias of an item (see Shepard et al., 1981, for example) must be attributed to the operational definitions that are employed with these two procedures. Since the validity of these procedures has not been established conclusively, the proper approach is to assess item bias using both procedures, and in the event of a disagreement, study the offending item carefully with the hope of resolving the issue.

A problem that is common to these two procedures is that the two groups under study may have ability distributions centered at the high and low ends of the ability continuum (figure 13-4). In this case the estimation of item parameters in each of the two groups may pose a problem. The c parameter will be estimated poorly in the high ability group. The estimation of the a and b parameters will also become a problem if the ability distributions of the groups are concentrated in different parts of the ability continuum. This problem is not unique to item response theory and occurs even in the estimation of linear regression models. The non-linearity of the item characteristic curve exacerbates the problem. A further problem is the number of observations available, particularly, in a minority group.

Problems with estimating item parameters have been documented in Shepard, et al. (1981). However, Lord (1977c, 1980a, p. 217) anticipated this problem and has suggested a possible solution. The steps in estimating the parameters are:

1. Combine the two groups and estimate the item and ability parameters, standardizing on the b_i (this places all the item parameters on the same scale).
2. Fix the c_i at the values determined in Step 1.
3. With the c_i values fixed, estimate the ability, the difficulty, and discrimination parameters separately for each group, standardizing on the b_i (this obviates the need for scaling the item parameter estimates).

When this procedure is followed, the c_i values are made equal for the two groups. Hence, in the item parameter comparison method, only the parameters a_i and b_i should be compared across groups.

Shepard et al. (1981) have reported problems with this approach. In their analysis with a combined sample of 1,593 examinees, almost 40% of the c parameters did not converge. A further problem encountered by these authors is that when the c_i estimates from the combined sample were taken as given values, the difficulty and discrimination parameters were poorly estimated in the lower ability group. One possible explanation for this is that the c_i values were too large for the low ability group and this affected the estimation of other parameters in that group (Shepard et al., 1981). The problem of estimation is indeed a perplexing one. Research that is being done with the development of improved estimation methods (see chapter 7) may provide the solution to this problem.

In addition to these two item response theory based procedures, a third procedure for assessing item bias has been suggested by Wright et al. (1976) and Linn and Harnisch (1981). This is based on comparing the fit of the model in the two groups.

Comparison of Fit

The procedures available for assessing the fit of an item response model to the data are described in chapter 8. The procedure for detecting item bias is to compare the item fit statistic across for the groups of interest. Differences in fit may indicate item bias (Wright et al., 1976).

Linn and Harnisch (1981) suggested the following procedure for assessing the fit of the model in two groups:

1. The two samples are combined and the item and ability parameters are estimated.
2. The probability of correct response P_{iag} ($g = 1, 2$) is computed for each person.
3. The average probability of correct response $P_{i.g}$ is computed for each group.
4. The observed proportion, $p_{i.g}$, of the individuals in a group responding correctly to the item is computed (this is the classical item difficulty index).
5. The quantity $P_{i.g}$ is compared with $p_{i.g}$ ($g = 1, 2$).
6. In addition the standard residual

$$Z_{iag} = (U_{iag} - P_{iag})/[P_{iag}(1 - P_{iag})]^{\frac{1}{2}}$$

is computed for each person, averaged within each group and compared across the two groups (Wright, et al., 1976 recommend using Z_{iag}^2, obtaining an average for each group and comparing them.)

The fit statistic may not provide meaningful comparisons. For the one-parameter model Shepard et al. (1981) found the statistic to show no evidence of convergent validity, i.e., the statistic was found to correlate poorly with other indices of bias. Furthermore, differential fit may be attributed to several factors such as failing to take into account guessing, and discrimination, other than item bias.

The fit statistic may provide reasonable assessment of bias in the three-parameter model (Linn & Harnisch, 1981). However, even here the meaning of the fit comparison is not entirely clear. Further evidence of the validity of this method is needed before it can be endorsed.

In summary, the bias in any item may be investigated more meaningfully with item response models than with conventional methods. The appropriate model for assessing bias appears to be the three-parameter model (Ironson, 1982, 1983; Shepard et al., 1981). However, estimation of parameters may pose a real problem unless the groups to be compared are large and have a large ability range.

The two procedures that can be recommended are: the "area" method and the parameter comparison method. These methods are logically equivalent in that the item characteristic curves are compared. The operational definition of these procedures, however, may result in inconsistent decisions regarding the bias of an item. Preferably both procedures should be used to accumulate evidence regarding bias and this should be followed by a detailed content analysis of the item.

13.3 Adaptive Testing

Almost all testing is done in settings in which a group of individuals take the same test (or parallel forms). Since these individuals will vary in the ability being measured by the test, it can be shown that a test would measure maximally the ability of each individual in the group if test items were presented to each individual such that the probability of answering each item correctly is .50. This, of course, is not possible using a single test; consequently, there is a need for "tailored tests" or "adaptive testing" (Lord, 1970b, 1971d, 1974b; Weiss, 1983; Wood, 1973). Item response models are particularly important in adaptive testing because it is possible to derive ability estimates that are independent of the particular choice of test items administered. Thus, examinees can be compared even though they may have taken sets of test items of varying difficulty.

In adaptive testing an attempt is made to match the difficulties of the test items to the ability of the examinee being measured. To match test items to ability levels requires a large pool of items whose statistical characteristics are known so that suitable items may be drawn. Ability scores can be estimated using the methods described in chapter 5. Since the item selection procedure does not lend itself easily to paper-and-pencil tests, the adaptive testing process is typically done by computer (exceptions to this rule are presented in the work of Lord (1971b, 1971c, 1971d). According to Lord (1974b), a computer must be programmed to accomplish the following in order to tailor a test to an examinee:

1. Predict from the examinee's previous responses how the examinee would respond to various test items not yet administered.
2. Make effective use of this knowledge to select the test item to be administered next.

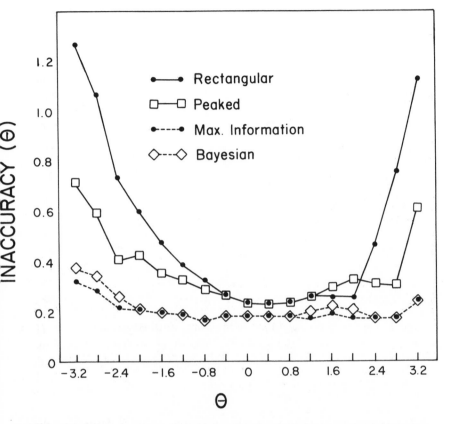

Figure 13-6.   Inaccuracy for 30-Item Rectangular and Peaked Conventional Tests and Maximum Information and Bayesian Adaptive Tests (From Weiss, D. J. Improving measurement quality and efficiency with adaptive testing. *Applied Psychological Measurement,* 1982, *6,* 473–492. Reprinted with permission.)

3.   Assign at the end of testing a numerical score that represents the ability of the examinee tested.

   Research has been done on a variety of adaptive testing strategies built on the following decision rule: If an examinee answers an item correctly, the next item should be more difficult; if an examinee answers incorrectly, the next item should be easier. These strategies can be broken down into *two-stage strategies* and *multistage strategies*. The multistage strategies are

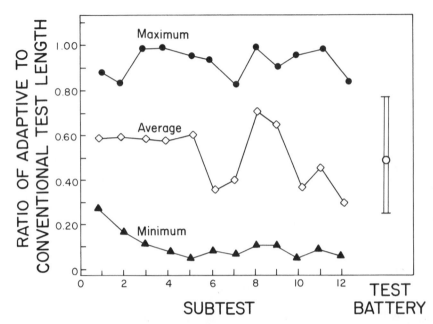

Figure 13-7. Ratio of Mean, Minimum, and Maximum Adaptive Test Lengths to Conventional Test Lengths for 12 Subtests and Total Test Battery (From Weiss, D. J. Improving measurement quality and efficient with adaptive testing. *Applied Psychological Measurement*, 1982, 6, 473-492. Reprinted with permission.)

either of the *fixed branching* variety or the *variable branching* variety. Weiss and Betz (1973) and Weiss (1974) have provided useful reviews of these strategies. Some of the adaptive testing advantages are reflected in some recent work by Weiss (1982) and reported in figures 13-6 and 13-7 and table 13-1.

In the two-stage procedure (Lord, 1971a; Betz & Weiss, 1973, 1974), all examinees take a routing test and based upon scores on this test, are directed to one of a number of tests constructed to provide maximum information at certain points along the ability continuum. Ability estimates are then derived from a combination of scores from the routing test and the optimum test (Lord, 1971a).

Whereas the two-stage strategy requires only one branching solution, from the routing to the optimum test, multistage strategies involve a branching decision after the examinee responds to each item. If the same item structure is used for all individuals, but each individual can move through the structure

Table 13-1. Percentage of Correct and Incorrect Mastery and Nonmastery Classifications Made by Conventional and Adaptive Mastery Tests Within Each of Five Content Areas.

	Testing Strategy	
Content Area and Classification	Conventional	Adaptive
Content Area 1		
Correct Nonmastery	45.3	50.7
Incorrect Nonmastery	41.1	30.5
Correct Mastery	12.6	16.0
Incorrect Mastery	.9	2.8
Total Correct	57.9	66.7
Total Incorrect	42.0	33.3
Content Area 2		
Correct Nonmastery	42.1	52.1
Incorrect Nonmastery	34.6	35.2
Correct Mastery	19.2	11.3
Incorrect Mastery	4.2	1.4
Total Correct	61.3	63.4
Total Incorrect	38.8	36.6
Content Area 3		
Correct Nonmastery	45.8	53.1
Incorrect Nonmastery	47.2	41.8
Correct Mastery	6.5	4.7
Incorrect Mastery	.5	.5
Total Correct	52.3	57.8
Total Incorrect	47.7	42.3
Content Area 4		
Correct Nonmastery	53.1	48.9
Incorrect Nonmastery	42.6	31.5
Correct Mastery	4.3	17.4
Incorrect Mastery	0	2.3
Total Correct	57.4	66.3
Total Incorrect	42.6	33.8
Content Area 5		
Correct Nonmastery	53.1	50.2
Incorrect Nonmastery	44.5	46.1
Correct Mastery	2.4	2.7
Incorrect Mastery	0	.9
Total Correct	55.5	52.9
Total Incorrect	44.5	47.0

Note: From Weiss (1983).

in a unique way, then it is called a *fixed-branching* model. The question of how much item difficulty should vary from item to item leads to considerations of structures with constant step size (Lord, 1970b) or decreasing step size (Lord, 1971b; Mussio, 1973).

For these multistage fixed-branching models, all examinees start at an item of median difficulty and based upon a correct or an incorrect response, pass through a set of items that have been arranged in order of item difficulty. After having completed a fixed set of items, either of two scores is used to obtain an estimate of ability: the difficulty of the (hypothetical) item that would have been administered after the nth (last) item, or the average of the item difficulties, excluding the first item and including the hypothetical $n + 1^{st}$ item (Lord, 1974b).

Other examples of fixed multistage strategies include the flexi-level test (Betz & Weiss, 1975) and the stratified-adaptive (stradaptive) test (Weiss, 1973; Waters, 1977). The flexi-level test, which can be represented in a modified pyramidal form, has only one item at each difficulty level. The decision rule for using this test is: Following a correct response, the next item given is the item next higher in difficulty that has not been administered. Following an incorrect response, the item next lower in difficulty that has not been administered is given. The stradaptive test, on the other hand, has items stratified into levels according to their difficulties. Branching then occurs by difficulty level across strata and can follow any of a number of possible branching schemes.

The *variable-branching* structures are multistage strategies that do not operate with a fixed item structure. Rather, at each stage of the process, an item in the established item pool is selected for a certain examinee in a fashion such that the item, if administered, will maximally reduce the uncertainty of the examinee's ability estimate. After administration of the item, the ability estimate is either recalculated using maximum likelihood procedures (Lord, 1980a) or Bayesian procedures (McBride, 1977; Swaminathan, in press; Wood, 1976).

There are a number of ways in which items can be tailored to ability, as well as ways of computing ability estimates. What is needed, however, is a mechanism for evaluating the results of studies obtained from these various procedures. The mechanism for evaluation should not be based on group statistics such as correlation coefficients because the crux of the problem is to determine the accuracy with which ability can be estimated for a single examinee. Almost all these studies have compared tests constructed using various procedures by making use of test information functions. Adaptive testing procedures provide more information at the extremes of ability distribution than do any of the standard tests used for comparative purposes, and they provide adequate information at medium-difficulty and -ability levels (where standard tests cannot be surpassed). Areas in need of research in adaptive testing are suggested by Lord (1977b), Weiss (1983), and Urry (1977).

13.4 Differential Weighting of Response Alternatives

Commonly believed among test developers is that it should be possible to construct alternatives for multiple-choice test items that differ in their degree of correctness. An examinee's test score could then be based on the degree of correctness of his or her response alternative selections, instead of simply the number of correct answers, possibly corrected for guessing. However, with few exceptions, the results of differential weighting of response alternatives have been disappointing (Wang & Stanley, 1970). Despite the intuitive beliefs of test developers and researchers, past research makes clear that differential weighting of response alternatives has no consistent effect on the reliability and validity of the derived test scores. However, using correlation coefficients to study the merits of any new scoring system is less than ideal, because correlation coefficients will not reveal any improvements in the estimation of ability at different regions of the ability scale. A concern for the precision of measurement at different ability levels is important. There is reason to believe that the largest gains in precision of measurement to be derived from a scoring system that incorporates scoring weights for the response alternatives will occur with low-ability examinees. High-ability examinees make relatively few errors on their test papers and therefore would make little use of differently weighted incorrect response alternatives. The problem with using a group statistic like the correlation coefficient to reflect the improvements of a new scoring system is that any gains at the low end of the ability continuum will be "washed out" when combined with the lack of gain in information at other places on the ability continuum. One way of evaluating a test scoring method is in terms of the precision with which it estimates an examinee's ability: The more precise the estimate, the more *information* the test scoring method provides. Birnbaum's concept of *information* introduced in chapter 5 provides a much better criterion than do correlation coefficients for judging the merits of new scoring methods.

Motivated by the contention of Jacobs and Vandeventer (1970) that there is information to be gained in the incorrect responses to the Raven's Progressive Matrices Test (a test in which the answer choices to each item can be logically ordered according to their degree of correctness), Thissen (1976) applied the nominal response model to a set of the test data. As shown in figure 11-1, the nominal response model produced substantial improvements in the precision of ability estimation in the lower half of the ability range. Gains in information ranged from one-third more to nearly twice the information derived from 0–1 scoring with the logistic test model. According to Bock (1972), most of the new information to be derived from weighted response scoring comes from distinguishing between examinees who choose plausible or partly correct answers from those who omit the items.

In a study of vocabulary test items with the nominal response model, Bock (1972) found that for below median ability there was one and one-half to two times more information derived from the nominal response model over the usual 0–1 test scoring method. In terms of test length, the scoring system associated with the nominal response model had, for about one-half of the examinee population, produced improvements in precision of ability estimation equal to the precision that could be obtained by a binary-scored test one and one-half to two times longer than the original one with the new method of scoring. Also encouraging was that the "curve" for each response alternative (estimated empirically) was psychologically interpretable. The Thissen and Bock studies should encourage other researchers to go back and reanalyze their data using the nominal response model and the measure of "information" provided by the item response models. The Thissen and Bock studies indicate that there is "information" that can be recovered from incorrect examinee responses to a set of test items and provide interesting applications of test information curves to compare different test scoring methods.

13.5 Estimation of Power Scores

A speeded test is defined as one in which examinees do not have time to respond to some questions for which they know the answers, while a power test is one in which examinees have sufficient time to show what they know. Most academic achievement tests are more speeded for some examinees than for others. Occasionally, the situation exists when a test that is intended to be a power test becomes a speeded test. An example of this situation is a test that has been mistimed, i.e., examinees are given less than the specified amount of time to complete the test. In this situation, it would be desirable to estimate what an examinee's score would have been if the test had been properly timed. This score is referred to as an examinee's *power score*. Lord (1973) had discussed a method using the three-parameter logistic model and applied it to the estimation of power scores for 21 examinees who had taken a mistimed verbal aptitude test. Lord's method requires not only the usual assumptions of the three-parameter logistic model, but also assumes that the students answer the items in order and that they respond as they would if given unlimited time.

The expected power score for an examinee with ability level θ on a set of n test items is the sum of the probabilities associated with the examinee answering the items correctly, i.e.,

$$E(X_a) = \sum_{i=1}^{n} P_i(\theta_a).$$

In practice, $\hat{\theta}_a$ is substituted for the unknown parameter θ_a. As long as the examinee completed a sufficient number of test items (n_a) to obtain a satisfactory ability estimate, then the examinee's expected total score (Lord calls this score *a power score*) can be estimated from

$$X_a + \sum_{i=n_a+1}^{n} \hat{P}_i(\hat{\theta}_a),$$

where X_a is the examinee's score on the attempted items and the second term is the examinee's expected score on the remaining items utilizing the ability estimate obtained from the attempted items and the ICCs for the unattempted items.

Lord (1973) obtained correlations exceeding .98 between power scores and number-right scores in two different studies. However, since several assumptions are involved, he cautions that a wide variety of empirical checks would have to be carried out before one could be sure of all the circumstances under which his method would produce satisfactory results.

13.6 Summary

The four applications described in this chapter are only a small subset of the number of IRT model applications that are presently under development. Other applications include the reporting of test performance over time for groups (Pandey & Carlson, 1983), mastery-nonmastery classifications within the context of competency testing (Hambleton, 1983c), detection of aberrant response patterns (Harnisch & Tatsuoka, 1983; Levine & Rubin, 1979), and modelling cognitive processes (Fischer & Formann, 1982; Whitely, 1980).

14 PRACTICAL CONSIDERATIONS IN USING IRT MODELS

14.1 Overview

The virtues of item response theory and the potential it holds for solving hitherto unsolvable problems in the area of mental measurement make item response theoretic procedures invaluable to practitioners. However, item response theory is mathematically complex, is based on strong assumptions, and its applicability is almost totally dependent on the availability of large computers. The basic question that arises then is: Under what circumstances should the practitioner take the plunge and apply item response theory procedures?

Several key decisions must be made before applying item response theory procedures. They are based upon the following considerations:

- Is the purpose to develop a test or analyze existing test data?
- Is the test unidimensional?
- Which model fits the data best?
- Should the data be trimmed to fit the model or the model chosen to fit the data?
- Is the sample size adequate?

- Are suitable computer programs available?
- Are sufficient resources available?
- Which estimation procedure is appropriate?
- How should test scores be reported?
- Does the application of item response theory methods provide the answers that are being sought?

The answers to these questions may be ambivalent in some cases. In other situations, answers may not be available. Only in a limited set of circumstances may clear-cut answers be available that indicate the directions along which one could proceed. Despite these dire statements, the very act of asking these questions may provide guides and answers regarding the problem at hand, the nature of the data, and the possibility of a solution.

The first question that has to be resolved is that of purpose. The purpose clearly dictates the direction along which one proceeds. We shall attempt to address the questions listed above with respect to this dichotomy: Is the purpose to develop a test or to solve a measurement problem with an existing test or tests?

14.2 Applicability of Item Response Theory

Current methodology is applicable only to unidimensional test data. Testing this basic assumption is therefore the first step. The procedures for assessing dimensionality have been described in chapter 8. The popular method of factor analysis is often not satisfactory. Factor analysis, being a linear procedure, may not yield a single dimension when there is considerable nonlinearity in the data. Since data that fit an item response model will almost surely be nonlinear, the results of a factor analysis will be a foregone conclusion.

Despite this drawback, a factor analysis should be routinely carried out. The appropriate item correlation to employ is the tetrachoric correlation since it is believed that the use of phi-coefficients may result in spurious factors though McDonald and Ahlawat (1974) have challenged this conjecture by pointing out that the spurious factors are a consequence of the nonlinearity in the data and not the result of the choice of a correlation coefficient. It stands to reason, therefore, that the existence of a single factor, extracted using conventional factor analysis of tetrachoric correlation coefficients, is a sufficient but not a necessary condition for a single underlying dimension. Hence, a dominant first factor may be taken as an indication of unidimensional data.

If the purpose is test development, it may be possible to delete items from the test in such a way that the resulting test possesses a dominant first factor. But when this approach is chosen, care must be taken to insure that the content domain of interest is still being measured. When it is not, the content domain measured by the test must be respecified. With the unidimensionality condition met, attempts to choose an appropriate item response model may be undertaken. If a dominant first factor is not available, the test may be divided into unidimensional subtests by grouping items that load on each factor. Each of these subtests must then be analyzed separately.

Linear factor analytic procedures may not be adequate for the analysis of nonlinear data. Nonlinear factor analysis may be more appropriate (Hambleton & Rovinelli, 1983; McDonald, 1967; McDonald and Ahlawat, 1974). It was pointed out earlier that local independence and unidimensional latent space (when this is the complete latent space) are equivalent concepts. Since local independence obtains at a each given level of θ and not for the entire groups of examinees, factor analytic procedures based on the responses of the entire groups of examinees may not be appropriate. Test of dimensionality based on the notion of local independence may be more appropriate. Considerably more research is needed before these procedures can be endorsed.

14.3 Model Selection

Assuming at this point that the latent space is unidimensional, the second step is to choose an appropriate item response model. Several factors must be taken into account in this stage before this decision is made. The first consideration is, *Should the model be chosen so that it fits the data well or should the data be edited so that the data fit the model desired?* Philosophical issues and the objectives of the project may be brought to bear on this question.

The Rasch model has the property of specific objectivity. If this property is deemed the most relevant, then the data may be edited to fit the model. When the primary purpose is test development, this editing of data to fit the model may be an integral part of the test development phase. However, if vertical equating of scores or detection of aberrant response patterns is a future objective, then the choice of the Rasch model may not be viable. Most likely, a two- or a three-parameter model must be chosen (Drasgow, 1982; Gustaffson, 1978; Loyd & Hoover, 1981; Slinde & Linn, 1977, 1979a, 1979b; Yen, 1981). Even in this situation, it may be necessary to edit the data to fit the model chosen when test development is mandated. In the event that test data are available and it is necessary to analyze the data, the investigator has little or no choice. The model must be chosen to fit the data.

A second consideration that is relevant for the choice of model is the *availability of sample* (see Ree, 1979, 1981). If a large sample is available, the fit of a one-, two-, or three-parameter model may be examined. If, however, less than 200 examinees are available, restrictions imposed by the accuracy with which the parameters may be estimated may dictate a one-parameter model (Lord, 1983). The inaccuracy with which the discrimination and chance-level parameters are estimated make the two-parameter or three-parameter models impractical.

A third consideration is the *quality of the data* available. The size of the sample is often given predominance over the nature of the sample. Size of the sample is certainly important but so is the nature of the available sample. For example, if a three-parameter model is chosen and the sample is such that only a few examinees at the low-ability level are available, then the chance-level parameter cannot be estimated well. The three-parameter model should not be chosen in this case. Alternatively, it may often be reasonable to choose a priori a constant value for the "c" parameter.

A fourth consideration is the *available resources*. Although, in one sense, it should not be a critical factor, it may become a practical consideration. If a three-parameter model analysis is extremely costly, then a lower-order model may be chosen as a compromise. It should be noted that cost may be confounded by the nature of the data. Lack of examinees at the lower ability levels may make the estimation of chance-level parameters difficult, and this may result in costly computer runs.

The fifth consideration is *the choice of estimation procedure*. Although apparently not directly related to the selection of models, it has considerable bearing on the issue. The cost considerations mentioned above may be ameliorated by the choice of a proper estimation procedure. For example, in some situations a Bayes estimation procedure may be sufficiently effective that the parameters of a three-parameter model may be estimated economically.

A related consideration is *the availability of computer programs*—indeed limiting in that currently only a few computer programs are available. When combined with the estimation procedures, the present choice is indeed very narrow. Joint maximum likelihood estimates for the three item response models are available. The conditional estimation procedure is applicable to and available for the Rasch model.

The seventh and final consideration is the *assessment of model fit*. A statistically justifiable procedure for the assessment of model fit is available only for the Rasch model when conditional estimators of item parameters are obtained. Fit assessment in other instances are based on heuristic and/or descriptive procedures. The descriptive procedures outlined in chapter 8 should be routinely carried out to assess model fit to supplement or replace statistical procedures. Innovative methods that suit the particular objective of the study may be used. For example, if the purpose of the study is to equate, then invariance of item parameters across samples of examinees must be examined. This condition being met may be taken as indication of model fit even if other indices provide ambiguous information, given the objective of the study.

These eight factors taken into account together may provide sufficient information for the selection of a model.

14.4 Reporting of Scores

For the most part, the main purpose behind using item response theory is to assess the performance level or ability of an examinee. An estimated value of θ, $\hat{\theta}$, will provide the information. The main advantage of this parameter is that it is invariant, while the main disadvantage is that it is on a scale that is not very well understood by test score users.

Lord (1980a) has suggested that the score metric may be a more useful metric than the ability scale. The estimated $\hat{\theta}$ may be transformed to the score metric through the test characteristic curve. The resulting transformed score ranges from zero to n, where n is the number of items. This transformation avoids the problem of not being able to estimate (using maximum likelihood method) the ability corresponding to a perfect score or a zero score.

14.5 Conclusion

Several practical issues that must be considered in applying item response theory have been discussed in this chapter. Once these issues have been addressed, item response theory methods may be applied to a variety of situations:

- Development of item banks;
- Test development;
- Equating of test scores;
- Detection of biased items;
- Adaptive testing.

While we have discussed the comparative merits of item response theory methods over classical methods, in most cases the two methods may be used jointly to great advantage. Classical item analysis procedures are especially powerful, easy to understand, and enable the investigator to better understand the results derived from using item response models methods. We encourage, therefore, the use of classical item analysis procedures to supplement item response theory methods and to aid in the understanding of the basic nature of test scores.

Appendix A: Values of $e^x/(1 + e^x)$ for $x = -4.0$ to 4.0 (.10)

x	$\dfrac{e^x}{1 + e^x}$	x	$\dfrac{e^x}{1 + e^x}$	x	$\dfrac{e^x}{1 + e^x}$
−4.0	.018	−1.0	.269	2.0	.881
−3.9	.020	−.9	.289	2.1	.891
−3.8	.022	−.8	.310	2.2	.900
−3.7	.024	−.7	.332	2.3	.909
−3.6	.027	−.6	.354	2.4	.917
−3.5	.029	−.5	.378	2.5	.924
−3.4	.032	−.4	.401	2.6	.931
−3.3	.036	−.3	.426	2.7	.937
−3.2	.039	−.2	.450	2.8	.943
−3.1	.043	−.1	.475	2.9	.948
−3.0	.047	.0	.500	3.0	.953
−2.9	.052	.1	.525	3.1	.957
−2.8	.057	.2	.550	3.2	.961
−2.7	.063	.3	.574	3.3	.964
−2.6	.069	.4	.599	3.4	.968
−2.5	.076	.5	.622	3.5	.971
−2.4	.083	.6	.646	3.6	.973
−2.3	.091	.7	.668	3.7	.976
−2.2	.099	.8	.690	3.8	.978
−2.1	.100	.9	.711	3.9	.980
				4.0	.982
−2.0	.119	1.0	.731		
−1.9	.130	1.1	.750		
−1.8	.142	1.2	.769		
−1.7	.154	1.3	.786		
−1.6	.168	1.4	.802		
−1.5	.182	1.5	.818		
−1.4	.200	1.6	.832		
−1.3	.214	1.7	.846		
−1.2	.231	1.8	.858		
−1.1	.250	1.9	.870		

REFERENCES

Andersen, E. B. Asymptotic properties of conditional maximum likelihood estimates. *The Journal of the Royal Statistical Society*, Series B, 1970, *32*, 283–301.

Andersen, E. B. The numerical solution of a set of conditional estimation equations. *The Journal of the Royal Statistical Society*, Series B, 1972, *34*, 42–54.

Andersen, E. B. Conditional inference in multiple choice questionnaires. *British Journal of Mathematical and Statistical Psychology*, 1973, *26*, 31–44. (a)

Andersen, E. B. A goodness of fit test for the Rasch model. *Psychometrika*, 1973, *38*, 123–140. (b)

Andersen, E. B., & Madsen, M. Estimating the parameters of the latent population distribution. *Psychometrika*, 1977, *42*, 357–374.

Andersen, J., Kearney, G. E., & Everett, A. V. An evaluation of Rasch's structural model for test items. *British Journal of Mathematical and Statistical Psychology*, 1968, *21*, 231–238.

Andrich, D. A binomal latent trait model for the study of Likert-style attitude questionnaires. *British Journal of Mathematical and Statistical Psychology*, 1978, *31*, 84–98. (a)

Andrich, D. A rating formulation for ordered response categories. *Psychometrika*, 1978, *43*, 561–573. (b)

Andrich, D. Applications of a psychometric rating model to ordered categories which are scored with successive integers. *Applied Psychological Measurement*, 1978, *2*, 581–594. (c)

Angoff, W. H. Scales, norms, and equivalent scores. In R. L. Thorndike (Ed.), *Educational measurement.* (2nd ed.) Washington, D. C.: American Council on Education, 1971.

Angoff, W. H. Summary and derivation of equating methods used at ETS. In P. W. Holland, & D. R. Rubin (Eds.), *Test equating.* New York: Academic Press, 1982. (a)

Angoff, W. H. Use of difficulty and discrimination indices for detecting item bias. In R. A. Berk (Ed.), *Handbook of Methods for Detecting Test Bias.* Baltimore, MD: The Johns Hopkins University, 1982.(b)

Angoff, W. H., & Ford, S. F. Item–race interaction on a test of scholastic aptitude. *Journal of Educational Measurement,* 1973, *10,* 95–106.

Baker, F. B. An intersection of test score interpretation and item analysis. *Journal of Educational Measurement,* 1964, *1,* 23–28.

Baker, F. B. Origins of the item parameters X_{50} and β and as a modern item analysis technique. *Journal of Educational Measurement,* 1965, *2,* 167–180.

Baker, F. B. Advances in item analysis. *Review of Educational Research,* 1977, *47,* 151–178.

Barton, M. A., & Lord, F. M. An upper asymptote for the three-parameter logistic item-response model. *Research Bulletin 81-20.* Princeton, NJ: Educational Testing Service, 1981.

Bejar, I. I. An application of the continuous response level model to personality measurement. *Applied Psychological Measurement,* 1977 *1,* 509–521.

Bejar, I. I. A procedure for investigating the unidimensionality of achievement tests based on item parameter estimates. *Journal of Educational Measurement,* 1980, *17,* 283–296.

Bejar, I. I. Introduction to item response models and their assumptions. In R. K. Hambleton (Ed.), *Applications of Item Response Theory.* Vancouver, BC: Educational Research Institute of British Columbia, 1983.

Berk, R. A. (Ed.) *Handbook of methods for detecting test bias.* Baltimore, MD: The Johns Hopkins University Press, 1982.

Betz, N. E. & Weiss, D. J. An empirical study of computer-administered two-stage ability testing. *Research Report 73-4.* Minneapolis: University of Minnesota, Psychometric Methods Program, Department of Psychology, 1973.

Betz, N. E. & Weiss, D. J. Simulation studies of two-stage ability testing. *Research Report 74-4.* Minneapolis: University of Minnesota, Psychometric Methods Program, Department of Psychology, 1974.

Betz, N. E. & Weiss, D. J. Empirical and simulation studies of flexi-level ability testing. *Research Report 75-3.* Minneapolis: University of Minnesota, Psychometric Methods Program, Department of Psychology, 1975.

Binet, A., & Simon, T. H. *The development of intelligence in young children.* Vineland, NJ: The Training School, 1916.

Birnbaum, A. Efficient design and use of tests of a mental ability for various decision-making problems. Series Report No. 58-16. Project No. 7755-23,USAF School of Aviation Medicine, Randolph Air Force Base, Texas, 1957.

Birnbaum, A. On the estimation of mental ability. Series Report No. 15. Project No. 7755-23, USAF School of Aviation Medicine, Randolph Air Force Base, Texas, 1958. (a)

Birnbaum, A. Further considerations of efficiency in tests of a mental ability. Technical Report No. 17. Project No. 7755-23, USAF School of Aviation Medicine, Randolph Air Force Base, Texas, 1958. (b)

Birnbaum, A. Some latent trait models and their use in inferring an examinee's ability. In F. M. Lord, & M. R. Novick, *Statistical theories of mental test scores*. Reading MA: Addison-Wesley, 1968.

Birnbaum, A. Statistical theory for logistic mental test models with a prior distribution of ability. *Journal of Mathematical Psychology*, 1969, *6*, 258–276.

Bock, R. D. Estimating item parameters and latent ability when responses are scored in two or more nominal categories. *Psychometrika*, 1972, *37*, 29–51.

Bock, R. D., & Aitkin, M. Marginal maximum likelihood estimation of item parameters: An application of an EM algorithm. *Psychometrika*, 1981, *46*, 443–459.

Bock, R. D. & Lieberman, M. Fitting a response model for n dichotomously scored items. *Psychometrika*, 1970, *35*, 179–197.

Bock, R. D., Mislevy, R. J., & Woodson, C. E. The next stage in educational assessment. *Educational Researcher*, 1982, *11*, 4–11.

Bock, R. D. & Wood, R. Test theory. In P. H. Mussen, & M. R. Rosenzweig (Eds.), *Annual Review of Psychology*. Palo Alto, CA: Annual Reviews Inc., 1971.

Choppin, B. H. Recent developments in item banking: A review. In D. DeGruijter & L. J. Th. van der Kamp (Eds.), *Advances in psychological and educational measurement*. New York: Wiley, 1976.

Cleary, T.A., & Hilton, T. L. An investigation of item bias. *Educational and Psychological Measurement*, 1968, *28*, 61–75.

Connolly, A. J., Nachtman, W., & Pritchett, E. M. *Key math diagnostic arithmetic test*. Circle Pines, MN: American Guidance Service, 1974.

Cook, L. L., & Eignor, D. R. Practical considerations regarding the use of item response theory to equate tests. In R. K. Hambleton (Ed.), *Applications of item response theory*. Vancouver, BC: Educational Research Institute of British Columbia, 1983.

Cook, L. L., & Hambleton, R. K. Application of latent trait models to the development of norm-referenced and criterion-referenced tests. *Laboratory of Psychometric and Evaluative Research Report No. 72*. Amherst: University of Massachusetts, School of Education, 1978. (a)

Cook, L. L. , & Hambleton, R. K. A comparative study of item selection methods utilizing latent trait theoretic models and concepts. *Laboratory of Psychometric and Evaluative Research Report No. 88*. Amherst, MA: University of Massachusetts, School of Education, 1978. (b)

Cronbach, L. J., & Warrington, W. G. Time-limit tests: Estimating their reliability and degree of speeding. *Psychometrika*, 1951, *16*, 167–188.

de Gruijter, D. N. M., & Hambleton, R. K. Using item response models in criterion-referenced test item selection. In R. K. Hambleton (Ed.), *Applications of item response theory.* Vancouver, BC: Educational Research Institute of British Columbia, 1983.

Dempster, A. P., Laird, N. M., & Rubin, D. B. Maximum likelihood from incomplete data via the EM algorithm (with discussion). *Journal of the Royal Statistical Society,* Series B, 1977, *39,* 1–38.

Divgi, D. R. Model free evaluation of equating and scaling. *Applied Psychological Measurement,* 1981, *5,* 203–208. (a)

Divgi, D. R. Does the Rasch model really work? Not if you look closely. Paper presented at the annual meeting of NCME, Los Angeles, l981. (b)

Donlon, T. F. An exploratory study of the implications of test speededness. Princeton, NJ: Educational Testing Service, 1978.

Drasgow, F. Choice of test model for appropriateness measurement. *Applied Psychological Measurement,* 1982, *6,* 297–308.

Durovic, J. Application of the Rasch model to civil service testing. Paper presented at the meeting of the Northeastern Educational Research Association, Grossingers, New York, November 1970. (ERIC Document Reproduction Service No. ED 049 305).

Fischer, G. H. *Einfuhrung in die theorie psychologischer tests.* Bern: Huber, 1974.

Fischer, G. H., & Formann, A. K. Some applications of logistic latent trait models with linear constraints on the parameters. *Applied Psychological Measurement,* 1982, *6,* 397–416.

Fischer, G. H., & Pendl, P. Individualized testing on the basis of the dichotomous Rasch model. In L. J. Th. van der Kamp, W. F. Langerak, & D. N. M. de Gruijter (Eds.), *Psychometrics for educational debates.* New York: Wiley, 1980.

Green, S. B., Lissitz, R. W., & Mulaik, S. A. Limitations of coefficient alpha as an index of test unidimensionality. *Educational and Psychological Measurement,* 1977, *37,* 827–838

Guion, R. M., & Ironson, G. H. Latent trait theory for organizational research. *Organizational Behavior and Human Performance,* 1983, *31,* 54–87.

Gulliksen, H. *Theory of mental tests.* New York: Wiley, 1950.

Gustafsson, J. E. The Rasch model in vertical equating of tests: A critique of Slinde and Linn. *Journal of Educational Measurement,* 1978, *16,* 153–158.

Gustafsson, J. E. A solution of the conditional estimation problem for long tests in the Rasch model for dichotomous items. *Educational and Psychological Measurement,* 1980, *40,* 377–385. (a)

Gustafsson, J. E. Testing and obtaining fit of data to the Rasch model. *British Journal of Mathematical and Statistical Psychology,* 1980, *33,* 205–233.(b)

Guttman, L. A basis for scaling qualitative data. *American Sociological Review,* 1944, *9,* 139–150.

Haberman, S. Maximum likelihood estimates in exponential response models. *Technical Report.* Chicago, IL: University of Chicago, 1975.

Haebara. T. Equating logistic ability scales by weighted least squares method. *Japanese Psychological Research,* 1980 *22,* 144–149.

Haley, D. C. Estimation of the dosage mortality relationship when the dose is subject to error. *Technical Report No. 15*. Stanford, Calif.: Stanford University, Applied Mathematics and Statistics Laboratory, 1952.

Hambleton, R. K. *An empirical investigation of the Rasch test theory model.* Unpublished doctoral dissertation University of Toronto, 1969.

Hambleton, R. K. Latent trait models and their applications. In R. Traub (Ed.), *Methodological developments: New directions for testing and measurement (No.4).* San Francisco, Jossey-Bass, 1979.

Hambleton, R. K. Latent ability scales, interpretations, and uses. In S. Mayo (Ed.), *New directions for testing and measurement: Interpreting test scores (No. 6).* San Francisco: Jossey-Bass, 1980.

Hambleton, R. K. Advances in criterion-referenced testing technology. In C. Reynolds & T. Gutkin (Eds.), *Handbook of school psychology.* New York: Wiley, 1982.

Hambleton, R. K. (Ed.) *Applications of item response theory.* Vancouver, BC: Educational Research Institute of British Columbia, 1983. (a)

Hambleton, R. K. Applications of item response models to criterion-referenced assessment. *Applied Psychological Measurement*, 1983, *6*, 33–44. (b)

Hambleton, R. K., & Cook, L. L. Latent trait models and their use in the analysis of educational test data. *Journal of Educational Measurement,* 1977, *14*, 75–96.

Hambleton, R. K., & Cook, L. L. The robustness of item response models and effects of test length and sample size on the precision of ability estimates. In D. Weiss (Ed.), *New Horizons in Testing.* New York: Academic Press, 1983.

Hambleton, R. K., & de Gruijter, D. N. M. Application of item response models to criterion-referenced test item selection. *Journal of Educational Measurement,* 1983, *20*, 355–367.

Hambleton, R. K., & Martois, J. S. Evaluation of a test score prediction system based upon item response model principles and procedures. In R. K. Hambleton (Ed.), *Applications of item response theory.* Vancouver, BC: Educational Research Institute of British Columbia, 1983.

Hambleton, R. K., & Murray, L. N. Some goodness of fit investigations for item response models. In R. K. Hambleton (Ed.), *Applications of item response theory.* Vancouver, BC: Educational Research Institute of British Columbia, 1983.

Hambleton, R. K., Murray, L. N., & Anderson, J. Uses of item statistics in item evaluation and test development. *Research Report 82-1.* Vancouver, BC: Educational Research Institute of British Columbia, 1982.

Hambleton, R. K., Murray, L. N., & Simon, R. Utilization of item response models with NAEP mathematics exercise results. Final Report (NIE-ECS Contract No. 02-81-20319). Washington, DC: National Institute of Education, 1982.

Hambleton, R. K., Murray, L. N., & Williams, P. Fitting item response models to the Maryland Functional Reading Tests. *Laboratory of Psychometric and Evaluative Research Report No. 139.* Amherst, MA: School of Education, University of Massachusetts, 1983. (ERIC REPORTS: ED 230 624)

Hambleton, R. K., & Rovinelli, R. A Fortran IV program for generating examinee response data from logistic test models. *Behavioral Science,* 1973, *17*, 73–74.

Hambleton, R. K., & Rovinelli, R. J. Assessing the dimensionality of a set of test items. A paper presented at the annual meeting of AERA, Montreal, 1983.

Hambleton, R. K., Swaminathan, H., Cook, L. L., Eignor, D. R., & Gifford, J. A. Developments in latent trait theory: Models, technical issues, and applications. *Review of Educational Research,* 1978, *48,* 467–510.

Hambleton, R. K., & Traub, R. E. Information curves and efficiency of three logistic test models. *British Journal of Mathematical and Statistical Psychology,* 1971, *24,* 273–281.

Hambleton, R. K., & Traub, R. E. Analysis of empirical data using two logistic latent trait models. *British Journal of Mathematical and Statistical Psychology,* 1973, *26,* 195–211.

Hambleton, R. K., & Traub, R. E. The effects of item order on test performance and stress. *Journal of Experimental Education,* 1974, *43,* 40–46.

Hambleton, R. K., & Traub, R. E. The robustness of the Rasch test model. *Laboratory of Psychometric and Evaluative Research Report No. 42.* Amherst: University of Massachusetts, School of Education, 1976.

Hambleton, R. K., & van der Linden, W. J. Advances in item response theory and applications: An introduction. *Applied Psychological Measurement,* 1982, *6,* 373–378.

Harnisch, D. L., & Tatsuoka, K. K. A comparison of appropriateness indices based on item response theory. In R. K. Hambleton (Ed.), *Applications of item response theory.* Vancouver, BC: Educational Research Institute of British Columbia, 1983.

Hattie, J. A. Decision criteria for determining unidimensionality. Unpublished doctoral dissertation, University of Toronto, 1981.

Hiscox, M., & Brzezinski, E. *A guide to item banking.* Portland, OR: Northwest Regional Educational Laboratory, 1980.

Horn, J.L. A rationale and test for the number of factors in factor analysis. *Psychometrika,* 1965, *30,* 179–185.

Hunter, J. E. A critical analysis of the use of item means and item-test correlations to determine the presence or absence of content bias in achievement test items. Paper presented at the National Institute of Education Conference on Test Bias, Annapolis, MD, December 1975.

Individualized Criterion-Referenced Test Manual. Tulsa: Educational Development Corporation, 1980.

Ironson, G. H. Use of chi-square and latent trait approaches for detecting item bias. In R. Berk (Ed.), *Handbook of Methods for Detecting Test Bias.* Baltimore, MD: The Johns Hopkins University Press, 1982.

Ironson, G. H. Using item response theory to measure bias. In R. K. Hambleton (Ed.), *Applications of item response theory.* Vancouver, BC: Educational Research Institute of British Columbia, 1983.

Isaacson, E., & Keller, H. *Analysis of numerical methods.* New York: Wiley, 1966.

Jacobs, P., & Vandeventer, M. Information in wrong responses. *Psychological Reports,* 1970, *26,* 311–315.

Jensema, C. J. A simple technique for estimating latent trait mental test parameters. *Educational and Psychological Measurement,* 1976, *36,* 705–715.

Keats, J. A. Test theory. *Annual Review of Psychology,* 1967, 217–238.

Kendall, M.G., & Stuart, A. *The advanced theory of statistics* (Vol.2) New York: Hafner, 1973.

Kolen, M. Comparison of traditional and item response theory methods for equating tests. *Journal of Educational Measurement,* 1981, *18,* 1–11.

Lawley, D. N. On problems connected with item selection and test construction. *Proceedings of the Royal Society of Edinburgh,* 1943, *6,* 273–287.

Lawley, D. N. The factorial analysis of multiple item tests. *Proceedings of the Royal Society of Edinburgh,* 1944, *62-A,* 74–82.

Lazarsfeld, P. F. The logical and mathematical foundation of latent structure analysis. In S.A. Stouffer et al., *Measurement and prediction.* Princeton: Princeton University Press, 1950.

Lazarsfeld, P. F., & Henry, N. W. *Latent structure analysis.* New York: Houghton Mifflin, 1968.

Levine, M. V., & Drasgow, F. Appropriateness measurement: Review, critique and validating studies. *British Journal of Mathematical and Statistical Psychology,* 1982, *35,* 42–56.

Levine, M. V., & Rubin, D. B. Measuring the appropriateness of multiple-choice test scores. *Journal of Educational Statistics,* 1979, *4,* 269–290.

Levine, M. V., Wardrop J. L., & Linn, R. L. Weighted mean square item bias statistics. Paper presented at the annual meeting of the American Educational Research Association, New York, 1982.

Lindley, D. V., & Smith, A.F.M. Bayesian estimates for the linear model. *Journal of the Royal Statistical Society,* 1972, *34,* 1–41.

Linn, R. L., & Harnisch D.L. Interactions between item content and group membership on achievement test items. *Journal of Educational Measurement,* 1981, *18,* 109–118.

Linn, R. L., Levine, M.V., Hastings, C.N., & Wardrop, J.L. An investigation of item bias in a test of reading comprehension. *Applied Psychological Measurement,* 1981, *5,* 159–173.

Lord, F. M. A theory of test scores. *Psychometric Monograph,* 1952, No. 7.

Lord, F. M. An application of confidence intervals and of maximum likelihood to the estimation of an examinee's ability. *Psychometrika,* 1953, *18,* 57–75. (a)

Lord, F. M. The relation of test score to the trait underlying the test. *Educational and Psychological Measurement,* 1953, *13,* 517–548. (b)

Lord, F. M. An analysis of the Verbal Scholastic Aptitude Test using Birnbaum's three-parameter logistic model. *Educational and Psychological Measurement,* 1968, *28,* 989–1020.

Lord, F. M. Estimating item characteristic curves without knowledge of their mathematical form. *Psychometrika,* 1970, *35,* 43–50. (a)

Lord, F. M. Some test theory for tailored testing. In W.H. Holtzman (Ed.), *Computer-assisted instruction, testing and guidance.* New York: Harper & Row, 1970. (b)

Lord, F. M. Robbins-Monro procedures for tailored testing. *Educational and Psychological Measurement,* 1971, *31,* 3–31. (a)

Lord, F. M. The self-scoring flexilevel test. *Journal of Educational Measurement,* 1971, *8,* 147–151. (b)

Lord, F. M. A theoretical study of the measurement effectiveness of flexilevel tests. *Educational and Psychological Measurement,* 1971, *31,* 805–813. (c)

Lord, F. M. A theoretical study of two-stage testing. *Psychometrika,* 1971, *36,* 227–242. (d)

Lord, F. M. Power scores estimated by item characteristic curves. *Educational and Psychological Measurement,* 1973, *33,* 219–224.

Lord, F. M. Estimation of latent ability and item parameters when there are omitted responses. *Psychometrika,* 1974, *39,* 247–264.(a)

Lord, F. M. Individualized testing and item characteristic curve theory. In D.H. Krantz, R.C. Atkinson, R.D. Luce, & P. Suppes (Eds.), *Contemporary developments in mathematical psychology, Vol. II.* San Francisco: Freeman, 1974. (b)

Lord, F.M. Practical methods for redesigning a homogeneous test, also for designing a multi-level test. *Research Bulletin 74-30.* Princeton, NJ: Educational Testing Service, 1974. (c)

Lord, F. M. Quick estimates of the relative efficiency of two tests as a function of ability level. *Journal of Educational Measurement,* 1974, *11,* 247–254.(d)

Lord, F. M. The relative efficiency of two tests as a function of ability level. *Psychometrika,* 1974, *39,* 351–358. (e)

Lord F. M. The "ability" scale in item characteristic curve theory. *Psychometrika,* 1975, *44,* 205–217. (a)

Lord, F. M. Evaluation with artificial data of a procedure for estimating ability and item characteristic curve parameters. *Research Bulletin 75-33.* Princeton, NJ: Educational Testing Service, 1975. (b)

Lord, F. M. Relative efficiency of number-right and formula scores. *British Journal of Mathematical and Statistical Psychology,* 1975, *28,* 46–50.(c)

Lord, F. M. A survey of equating methods based on item characteristic curve theory. *Research Bulletin 75-13.* Princeton, NJ: Educational Testing Service, 1975. (d)

Lord, F. M. A broad-range tailored test of verbal ability. *Applied Psychological Measurement,* 1977, *1,* 95–100.(a)

Lord, F. M. Practical applications of item characteristic curve theory. *Journal of Educational Measurement,* 1977, *14,* 117–138. (b)

Lord, F. M. A study of item bias, using item characteristic curve theory. In Y.H. Poortinga (Ed.), *Basic problems in cross-cultural psychology.* Amsterdam: Swets & Zeitlinger, 1977. (c)

Lord, F. M. *Applications of item response theory to practical testing problems.* Hillsdale, NJ: Erlbaum, 1980. (a)

Lord, F. M. Some how and which for practical tailored testing. In L.J. Th. van der Kamp, W.F. Langerak, & D.N.M. de Gruijter (Eds.), *Psychometrics for Educational Debates.* New York: Wiley, 1980. (b)

Lord, F. M. Small *N* justifies Rasch methods. In D. Weiss (Ed.), *New Horizons in Testing.* New York: Academic Press, 1983.

Lord, F. M. & Novick, M.R. *Statistical theories of mental test scores.* Reading Mass: Addison-Wesley, 1968.

Lord, F. M., & Wingersky, M.S. Comparison of IRT observed-score and true-score "equatings." *Research Bulletin 83-26.* Princeton, NJ: Educational Testing Service, 1983.

Loyd, B. H., & Hoover, H.D. Vertical equating using the Rasch model. *Journal of Educational Measurement,* 1981, *18,* 1–11.

Lumsden, J. The construction of unidimensional tests. *Psychological Bulletin,* 1961, *58,* 122–131.

Lumsden, J. Test theory. In M.R. Rosenzweig, & L.W. Porter (Eds.), *Annual Review of Psychology.* Palo Alto, CA: Annual Reviews Inc., 1976.

Marco, G. Item characteristic curve solutions to three intractable testing problems. *Journal of Educational Measurement,* 1977, *14,* 139–160.

Masters, G. N. A Rasch model for partial credit scoring. *Psychometrika,* 1982, *47,* 149–174.

McBride, J. R. Some properties of a Bayesian adaptive ability testing strategy. *Applied Psychological Measurement,* 1977, *1,* 121–140.

McDonald, R. P. Non-linear factor analysis. *Psychometric Monographs,* No. 15, 1967.

McDonald, R. P. The dimensionality of tests and items. *British Journal of Mathematical and Statistical Psychology,* 1980, *33,* 205–233. (a)

McDonald, R. P. Fitting latent trait models. In D. Spearitt (Ed.), *The Improvement of Measurement in Education and Pyschology.* Proceedings of the Invitational Seminar for the Fiftieth Anniversary of the Australian Council of Educational Research, Melbourne, 1980. (b)

McDonald, R. P. Linear versus non-linear models in item response theory. *Applied Psychological Measurement,* 1982, *6,* 379–396.

McDonald, R. P., & Ahlawat, K.S. Difficulty factors in binary data. *British Journal of Mathematical and Statistical Psychology,* 1974, *27,* 82–99.

McKinley, R. L., & Reckase, M.D. A comparison of the ANCILLES and LOGIST parameter estimation procedure for the three-parameter logistic model using goodness of fit as a criterion. *Research Report 80-2.* Columbia, MD: University of Missouri, 1980.

Mead, R. Assessing the fit of data to the Rasch model. A paper presented at the annual meeting of AERA, San Francisco, 1976.

Mislevy, R. J., & Bock R.D. *BILOG: Maximum likelihood item analysis and test scoring with logistic models for binary items.* Chicago: International Educational Services, 1982.

Mulaik, S. A. *The foundations of factor analysis.* New York: McGraw-Hill, 1972.

Murray, L. N., & Hambleton, R.K. Using residual analyses to assess item response model-test data fit. *Laboratory of Psychometric and Evaluative Research Report No. 140.* Amherst, MA: School of Education, University of Massachusetts, 1983.

Mussio, J. J. *A modification to Lord's model for tailored tests.* Unpublished doctoral dissertation, University of Toronto, 1973.

Neyman, J., & Scott, E. L. Consistent estimates based on partially consistent observations. *Econometrika*, 1948, *16*, 1–32.

Novick, M. R., Lewis, C., & Jackson, P.H. The estimation of proportion in m groups. *Psychometrika*, 1973, *3*, 19–46.

Owen, R. A Bayesian sequential procedure for quantal response in the context of adaptive mental testing. *Journal of the American Statistical Association*, 1975, *70*, 351–356.

Panchapakesan, N. *The simple logistic model and mental measurement.* Unpublished doctoral dissertation. University of Chicago, 1969.

Pandey, T. N., & Carlson, D. Application of item response models to reporting assessment data. In R.K. Hambleton (Ed.), *Applications of item response theory.* Vancouver, BC: Educational Research Institute of British Columbia, 1983.

Pine, S. M. Applications of item response theory to the problem of test bias. In D.J. Weiss (Ed.), *Applications of computerized adaptive testing* (Research Report 77-1). Minneapolis: University of Minnesota, Psychometric Methods Program, Department of Psychology, 1977.

Popham, W. J. *Criterion-referenced measurement.* Englewood Cliffs, NJ: Prentice-Hall, 1978.

Popham, W. J. *Modern educational measurement.* Englewood Cliffs, NJ: Prentice-Hall, 1980.

Rao, C. R. *Linear statistical inference and its application.* New York: Wiley, 1965.

Rasch, G. *Probabilistic models for some intelligence and attainment tests.* Copenhagen: Danish Institute for Educational Research, 1960.

Rasch, G. An item analysis which takes individual differences into account. *British Journal of Mathematical and Statistical Psychology*, 1966, *19*, 49–57. (a)

Rasch, G. An individualistic approach to item analysis. In P. Lazarsfeld, & N.V. Henry (Eds.), *Readings in Mathematical social science.* Chicago: Science Research Association, 1966, 89–107. (b)

Reckase, M. D. Unifactor latent trait models applied to multifactor tests: Results and implications. *Journal of Educational Statistics*, 1979, *4*, 207– 230.

Ree, M. J. Estimating item characteristic curves. *Applied Psychological Measurement*, 1979, *3*, 371–385.

Ree, M. J. The effects of item calibration sample size on adaptive testing. *Applied Psychological Measurement*, 1981, *5*, 11–19.

Rentz, R. R., & Bashaw, W.L. *Equating reading tests with the Rasch model, Volume I final report, Volume II technical reference tables.* Athens: University of Georgia, Educational Research Laboratory, 1975.

Rentz, R. R., & Bashaw, W.L. The national reference scale for reading: An application of the Rasch model. *Journal of Educational Measurement*, 1977, *14*, 161–180.

Rentz, R. R., & Rentz, C.C. *Does the Rasch model really work? A synthesis of the literature for practitioners.* Princeton, NJ: ERIC Clearinghouse on Tests. Measurement and Evaluation, Educational Testing Services, 1978.

Rentz, R. R., & Ridenour, S.E. The fit of the Rasch model to achievement tests. A paper presented at the annual meeting of the Eastern Educational Research Association, Williamsburg, VA, March 1978.

Richardson, M. W. The relationship between difficulty and the differential validity of a test. *Psychometrika,* 1936, *1,* 33–49.

Ross, J. An empirical study of a logistic mental test model. *Psychometrika,* 1966, *31,* 325–340.

Rudner, L. M. An approach to biased item identification using latent trait measurement theory. Paper presented at the annual meeting of the American Educational Research Association, New York, April 1977.

Samejima, F. Estimation of latent ability using a response pattern of graded scores. *Psychometric Monograph,* 1969, No. 17.

Samejima, F. A general model for free-response data. *Psychometric Monograph,* 1972, No. 18.

Samejima, F. A comment on Birnbaum's three-parameter logistic model in the latent trait theory. *Psychometrika,* 1973, *38,* 221–223. (a)

Samejima, F. Homogeneous case of the continuous response model. *Psychometrika,* 1973, *38,* 203–219. (b)

Samejima, F, Normal ogive model on the continuous response level in the multidimensional latent space. *Psychometrika,* 1974, *39,* 111–121.

Samejima, F. A use of the information function in tailored testing. *Applied Psychological Measurement,* 1977, *1,* 233–247. (a)

Samejima, F. A method of estimating item characteristic functions using the maximum likelihood estimate of ability. *Psychometrika,* 1977, *42,* 163–191. (b)

Scheuneman, J. A method of assessing bias in test items. *Journal of Educational Measurement,* 1979, *16,* 143–152.

Schmidt, F. L. The Urry method of approximating the item parameters of latent trait theory. *Educational and Psychological Measurement,* 1977, *37,* 613–620.

Shepard, L. A., Camilli, G., & Averill, M. Comparison of procedures for detecting test-item bias with both internal and external ability criteria. *Journal of Educational Statistics,* 1981, *6,* 317–375.

Slinde, J. A., & Linn, R.L. Vertically equated tests: Fact or phantom? *Journal of Educational Measurement,* 1977, *14,* 23–32.

Slinde, J.A., & Linn, R.L. An exploration of the adequacy of the Rasch model for the problem of vertical equating. *Journal of Educational Measurement,* 1978, *15,* 23–35.

Slinde, J. A., & Linn, R.L. A note on vertical equating via the Rasch model for groups of quite different ability and tests of quite different difficulty. *Journal of Educational Measurement,* 1979, *16,* 159–165. (a)

Slinde, J. A., & Linn, R.L. The Rasch model, objective measurement, equating and robustness. *Applied Psychological Measurement,* 1979, *3,* 437–452. (b)

Soriyan, M. A. Measurement of the goodness-of-fit of Rasch's probabilistic model of item analysis to objective achievement test of the West African Certification Examination. Unpublished doctoral dissertation, University of Pittsburgh, 1977.

Stocking, M. L., & Lord, F.M. Developing a common metric in item response theory. *Applied Psychological Measurement*, 1983, *7*, 201–210.

Swaminathan, H. Parameter estimation in item-response models. In R.K. Hambleton (Ed.), *Application of item response theory*. Vancouver, BC: Educational Research Institute of British Columbia, 1983.

Swaminathan, H. Bayesian estimation in the two-parameter logistic model. *Psychometrika*, in press.

Swaminathan, H., & Gifford, J.A. Estimation of parameters in the three-parameter latent trait model. *Laboratory of Psychometric and Evaluative Research Report No. 93*. Amherst, Mass.: School of Education, University of Massachusetts, 1981.

Swaminathan, H., & Gifford, J.A. Bayesian estimation in the Rasch model. *Journal of Educational Statistics*, 1982, *7*, 175–192.

Swaminathan, H., & Gifford, J.A. Estimation of parameters in the three-parameter latent trait model. In D. Weiss (Ed.), *New Horizons in Testing*. New York: Academic Press, 1983.

Thissen, D. M. Information in wrong responses to Raven's Progressive Matrices. *Journal of Educational Measurement*, 1976, *13*, 201–214.

Thissen, D. M. Marginal maximum likelihood estimation for the one-parameter logistic model. *Psychometrika*, 1982, *47*, 175–186.

Tinsley, H. E. A., & Dawis, R. V. An investigation of the Rasch simple logistic model: Sample free item and test calibration. *Educational and Psychological Measurement*, 1974, *11*, 163–178.

Tinsley, H. E. A., & Dawis, R. V. Test-free person measurement with the Rasch simple logistic model. *Applied Psychological Measurement*, 1977, *1*, 483–487. (a)

Tinsley, H. E. A., & Dawis, R. V. Test-free person measurement with the Rasch simple logistic model. *Applied Psychological Measurement*, 1977, *1, 483–487.* (b)

Torgerson, W. S. *Theory and methods of scaling*. New York: Wiley, 1958.

Traub, R. E. A priori considerations in choosing an item response model. In R. K. Hambleton (Ed.), *Applications of item response theory*. Vancouver, BC: Educational Research Institute of British Columbia, 1983.

Traub, R. E., & Wolfe, R. G. Latent trait theories and the assessment of educational achievement. In D. C. Berliner (Ed.), *Review of research in education (vol.9)*. Washington: American Educational Research Association, 1981.

Tucker, L. R. Maximum validity of a test with equivalent items. *Psychometrika*, 1946, *11*, 1–13.

Urry, V. W. Approximations to item parameters of mental test models and their uses. *Educational and Psychological Measurement*, 1974, *34*, 253–269.

Urry, V. W. Ancilliary estimators for the item parameters of mental tests. Washington, D.C.: Personnel Research and Development Center, U.S. Civil Service Commission, 1976.

Urry, V. W. Tailored testing: A successful application of latent trait theory. *Journal of Educational Measurement*, 1977, *14*, 181–196.

Wainer, H., Morgan, A., & Gustafsson, J. E. A review of estimation procedures for the Rasch model with an eye toward longish tests. *Journal of Educational Statistics*, 1980, *5*, 35–64.

Waller, M. I. A procedure for comparing logistic latent trait models. *Journal of Educational Measurement*, 1981, *18*, 119–125.

Wang, M. W. & Stanley, J. C. Differential weighting: A review of methods and empirical studies. *Review of Educational Research*, 1970, *40*, 663–706.

Waters, B. K. An empirical investigation of the stratified adaptive computerized testing model. *Applied Psychological Measurement*, 1977, *1*, 141–152.

Weiss, D. J. The stratified adaptive computerized ability test. *Research Report 73-3*. Minneapolis: University of Minnesota, Psychometric Methods Program, Department of Psychology, 1973.

Weiss, D. J. Strategies of adaptive measurement. *Research Report 74-5*. Minneapolis: University of Minnesota, Psychometric Methods Program, Department of Psychology, 1974.

Weiss, D. J. Adaptive testing research at Minnesota: Overview, recent results, and future directions. In C. L. Clark (Ed.), *Proceedings of the First Conference on Computerized Adaptive Testing*. Washington, D.C.: United States Civil Service Commission, 1976.

Weiss, D. J. (Ed.). *Proceedings of the 1979 Computerized Adaptive Testing Conference*. Minneapolis: University of Minnesota, 1978.

Weiss, D. (Ed.). *Proceedings of the 1979 Computerized Adaptive Testing Conference*. Minneapolis: University of Minnesota, 1980.

Weiss, D. J. Improving measurement quality and efficiency with adaptive testing. *Applied Psychological Measurement*, 1982, *6*, 379–396.

Weiss, D. J. (Ed.) *New horizons in testing*. New York: Academic Press, 1983.

Weiss, D. J., & Betz, N. E. Ability measurement: Conventional or adaptive? *Research Report 73-1*. Minneapolis: University of Minnesota, Psychometric Methods Program, Department of Psychology, 1973.

Weiss, D. J., & Davidson, M. L. Test theory and methods. In M. R. Rosenzweig, & L.W. Porter (Eds.), *Annual Review of Psychology*. Palo Alto, CA: Annual Reviews Inc., 1981.

Whitely, S. E. Multicomponent latent trait models for ability tests. *Psychometrika*, 1980, *45*, 479–494.

Wilcox, R. A note on the length and passing score of a mastery test. *Journal of Educational Statistics*, 1976, *1*, 359–364.

Wingersky, M. S. LOGIST: A program for computing maximum likelihood procedures for logistic test models. In R.K. Hambleton (Ed.), *Applications of item response theory*. Vancouver, BC: Educational Research Institute of British Columbia, 1983.

Wingersky, M. S., Barton, M. A., & Lord, F. M. *LOGIST user's guide*. Princeton, NJ: Educational Testing Service, 1982.

Wollenberg, A. L. van den. On the Wright-Panchapakesan goodness of fit test for the Rasch model. *Internal Report 80-MA-02*. Nijmegen, The Netherlands: Katholieke Unversiteit Nijmegen, Vakgroep Mathematische Pyschologie, Psychologisch

Laboratorium, 1980.

Wollenberg, A. L. van den. Two new test statistics for the Rasch model. *Psychometrika*, 1982, *47*, 123–140. (a)

Wollenberg, A. L. van den. A simple and effective method to test the dimensionality axiom of the Rasch model. *Applied Psychological Measurement*, 1982, *6*, 83–91. (b)

Wood, R. Response-contingent testing. *Review of Educational Research*, 1973, *43*, 529–544.

Wood, R. Adaptive testing: A Bayesian procedure for efficient measurement of ability. *Programmed Learning and Educational Research*, 1976, *13*, 34–48.

Wood, R. Fitting the Rasch model—A heady tale. *British Journal of Mathematical and Statistical Psychology*, 1978, *31*, 27–32.

Woodcock, R. W. *Woodcock reading mastery test*. Circle Pine, MN: American Guidance Service, 1974.

Woodcock, R. W. Development and standardization of the *Woodcock-Johnson Psycho-Educational Battery*. Hingham, MA: Teaching Resources Corporation, 1978.

Wright, B. D. Sample-free test calibration and person measurement. *Proceedings of the 1967 Invitational Conference on Testing Problems*. Princeton, NJ: Educational Testing Service, 1986.

Wright, B. D. Solving measurement problems with the Rasch model. *Journal of Educational Measurement*, 1977, *14*, 97–166. (a)

Wright, B. D. Misunderstanding of the Rasch model. *Journal of Educational Measurement*, 1977, *14*, 219–226. (b)

Wright, B. D., & Douglas, G. A. *Best test design and self-tailored testing* (Research Memorandum No. 19). Chicago: University of Chicago, Statistical Laboratory, Department of Education, 1975.

Wright, B. D., & Douglas, G. A. Best procedures for sample-free item analysis. *Applied Psychological Measurement*, 1977, *1*, 281–295. (a)

Wright, B. D., & Douglas, G. A. Conditional versus unconditional procedures for sample-free analysis. *Educational and Psychological Measurement*, 1977, *37*, 573–586. (b)

Wright, B. D., & Mead, R. J. *BICAL Calibrating rating scales with the Rasch model. Research Memorandum No. 23*. Chicago: Statistical Laboratory, Department of Education, University of Chicago, 1976.

Wright, B. D., Mead, R., & Draba, R. *Detecting and correcting item bias with a logistic response model*. Research Memorandum No. 22. Chicago: University of Chicago, Statistical Laboratory. Department of Education, 1976.

Wright, B. D., & Panchapakesan, N. A procedure for sample-free item analysis. *Educational and Psychological Measurement*, 1969, *29*, 23–48.

Wright, B. D., & Stone, M. H. *Best test design*. Chicago: MESA, 1979.

Yen, W. M. The extent, causes and importance of context effects on item parameters for two latent trait models. *Journal of Educational Measurement*, 1980, *17*, 297–311.

Yen, W. M. Using simulation results to choose a latent trait model. *Applied Psychological Measurement*, 1981, 5, 245–262.

Yen, W. Use of the three-parameter model in the development of a standardized achievement test. In R. K. Hambleton (Ed.), *Applications of item response theory*. Vancouver, BC: Educational Research Institute of British Columbia, 1983.

Zellner, A. *An introduction to Bayesian inference in econometrics*. New York: Wiley, 1971.

Author Index

328

Zellner, A., 127, 141, 142

Subject Index